The Archaeological Excavations in the Castel Corno Caves (Isera, Trento, Italy)

The Archaeological Excavations in the Castel Corno Caves (Isera, Trento, Italy)

Burial Places and Settlement of a Small Alpine Community between the 25th and 17th Centuries BC

Maurizio Battisti, Umberto Tecchiati

Archaeopress Archaeology

Archaeopress Publishing Ltd
Summertown Pavilion
18-24 Middle Way
Summertown
Oxford OX2 7LG

www.archaeopress.com

ISBN 978-1-80327-193-4
ISBN 978-1-80327-194-1 (e-Pdf)

Cover: Image from Ausserer, K. 1911. *Die Herren von Schloss und Gericht Castelcorno im Lagertale (Vallagarina)*, Wien. The original image shows the inscription '1906 TS' in the lower left corner.

AUTHORS

Maurizio Battisti - Fondazione Museo Civico di Rovereto
Umberto Tecchiati - Professor of Prehistory and Protohistory at the State University of Milan.
The authors contributed equally to this work.

TRANSLATION

Janet Kilkenny

GRAPHIC ELABORATION

Maurizio Battisti (unless otherwise specified)

AKNOWLEDGEMENTS

We would like to thank for the availability, collaboration, support or for the useful advice: Mark Pearce, Marco Avanzini, Fabrizio Bizzarini, Michela Canali, Dario Candioli, Simone Cavalieri, Franco Marzatico, Valentina Coia, Viviana Conti, Andrea Fogolari, Alex Fontana, Stefano Marconi, Barbara Maurina, Alice Paladin, Tullio Pasquali, Barbara Proserpio, Elena Regola, Virginia Trinco, Fabiana Zandonai, Michele Zandonati, il Gruppo Grotte E. Roner CAI SAT Rovereto, l'istituto I.T.E.T. F.lli Fontana di Rovereto and all the students and volunteers who participated in the excavations.

fondazione museo civico di rovereto 107th Publication of Rovereto Civic Museum

Contents

List of Figures ... iii

1 – Historical and Geographical Introduction ... 1

Geographic and geomorphological framework ... 3

History of the research ... 5

Summary of research, excavations and surveys in Castel Corno Caves ... 9

2 – The Rovereto Civic Museum Excavations ... 10

Excavation campaign 1998 ... 10

The stratigraphy ... 11

Excavation campaign 1999 ... 15

Inspections between 2016 and 2018 ... 18

3 – The Material Culture ... 21

The pottery ... 21

Forms, accessories and typology ... 22

Pottery technology ... 27

Fired and baked clay ... 28

Stone tools ... 31

Artefacts made out of stone other than flint ... 33

Shell, bone and antler artefacts ... 35

Metals ... 36

4 – The Burial Places ... 37

5 – Paleoenvironmental and Economic Aspects ... 45

Archaeozoology ... 45

Archaeobotany ... 46

Reconstruction of the environment ... 49

6 – General Discussion and Conclusions ... 52

Settlement, cemetery or place of worship? ... 54

Settlement in Vallagarina between the Copper and Early Bronze Ages ... 58

The cultural context ... 61

Catalogue of Finds ... 64

Catalogue Entries ... 65

Plates ... 95

Appendix ... 133

Bibliography ... 136

List of Figures

Figure 1: Localization of the site of the Castel Corno Caves. 2
Figure 2: Panoramic view of Castel Corno and localization of the caves 3
Figure 3: Chambers plans and cross sections 4
Figure 4: Excavation photos from 1974 (left: Chamber 1; right: Sondage 1 in Chamber 1). 7
Figure 5: Chamber 3, Zone 1: cavity entrance 11
Figure 6: Chamber 3, Zone 1: Tomb 1 plan 14
Figure 7: Chamber 3, Zone 1: cumulative section 14
Figure 8: Chamber 3, Zone 1: Harris matrix 14
Figure 9: Access corridor to Chamber 1 15
Figure 10: Chamber 1, 1999 sondage: composite plan 17
Figure 11: Chamber 1, 1999 sondage: sections A-B and C-D 18
Figure 12: Chamber 1, 1999 sondage: Harris matrix. 18
Figure 13: Chamber 1: cave plan with placement of 1974 and 1999 sondages (black dot-dashed line) and of the recent illegal excavation (red dashed line) 19
Figure 14: Correlation between surfaces and fabrics color 22
Figure 15: Correlation between vessel and quality classes. 24
Figure 16: Mug from Chamber 1, US 5 24
Figure 17: Baked clay platform fragments (a: from Riparo del Santuario (Lasino), b and c: from the Chamber 3 of Castel Corno) 29
Figure 18: Baked clay platform fragment with traces of vegetal interweaving 30
Figure 19: Shapeless baked clay lump with traces of handling 30
Figure 20: Place of discovery of flint tools 31
Figure 21: Colour of flint tools and chips 32
Figure 22: Metal artefacts. a: small copper residue (or of a copper alloy), b: piece of smelting slag 36
Figure 23: Distribution of human bones 39
Figure 24: Individual 3's skull and hypothetical position of it at the time of burning 41
Figure 25: Reconstruction of the original position of individual 3's skeletal remains 41
Figure 26: Calibration made with the software Oxcal v.4.3.2 (Bronk Ramsey 2017) and IntCal13 atmospheric curve (Reimer *et al.* 2013) 43
Figure 27: Determination of tree species of US 9 and 10 (Chamber 3) 47
Figure 28: Determination of cereal plants of US 9 and 10 (Chamber 3) 48
Figure 29: Determination of fruit remains of US 9 and 10 (Chamber 3) 48
Figure 30: Localization of hypothetical flat cultivable fields near the site 50
Figure 31: Vessel potsherds from US 9 and 10 (Chamber 3) 52
Figure 32: Vessel potsherds from Chamber 1 in order of excavation: US 5, 2 and 3 53
Figure 33: Distribution of the vessel classes in the site 57
Figure 34: Distribution map of Copper Age finds (orange) and sites (yellow). 1. Le Corone, 2. Vico e Bojom, 3. M. Altissimo, 4. Bersaglio, 5. Lizzana, 6. La Torretta e Dos Pipel, 7. Grotte di Castel Corno, 8. Passo Bordala, 9. M. Stivo, 10. Balteri e Laste Rosse, 11. Paludei, 12. Acquaviva, 13. S. Andrea Island 59
Figure 35: Distribution map of Early Bronze Age finds (orange) and sites (yellow). 1. Serravalle, 2. Castel Tierno e Montecatini, 3/4. Bersaglio e Colombo, 5. Monte Albano, 6. Molina, 7. Castel Pradaglia, 8. Grotte di Castel Corno, 9. Dosso Alto, 10. Rovereto city centre, 11. San Colombano, 12. Pizzini di Castellano, 13/14/15. Le Ville, San Rocco e Dos Destor, 16. Monte Corona, 17. Dos Alt (Nomi), 18. Castel Beseno, 19. Corona di Sachiel, 20. Becchetta 60
Figure 36: Facial reconstruction of Individual 3 created by Viviana Conti 62

1 – Historical and Geographical Introduction

Wenn sich aber die Nebel zwischen die Felswand und den Sclossberg schieben, dann hebt sich dieser zerrissene Felszacken mit den Ruinen, wie ein Riesenzahn, als Silhouette von der hellen Wolkenbanck ab.

But when the fog pushes between the cliff and the castle, then this steep boulder comes out with its ruins, like a giant tooth, and outlines its profile against the clear background of the clouds.[1]

The ruins of Castel Corno are to be found in the eastern Alps, along the Adige valley (province of Trento, Italy) near Isera, on the mountain side to the right of the river at an altitude of about 800 metres above sea level (**Figure 1**). It was a well-fortified castle, skilfully built on gigantic, upwardly stretching teeth of rock. At the foot of the castle, amid the boulders of the great landslide on which the castle proudly stands, there open numerous cavities, chambers, gullies and tunnels from which archaeological evidence has emerged showing them to have been occupied between the end of the 3rd and beginning of the 2nd millennium BC.

The first superficial investigations go back to the end of the nineteen-sixties, but up until 1999 a great number of excavations of varied importance and approach were carried out. The finds recovered in the various investigations and during the excavations are all preserved at the Civic Museum at Rovereto.

In this volume we wish to provide a complete picture of all the interventions so far undertaken on the site, analysing the stratigraphy, the chrono-typological aspects of the materials found and, in general, all the archaeological evidence emerged.

The work in question has been hampered by the poor quality of documentation due to the poor integrity of the contexts, disturbed and seriously compromised by an intense and highly visible looting activity, but also by the arduous conditions in which the excavations were carried out: artificial light, high humidity, extremely restricted space, difficulty in moving the earth and relative slowness of the operations. This difficulty was in part compensated for by the exceptional state of preservation of both artefacts and bones, maintained by the stable microclimate typical of cave settings.

The Vallagarina, a stretch of the valley of the river Adige which, starting from the village of Besenello (10 kilometers south of Trento) reaches almost to the gates of Verona, has given us important evidence of the prehistoric settlement from the Middle Paleolithic to the Iron Age. As regards specifically the basin today occupied by the town of Rovereto, overlooked by Castel Corno, very few sites have been the subject of modern and methodological archaeological investigations. Most of the finds, in fact, were made in the nineteenth century and, later, between the 1960s and 1970s. Regarding the site in question, study of the documentation which emerged in the excavations conducted by the Civic Museum of Rovereto between 1998 and 1999, occupies therefore a significant role in the attempt to organize the sporadic and incomplete data previously collected and published about the site.

This study starts from the data which emerged in Elena Regola's degree thesis,[2] expanding the field of investigation with new research, laboratory analyses, radiocarbon dating and reassessment of the resulting data.

[1] Ausserer 1911, p. 5.
[2] Regola 2005.

Figure 1: Localization of the site of the Castel Corno Caves.

Considering the limited number of archaeological evidences referring to the Copper Age and the rare edited documentation for the Bronze Age from the lower Adige valley, we hope that this volume, partly bridging this gap, may make a useful contribution to the reconstruction of the settlement dynamics and funerary practices between the end of the Copper Age and beginning of the Bronze Age in an area of particular interest, an important point of contact and exchange between northern Italy and central Europe.

Geographic and geomorphological framework

The site of the Castel Corno Caves is found just to the south of the castle of that name, on the hydrographic right of the river Adige near Isera (Trento, Italia), on a terrace a little over 800 masl, precisely half way between the villages of Isera and Patone.

The origin of the caves of Castel Corno is not to be traced back to the destructive or constructive action of exogenous or endogenous agents as usually happens in the formation of natural cavities, but rather was due to the effects of a landslide of great proportions, detaching itself from the western slope above the castle (Croz de Naranc, at the foot of mount Biaena). This caused enormous blocks of calcareous rock to pile on top of each other and consequently the creation of a maze of chambers and gullies, often inter-connected, and numerous rock shelters. The castle itself was erected on cyclopean vertical boulders which had fallen from mount Biaena and slid to here, now soaring skywards like mighty teeth or, exactly, stone horns (meaning of '*corno*').

Figure 2: Panoramic view of Castel Corno and localization of the caves. (Image taken from Google Earth Pro V. 7.3.4.8642, on 31 August 2021).

Mount Biaena is a mountain situated to the north-east of Lake Garda on the slope of which can be seen landslide niche and, at its feet, the commensurate heaps of rock. Around 13,000 years ago, when the glaciers retreated, the valley sides underwent alterations: deep effects of erosion and collapse followed consequently by instability when the glacial mass ceased to push.[3] The origin of the landslide of Castel Corno is thus traceable to this phenomenon: it is probable that a mass of rock, already destabilized, fell from the slopes of mount Biaena and slid to the valley side,[4] leading, as a consequence, to the formation of the caves.

Observing the area in question, an elongated ridge can be noted with two prominences at either end: the higher one to the north is the one the actual castle was built on; the lower one to the south is where we find the complex of caves and underground tunnels which are the subject of this book (**Figure 2**).

The four chambers so far investigated (see **Figure 3**) are linked together by tunnels, pits and narrow passages. Access to the area of the caves is possible by road from the villages of Lenzima or Patone, near Isera. Once the castle has been reached, continuing to the south, in the small valley between the slopes of mount Biaena and the top of the landslide, an imposing mass of boulders with its system of caves is arrived at.

From the first chamber (Chamber 1), the easiest to access, you enter the second (Chamber 2) through a passage which opens out at the end. Chamber 2 also has a direct access to the outside which, though very tight (entered by crawling), was used during the most recent excavations. This chamber, much narrower than the first, is positioned slightly higher and proceeds in a northern direction. The third chamber (Chamber 3) can be reached via a narrow, vertical pit, which from the second chamber drops

[3] Perna 1974.
[4] Avanzini *et al.* 1987.

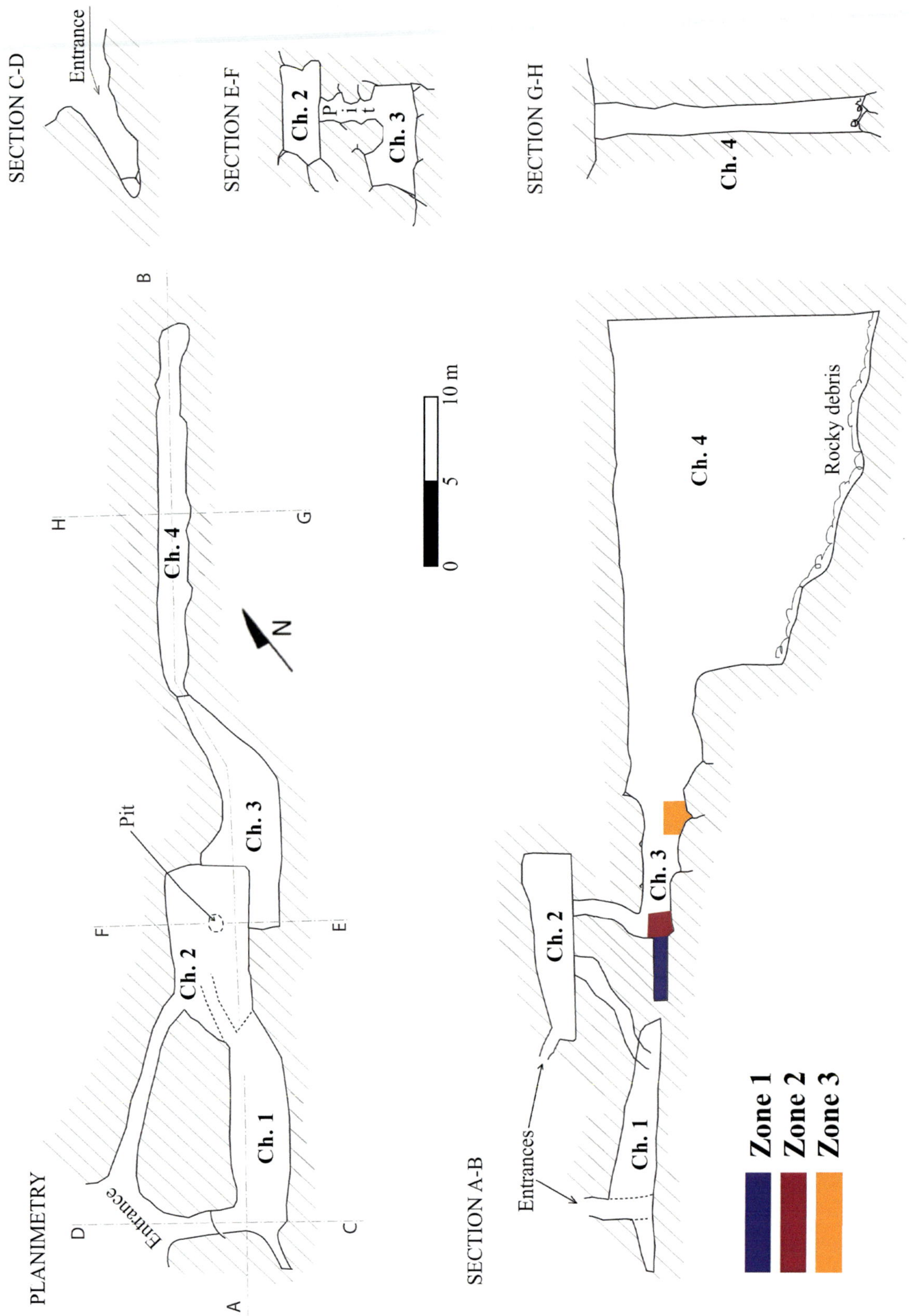

Figure 3: Chambers plans and cross sections (image modified from Chiocchetti 1985).

vertically towards the third. Finally, at the end of the third chamber, the fourth and last chamber (Chamber 4) opens out, in reality a deep, long, narrow gully.

More innumerable small caves exist around this area, rock shelters, narrow clefts and cavities of various dimensions, largely till now unexplored, also because they are almost entirely full of earth and covered with vegetation.

History of the research

The research into this archaeological site has been quite sporadic, often occasional and, in many cases, not so well documented. Furthermore, the site also has its own 'history of looting', unfortunately not quite as discontinuous, parallel to more or less official studies; looting that continues to this day. These illicit activities have caused serious damage to the original stratigraphy and made the task of those who tried to conduct more methodical digs even harder in a situation which was already difficult because of the extreme environmental conditions typical of the caves.

Here it has been attempted to reconstruct, as in a puzzle, the events which have characterized the troubled history of the studies of these caves. It has thus been possible to reassemble a synthetic chronological outline at least concerning the interventions which have left some documentary evidence.[5]

Altogether, in a period of time going from 1960 to 1999, at Castel Corno Caves a good fifteen different interventions were documented, between proper archaeological excavations, chance finds, and field surveys.

The discovery of the site happened by chance, at the end of the 60s, thanks to Dario Candioli, at the time just a boy. Immediately some more intense research followed, carried out by Valentino Chiocchetti, professor of philosophy, interested in archaeology, who became, in 1969, curator at the Civic Museum of Rovereto. To this first research is owed not only the recovery of archaeological artefacts,[6] but also the realization of a map and a cross-section of the caves.[7] The finds recovered all come from Zone 1 of Chamber 3.[8] Among the various artefacts, the most important are a fragmentary truncated-cone shaped tuyère (**265**)[9] and a fragmentary loom weight with a sub-cylindric body (**264**). Few flint tools and animal bones were found: among these were some flint sickle blades and teeth and joints, mostly belonging to herbivores. Of great importance is the find, again in Chamber 3, of the first human bones and the only complete skull, which was found entirely covered by stones. Exactly next to the human bones were found the terracotta tuyére previously mentioned.

Further investigations, begun in the 1970s by local associations of amateurs, were more methodical and systematic. In 1970, in fact, is dated the first of numerous interventions promoted and carried out by the Roveretan Archaeological Group (G.A.R., an association which then took the name Centre of Studies Lagarini - C.S.L.) under the guidance of Adriano Rigotti. These explorations, all undertaken inside the caves, led to the discovery of mostly ceramic finds with some flint tools, a jaw and teeth of herbivores.[10] The fragment of red deer antler, cut and burnished with a small through hole (**308**) found in Chamber 3, is particularly noteworthy.

[5] List of the documents, for the most part unpublished, conserved at the Civic Museum Foundation of Rovereto through which it was possible to reconstruct the history of the research into the site: two work journal books of the Roveretan Archaeological Group, dated 1972 and 1974; archaeological site recording sheet of Castel Corno Caves of the Centre of Studies Lagarini, dated 22 September 1974; letters registered 3/8/AR and 3/9/AR with the Autonomous Province of Trento – Office for Cultural Activities, dated 1 October 1974; Article from the newspaper l'Alto Adige, dated 3 October 1974; Articolo from the newspaper l'Adige, dated 4 October 1974; Report, unpublished, of the investigation by Marco Avanzini in 1985; Protocol 5/5/AR of the Autonomous Province of Trento – Office for Cultural Activities, dated 5 November 1974; Protocol 5/6/AR of the Autonomous Province of Trento – Office for Cultural Activities, dated 11 November 1974; Inventary of entries Civic Museum of Rovereto; Inventary archaeological finds Civic Museum of Rovereto (Regola 2005).

[6] See in the Plates finds 4, 31, 35, 36, 45, 72, 86, 130, 134, 227, 228, 229, 230, 233, 264, 265.

[7] Chiocchetti 1985.

[8] See map and general cross section in **Figure 3**, extrapolated by Chiocchetti 1985, modified by the authors.

[9] The identification number of the find is indicated in bold and in brackets (Catalogue entries and Plates).

[10] See finds 8, 9, 41, 44, 71, 125, 137, 164, 171, 234, 276, 308.

In 1972 two different interventions made by the Cave Group (Gruppo Grotte) of the S.A.T. of Rovereto (G.G.R.)[11] were documented: these involved an in-depth exploration of the caves and removal of several artefacts. These explorations are documented not only in the entry register at the Civic Museum of Rovereto (n.1078/1972), to which the finds were eventually consigned,[12] but also in some unpublished notes of the G.A.R. which, in the person of Adriano Rigotti, monitored the situation. The valuable activity of inspection on land carried out by the latter and his association permitted, in many cases, the documentation of the activities of other interested groups or associations in Vallagarina. It also resulted in the Civic Museum of Rovereto being indicated as the place for collection and conservation of the finds otherwise dispersed among private collections and those of various associations and minor institutions unable to guarantee their conservation, inventory and research. The research involved above all Chamber 2 and, secondly, Chamber 3. It is thought to have been in this phase that the narrow access passage connecting Chamber 2 with the outside was opened.

Two documents of the Autonomous Province of Trento (protocol numbers 5/5/AR of 5 November 1974 and 5/6/AR of 11 November 1974), mention, among the activities conducted by the C.S.L. in 1973, investigations at Castel Corno, preliminary to and serving the excavation to be carried out the following year.

In fact, in 1974 the first real archaeological and stratigraphic survey took place. On the 22nd of September 1974, with the authorization of the Superintendence and on the indication of Dr Bernardino Bagolini, the first registration of 'archaeological site' was compiled for the area of Castel Corno. The ground was defined as '*steep wooded zone 50 metres south of the ruins of the castle of Castel Corno*' and localized '*at an altitude of c. 800 masl, above Isera, half way between Patone and Lenzima as the crow flies*'.[13] Following the recognition of this zone's archaeological importance, a collaboration between the Cave Group of the SAT and the Centre for Studies Lagarini (ex G.A.R.) was set up to implement an excavation campaign, this cooperation was also made official approved by the Autonomous Province of Trento.[14]

The excavations of 1974, carried out in the last ten days of September under the direction of Adriano Rigotti, concerned above all Chamber 1, even if a further exploration with a consequent field survey involved all the other chambers, as well as the terrace above them (top of the landslide) and some cavities in the immediate vicinity. Inside Chamber 1 two small sondages were performed: the first (80×50×110 cm) near the entrance to the chamber, the second (100×100×40 cm) at the end of it, inside a small cavity opening to the east (see **Figures 4 and 13**).

The dig, made in spits (arbitrary levels), revealed a carbonaceous level rich in pottery, flint and bone finds. Among the numerous potsherds found during this brief research there was to be noted a small bowl with three handles vertically developed, two of which were pierced horizontally (**77**), found in an upper layer of Chamber 3. The works of 1974, which led to the recovery of several artefacts,[15] contributed substantially to a greater knowledge regarding the human presence in the zone under examination and in general to the Early Bronze Age (hereafter referred to as EBA) in Vallagarina. The event had a certain resonance locally, reawakening an interest in the prehistory and protohistory of the place, such that it was reported in articles in the major newspapers of Trentino.[16] The systematic and careful approach with which this intervention was executed led to a better, more detailed identification and description of the finds, and consequently to the compilation of a more complete documentation of the excavation phases.

[11] The Gruppo Grotte 'Emilio Roner' was officially founded in 1927 as an organ of the S.A.T. Centrale and of the then Natural History Museum of Trento. Later, since essentially constituted by Roveretan speleologists, it passed into the section S.A.T. of Rovereto.

[12] See finds 2, 5, 46, 61, 64, 65, 68, 78, 80, 85, 96, 136, 203, 206, 210, 215, 222, 224, 235, 306.

[13] Unpublished report of the archaeological site n. 9/74 of the Centre for Studies Lagarini.

[14] Protocols 3/8 /AR and 3/9/AR of 1st October 1974 of the Autonomous Province of Trento – Office for cultural activities.

[15] See finds 7, 9, 34, 40, 41, 77, 88, 95, 98, 108, 131, 169, 238.

[16] 'Alto Adige', Thursday 3rd October 1974; 'Adige', Friday 4th October 1974, p. 9.

Figure 4: Excavation photos from 1974 (left: Chamber 1; right: Sondage 1 in Chamber 1).

In 1975 more research followed, carried out by Tullio Pasquali, a local amateur archaeologist who worked in collaboration with the Civic Museum of Rovereto. The investigations were related to a zone outside the caves, in the open, enclosed by two boulders, overhanging Chamber 1: brought to light were potsherds, lithic tools and animal bone remains, mainly of domestic herbivores.[17] We have no written documentation of these small sondages but fortunately all the objects found here were marked and are easily identifiable. Moreover, the investigations made in the area by one of the authors of this contribution (M.B.) have permitted the identification of superficial, still present, traces of the sondages conducted in the southern part of the natural corridor formed by the rock walls at the side.

Further surveys, of both inside and outside the caves, were carried out some years later, in 1983, by Pasquali and his collaborator and member of the Society Civic Museum of Rovereto, Barbara Rauss, who also made the first technical drawings of the finds from this site.[18] The surveys involved both the interior and exterior of the caves and the finds, exclusively pottery, were consigned to the Civic Museum of Rovereto.

Another exploration took place in August 1985[19] carried out by Marco Avanzini, a geologist interested in history and archaeology, now curator at the Museum of Sciences in Trento (MUSE). On that occasion potsherds and two human jaw bones identified as burial remains belonging to two young people were found. The report on this exploration,[20] together with graphic and photographic documentation, also reveals the location in Chamber 3, of a further burial of a youth *in situ*. Visible among the human bones were forearms, part of the rib cage and the spine, fragments of the pelvis and the proximal part

[17] See finds 1, 6, 33, 39, 63, 73, 91–93, 112, 113, 115, 116, 126, 138, 154, 160, 231, 232, 266–275, 284, 287, 292, 293.
[18] Entry register number of the Civic Museum of Rovereto:1083/1986; e.g. find 94.
[19] Entry register number of the Civic Museum of Rovereto: 1054/1986.
[20] Avanzini 1985.

of a femur. These latter human remains, clearly still partially connected, were left *in situ* for future investigations.

Between 1986 and 1987 two more explorations were carried out by Tullio Pasquali and Barbara Rauss outside the caves and one by Marco Avanzini in Chamber 3. Those explorations taking place externally led to the find of numerous flint artefacts, comprising several sickle blades and some arrowheads, of a carved bones and a few potsherds.[21] Avanzini's exploration produced a spindle whorl and a potsherd (a wall with an elbow handle[22]).

In 1988 a new exploration by Pasquali-Rauss involved the area outside the castle, adjacent to the eastern walls. Among the Medieval finds brought to light, there were also two prehistoric artefacts, coming from the place defined as 'Dumping places A and B'.[23]

Between 1995 and 1997 the Civic Museum of Rovereto undertook a series of preliminary explorations in the field, authorized by the Superintendence for Archaeological Heritage of the Province of Trento, in order to make a complete plan of action for the excavation. The first took place in 1998, under the direction of Umberto Tecchiati, one of the authors of this contribution and at the time curator of the museum for the Archaeology section. Surveys was carried out both outside and inside the caves and a sondage was made for the interior of Chamber 3, in the area already involved in the find of human bones in previous decades.

The excavation in 1999 was directed by the curator Barbara Maurina with the collaboration of Maurizio Battisti, the other author of this contribution, and of Simone Cavalieri. In this case a sondage was opened in the interior of Chamber 1, an area where it was possible to put a more complete and detailed documentation together, thanks to better accessibility, greater available space, better environmental conditions and a stratigraphy less damaged by looting.

The preliminary results of these two excavations were, between 2004 and 2005, the subject of a degree thesis in which all the artefacts found in previous excavations, from 1969 on, were examined.[24]

In the first twenty years of the 21st century several investigations on the part of one of the authors of this contribution (M.B.) have been carried out, partly in order to monitor the possible prosecution of looting activities. Between 2016 and 2020, in particular, while carrying out examinations for technical and cartographic reasons in order to improve the graphic documentation for the publication of the archaeological site, the presence of some new illegal activities was discovered and reported (see the following chapter).

As regards printed publications about the site of the Castel Corno Caves until now, the first article appeared in 1980, written by Corrain and De Marchi.[25] In this brief contribution of an anthropological nature the human bones found during the excavations of 1969 were examined. After five years another brief article came out, in which were published, as already mentioned, plans and sections of the caves, written by Valentino Chiocchetti. Besides the publication of the studies on the ruins of the nearby castle, which includes various contributions,[26] between 1996 and 2007 the archaeological site of the nearby caves was previously described in two notes written by one of the authors of this volume (U.T.)[27] and was the subject of two degree theses.[28] Furthermore, between 2010 and 2012 an archaeozoological

[21] Numbers of entry register of the Civic Museum of Rovereto: 1083/1986 and 1166/1987; see finds 55, 161, 163, 277–279, 298, 299.
[22] Entry register number of the Civic Museum of Rovereto: 1096/1986 (finds 51, 259).
[23] Pasquali and Rauss 1988, fig. 3:1; Pasquali and Rauss 1990, 60–63, fig. 4:31, fig. 5:43.
[24] Regola 2005.
[25] Corrain and De Marchi 1980.
[26] Avanzini *et al.* 1987; Pasquali and Rauss 1987; Avanzini 1988; Avanzini *et al.* 1988; Pasquali and Rauss 1988; Avanzini 1990; Chelidonio 1990; Pasquali and Rauss 1990.
[27] Tecchiati 1996b; Tecchiati 2005.
[28] Regola 2005; Fontana 2007.

study was published on the animal remains found inside the caves.[29] Finally, recently an article has been published which analyzes the human remains found from an anthropological point of view[30] and anthracological and botanical analyses of the remains found with flotation and sifting are in press.

Summary of research, excavations and surveys in Castel Corno Caves

1969: research Candioli (Grotta 3);

1970: research Rigotti (survey in Chambers 1, 2, 3 and overlooking terrace);

1972: research of the Gruppo Grotte E. Roner di Rovereto (chiefly inside Chamber 2);

1973: preliminary investigations of the Centro Studi Lagarini (Rigotti) for excavations in the following year (for the first time they had the authorization of the Superintendence of Padova);

1974: excavations by the Centro Studi Lagarini in collaboration with the Gruppo Grotte Roner (Rigotti is the director of the excavation. They only excavate in Chamber 1; survey in the other chambers, outside and above the caves);

1975: research Pasquali (external zone);

1983: research Pasquali-Rauss (a few potsherds probably from the caves);

1985: research and documentation of Marco Avanzini (Chamber 3, Tomb 1);

1986: research Pasquali-Rauss (terrace overlooking the caves); research and documentation of Avanzini (Chamber 3, Tomb 1);

1987: research Pasquali-Rauss;

1988: research Pasquali-Rauss (at the foot of the castle);

1998: Excavations by the Civic Museum of Rovereto (in particular Chamber 3, Tomb 1);

1999: Excavations by the Civic Museum of Rovereto (Chamber 1);

2005: inspection by the Civic Museum of Rovereto (Battisti-Regola); collection of a few finds on the surface inside the caves and verification of continuing looting activity);

2016 and 2020: inspection by the Civic Museum Foundation of Rovereto (M.B.). The continuation of looting in the caves was verified and several potsherds and bones abandoned by the diggers, left at the sides were picked up. Laser surveys made for 3D mapping inside the caves and a topographical survey made of the area of access to them. [31]

[29] Fontana *et al.* 2010; Fontana *et al.* 2012.
[30] Mazzucchi *et al.* 2020.
[31] Measurements made by Michele Zandonati of the Gruppo Grotte E. Roner CAI SAT Rovereto and the I.T.E.T. F.lli Fontana of Rovereto.

2 – The Rovereto Civic Museum Excavations

The research by the Civic Museum of Rovereto carried out between 1998 and 1999 involved principally Chambers 1, 2 and 3, as stated. Chamber 4 was not explored due to logistic difficulties and the enormous quantity of stone of various dimensions requiring removal. The latter, in fact, is in the form of a long deep gully opening out from Chamber 3 (see **Figure 3**).

The stratigraphy of Chambers 2 and 3 already appeared partially damaged by decades of looting activity. The sondages effected by amateurs since the 1960s, described in the previous chapter, even if partially documented, have further complicated the situation, making it difficult to interpret the stratigraphy correctly.

In the course of the excavation campaign of 1998, which primarily concerned Chamber 3, precarious environmental conditions were added to the problems just described. In fact, it entailed a laborious excavation inside an intricate labyrinth of caves. The narrow passages, the extreme humidity and the difficulties encountered in setting up adequate lighting complicated both the logistics for transporting the earth and excavation tools and the making of precise, complete graphic and photographic documentation. Burial remains were spotted, for example, within a cavity where it was only possible to dig lying down or on all fours (the height of the vault was no greater than 50–60 cm; see **Figure 5**).

During the second excavation campaign, in the summer of 1999, inside Chamber 1, conditions were decidedly better. The haphazard accumulation of landslide boulders in this place generated an ample, sub-rectangular space of about 40 square metres affording comfortable standing chamber and a direct exit to the outside (**Figures 4 and 13**). Given this ease of access (**Figure 9**), the lower humidity and ample space available, a more accurate documentation of the excavation could be made.

All the earth removed in both excavation campaigns was sieved in water with mesh of 0.5 cm and then submitted to flotation.

Excavation campaign 1998

During the first excavation campaign research on the surfaces outside the caves complex and inside Chambers 1, 2 and 3 was carried out beforehand. A small sondage was made in the latter chamber inside a low, narrow cavity which extended towards the south (defined as Chamber 3 - Zone 1), the selfsame area which yielded the burial remains already found in 1969 (see **Figure 3**). Inside, two distinct areas have been identified, containing an abundance of human bones, which were defined Tomb 1 and Tomb 2. In the first case various bones still partially anatomically connected were clearly visible. Tomb 2 on the other hand, looked like an apparently random accumulation of human bones just at entrance of the cavity that houses Tomb 1.

Tomb 1, as already stated, previously disturbed and partly damaged by interventions in the 1960s and 1970s and by looters, was found partially covered with dislodged stones, no longer in their original position. Reports from the period of the first discoveries however refer to a small mound of stones which covered human remains. When completely excavated it revealed bones belonging to a youth and anatomically disconnected bones of other individuals.[1] Besides bone remains, numerous fragments of potsherds were found, including Polada-type mug sherds and truncated cone pottery beakers; three pottery spindle whorls; flint flakes and flint tools, many altered by heat; a smelting slag; some shell and stone necklace beads and many baked clay fragments.

[1] For further information on burials and the human remains discovered see Chapter 4.

Figure 5: Chamber 3, Zone 1: cavity entrance.

The so called 'Tomb 2' (US 18),[2] which emerged from the eastern section of the old excavations, appeared as a small heap of stones of various sizes mixed with human and animal remains, as well as potsherds and flint flakes.

Inside the same chamber (Chamber 3), just outside the cavity known as 'Zone 1' in an area called 'Zone 2', there were found numerous potsherds (rims, walls, bottoms, handles), a red deer antler fragment, flint waste (including also numerous flint flakes altered by heat), a hollow-based arrowhead and some baked clay fragments.

The stratigraphy

At the beginning of the excavation campaign of the Civic Museum of Rovereto the cavity known as Zone 1, inside Chamber 3, appeared extensively excavated. Before proceeding with the excavation therefore the exposed section at the bottom of the cavity had to be cleaned and straightened. Here a succession of eight layers superimposed one over the other were visible, distinguishable mainly thanks to the different quantities of charcoal fragments present within a silty sand matrix as they were otherwise relatively uniform. At its base were found the human bones already referred to, some of which were still anatomically connected.

The excavation of the grave could then proceed: this appeared still partly bordered by a series of medium-sized (10 to 50 cm axis) limestone pebbles. The sepulchral structure was made up of both a small mound of stones (almost entirely demolished already in 1969), and a shallow trench (max 15 cm) in which the human bones lay.

[2] The abbreviation 'US', which in Italian means 'Unità Stratigrafica', refers to an archaeological context/layer.

Almost all the layers covering the small mound had a slight concavity in their centre, where the thickness was greater, and tended to taper off and rise towards the sides of the cavity. All the layers above the grave, that is from US 1 to US 8, have yielded numerous charcoal fragments and several finds of pottery and bones, characterized by their high rate of fragmentation, particularly if compared with those found in the context of the grave (US 9 and US 10). In these last layers, in fact, the potsherds were found to be well preserved and without trace of post-depositional destructive episodes of either natural or anthropic origin.

In this sequence the only strata not to have been contaminated in any way by excavation activities preceding the campaign of the Civic Museum of Rovereto in 1998 are US 10, carbonaceous layer rich in finds, on which the graves were placed, and US 11, a sterile layer of natural origin positioned directly above the great mass of the landslide which serves as the floor of Chamber 3. Fortunately, however the human bones (US 14), the sepulchral structure (US 15 and 16) and a carbonaceous layer formed in contact with the bones directly beneath the tumulus of stones (US 9) were marginally intact, thus preserving the possibility of a realistic reading of the original stratigraphy.

Here follows the list of the layers, a concise description of them, the planimetry, the section and the corresponding Harris matrix diagram (**Figures 6, 7, 8**). It must be remembered that some data have only been obtained from observation and from cleaning the section already exposed at the beginning of the excavations by the Civic Museum of Rovereto. The first seven layers were visible only in section; the eighth was visible in section and was also excavated stratigrafically; layers 9, 10 and 11, related to the grave, were not visible in the section of the bottom of the cavity because it was about 35 cm in front of the section. For this reason, the reconstruction proposed here is a cumulative section that unites the upper portion, excavated between the 1960s and 1980s, to the lower portion, excavated in 1998 (**Figure 7**). In the drawing the original cover of stones has also been reconstructed following the descriptive accounts of the first excavations, the excavations of the 1980s and the visible traces still well preserved in 1998. However, not represented here is the great cut US 13, effected in 1969 to partly empty the cavity called Zone 1. At the time this cavity must have appeared almost entirely full and was not excavated in a stratigraphic way.

List US of Zone 1 in Chamber 3

US 1 Pale grey layer of plastic consistency in contact with the vault, maximum thickness 4.5 cm.
Cut by US 12; covers US 2.

US 2 Grey carbonaceous layer of variable thickness (maximum thickness at centre: 25 cm).
Cut by US 12; covered by US 1; covers US 3.

US 3 A grey level definitely paler than the one above (US 2). Abrupt upper limit. An anthropic layer of maximum thickness 7.5 cm. At the interface with the layer below a note indicates the presence of a slim brown-coloured lens which probably signifies the presence of a further layer, not however numbered in the documentation.
Cut by US 12; covered by US 2; covers US 4.

US 4 Thick earthy layer full of pottery and fauna, maximum thickness 15 cm. Very rich in charcoals, unlike the previous ones contains stones.
Cut by US 12; covered by US 3; covers US 5.

US 5 Layer similar to US 3 in colour and consistency. Maximum thickness 9 cm. Sunken and divided at the centre by a carbonaceous lens which implies an origin distinguished by two different phases, difficult to differentiate because of the homogeneity of the matrix.
Cut by US 12; covered by US 4; covers US 6.

US 6 An anthropic layer, greyish brown in colour darker than the previous one, 6–7 cm. in thickness. It contains charcoal (in very small fragments).

Cut by US 12; covered by US 5; covers US 7.

US 7 Layer of silty sand matrix with large fragments of charcoal evident, up to 6 cm axis. It tapers towards the right. Probably eroded or damaged by the layer above.

Cut by US 12; covered by US 6; covers US 8.

US 8 Anthropic layer, grey, silty clay, quite compact, full of small charcoals. Maximum thickness 16 cm. Also damaged by the cut US 12.

Cut by US 12; covered by US 7; covers US 16.

US 9 Carbonaceous level that directly covers the bones of Tomb 1 (US 14). Partially damaged by previous excavations (US 12). Maximum thickness circa 10 cm.

Cut by US 12; covered by US 16; covers US 10 and 14.

US 10 Anthropic layer containing many human bones and artefacts. Maximum thickness circa 8 cm.

Covered by US 9 and 14; fills US 15.

US 11 Sterile layer, clayey greyish yellow, rich in stone debris due to the natural exfoliation of the limestone rock. It represents the original floor of the chamber before anthropic presence. Maximum thickness 12 cm circa.

Cut by US 15; covers US 17.

US 12 Cut of ample dimensions due to excavations carried out between the 1960s and 1980s. The cut also partially damaged the graves in Tomb 1 from which some bones were removed then delivered to the Civic Museum of Rovereto, including the complete skull of a young individual circa 8–10 years old.

Filled by US 13; cut US 1, 2, 3, 4, 5, 6, 7, 8, 9, 14, 16.

US 13 Layer of recent formation resulting from the excavations carried out from 1969 onwards. It partly fills the cut US 12. Mixed up layer rich in charcoals, pottery, animal and human bones. Inside was found a fragment of nylon used as a temporary cover of the old excavations.

Fills US 12.

US 14 Human bones partially connected anatomically deposited in Tomb 1. The bones appear in an excellent state of conservation.

Cut by US 12; covered by US 9; covers US 10.

US 15 Cut of the grave trench. An ovoid shape, it reached a maximum depth of circa 15 cm, a maximum length of circa 120 cm and width of circa 80 cm.

Filled by US 9, 10, 16; Cut US 11.

US 16 Stone structure which delimits the grave trench of Tomb 1. Originally this structure served as a cover thus assuming a tumulus structure.

Cut by US 12; covered by US 8; fills US 15; covers US 9.

US 17 Landslide boulder which served as a floor for the whole of Chamber 3.

Covered by US 11.

US 18 At first (during the excavation) it was defined as 'Tomb 2'. Is a small concentration of stones, artefacts, human and animal bones just at the entrance to the narrow cavity that houses Tomb 1. This layer was only partially excavated during the 1998 excavations. Unfortunately, subsequent illegal excavations have totally erased what remained.

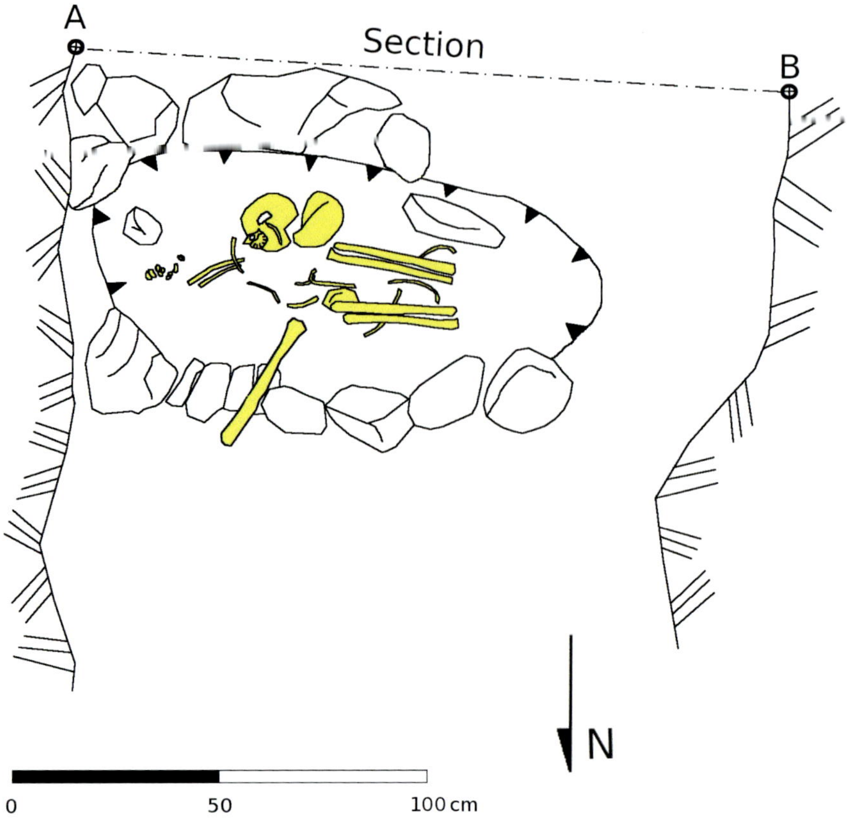

Figure 6: Chamber 3, Zone 1: Tomb 1 plan (A and B are the reference points of the section represented in Figure 7).

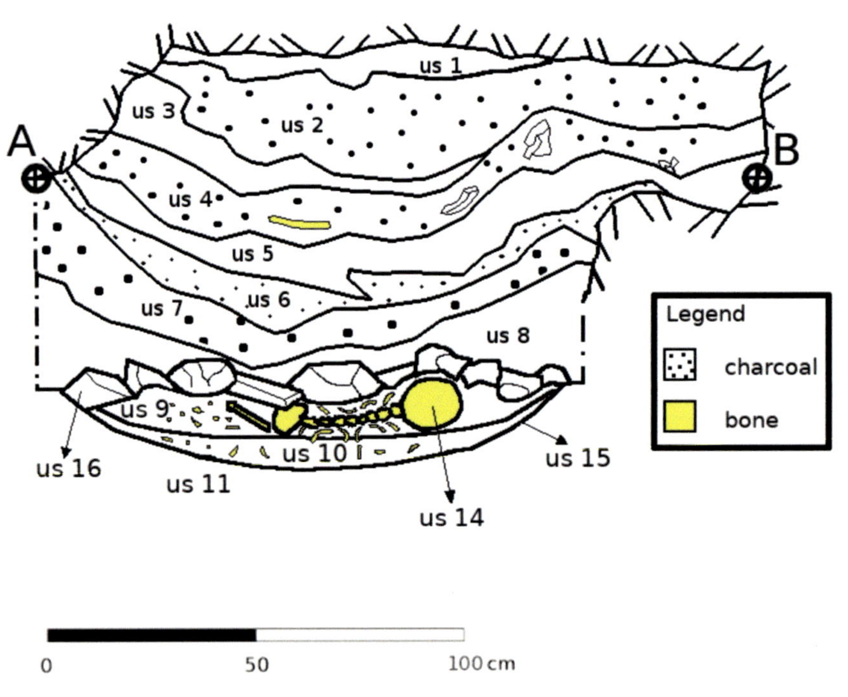

Figure 7: Chamber 3, Zone 1: cumulative section (see Figure 6).

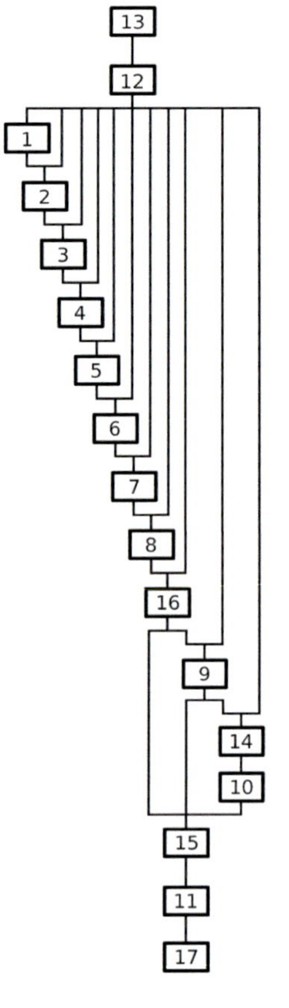

Figure 8: Chamber 3, Zone 1: Harris matrix.

Figure 9: Access corridor to Chamber 1.

Excavation campaign 1999

In 1999 attention was exclusively concentrated on Chamber 1. A sondage two metres by three was performed just inside the entrance (see **Figure 13**, sondage 1999). The chamber floor was circa 40–50 cm lower than the height at which it was before the excavations of the 1970s.[3]

While the demarcation of the sondage (200 × 300 cm) was taking place, a survey was carried out which involved all of Chamber 1 (US 0). Among the numerous artefacts which emerged were several fragments of pottery vessels definitely ascribable to the EBA and some tools in stone and bone.

Before starting on the excavation, all the southern part of the chamber was covered by a virtual grid made up of one metre sided squares, indicated with letters on a N-S line and numbers going E-W (see the green grid with dashed line in **Figure 13**).

Within the sondage, after removing some densely carbonaceous levels rich in artefacts, two layers containing numerous stones of great dimensions came to light. One (US 8) with every probability referable to a partial natural collapse of the vault, the other (US 4), semicircular in form, was most probably of artificial origin (see **Figures 10, 11, 12**).

The first layer removed, thickness circa 5–10 cm (US 1), certainly mixed up several times and trodden on by random explorers, consisted of a disturbed heap of stones in a silty sand matrix and presented many prehistoric pottery artefacts typified by a high degree of fragmentation.

Below this there was a dark silty clay level, highly organic, almost without stones, with an abundant amount of flint, bones and pottery remains (US 2) which covered a greyish sandy matrix with small clasts inside (US 5). Two charcoal lenses, US 9 and 10, found inside US 2, suggest that the layer is really the result of different successive accumulations, difficult to distinguish in detail because of the uniformity of the matrix and inclusions. Moving down through the stratigraphy of the sondage, a dark layer of ash and a large concentration of artefacts was found (US 3). US 2 and 3 were observed to be inclined from south to north (they dropped in height from the entrance to the chamber towards the back) having accumulated following the formation of the stony layer beneath (US 4), this too steeply sloping. The latter formed a conoid with its highest apex facing south-west, that is in the direction of the entrance to the chamber. The difference in height between the apex and the base was 60 cm, while the greatest radius identified was 1,80 cm. The layer directly in contact with this heap of stones, very carbonaceous and rich in artefacts (US 3), as already stated, yielded also a perfectly intact stone wrist guard in serpentinite (**305**).

US 11, the last layer identified but not excavated, apparently covered by US 4, was light grey in colour with a horizontal trend. At the northern edge of the sondage, finally, two large holes were visible (US 6 and 7) partly filled by some big rocks (US 8) which may, for natural reasons, have fallen

[3] Data obtained from documentation of excavation of the Centro Studi Lagarini (unpublished documents kept by the Rovereto Civic Museum Foundation).

from the sides of the chamber. Later US 5 went to fill what remained and also partly cover the rocks on the ground. In the lower left of the section C-D (**Figure 11**) US 2 also seems to partially cover the base of one of the rocks. This would create a stratigraphic paradox unless we consider the fact that the weight of a rock of such proportions could have compressed the layer below US 2 partially sinking into it.

In total thirteen stratigraphic units were documented. At first the abrupt external limit of the US 4, the position of the stones, the quantity and quality of the material discovered led to surmising that it could have been a great funerary mound. But its orientation and inclination suggested also the hypothesis of an artificial accumulation produced by the dumping of material from the inhabited area outside the chamber. In fact, its semicircular shape could be attributed to a typical conoid made of debris.

The interruption of the campaign of 1999 prevented further in-depth study or broadening the excavation area. Since all the stratigraphic sequence is strongly inclined towards the inside of the chamber, the oldest level brought to light remains in any case precisely the deposit US 4 in the south-west corner and the greyish level beneath (US 11), neither of which have yet been investigated.

Here follows a complete list of the stratigraphic units and a brief description, completed by a composite plan, two sections of the sondage and the Harris matrix (**Figures 10, 11, 12**).

List US of the sondage carried out in 1999 in Chamber 1

US 0 Collection of artefacts resulting from a first superficial cleaning.

US 1 Superficial layer characterized by a displaced heap of stones in a silty sandy matrix, thickness 5–10 cm. Abundant pottery remains present.

Covers US 2, 5, 8.

US 2 Layer with silty clay matrix, highly organic dark grey in colour. Tends to increase in thickness from west to east (from few cm to half a metre). Almost without inclusions. The few calcareous stones present are no greater than 10–20 cm in diameter. Flints, bones and abundant pottery remain present. The US was completely excavated only in the eastern portion of the sondage (see section C-D, **Figure 10**).

Covered by US 1, 5 and 8; cut by US 6 and 7; covers US 3.

US 3 Similar layer to US 2 but with greater concentration of artefacts and abundant charcoals and ash. Thickness between 6 and 18 cm.

Covered by US 2; covers US 4 and US 11.

US 4 Semicircular structure consisting of sharp-edged limestone fragments of various dimensions, which reach 50 cm at maximum length. The layer is of a conoidal shape with its apex in the direction of the entrance to the chamber (S-O). The difference in height between the apex and the base is circa 60 cm. The southern and western sides of the structure were not excavated since they were outside the limits of the sondage.

Covered by US 3; covers US 11.

US 5 Layer with greyish sandy matrix with small stone inclusions. It starts at about the centre of the sondage and develops towards the south-east, where it reaches a thickness of circa 50 cm. The layer is clearly visible in section C-D whereas absent in the western section A-B (**Figure 11**).

Covered by US 1; covers US 2 and 8; fills US 6 and 7.

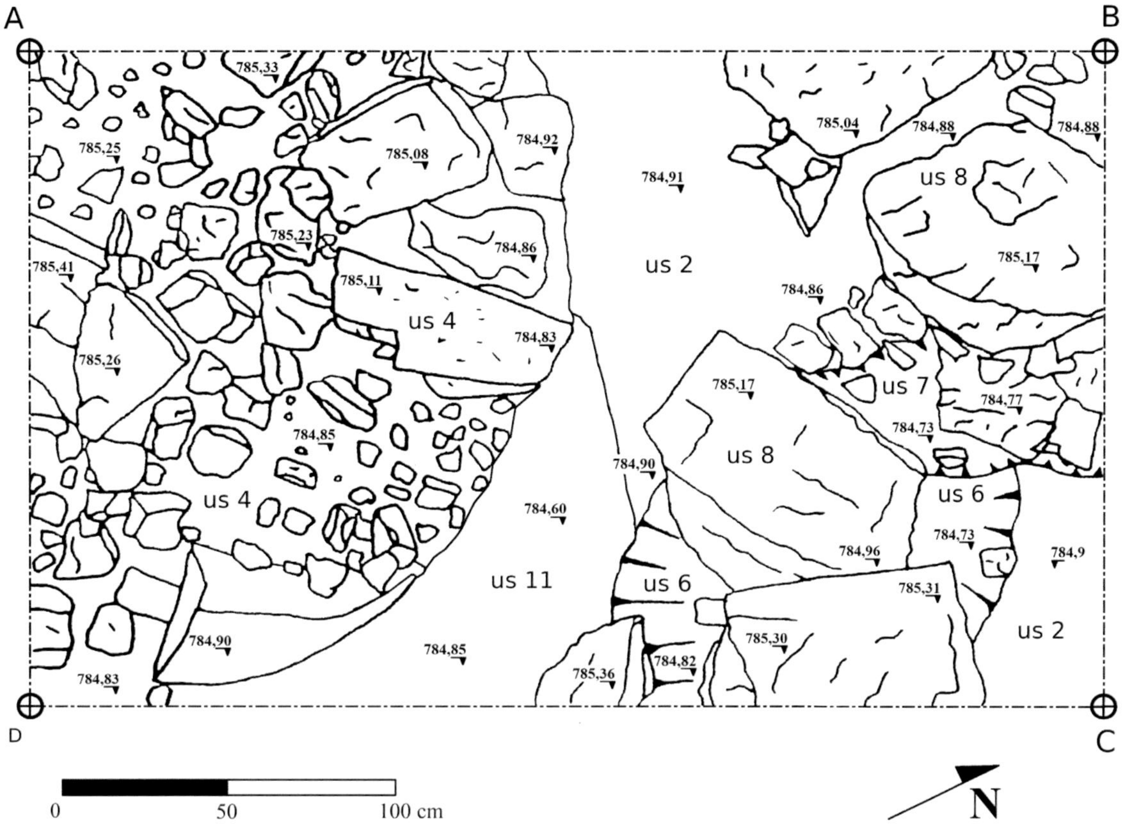

Figure 10: Chamber 1, 1999 sondage: composite plan (the elevations indicated are in meters above sea level).

US 6 Large hole of sub-circular shape in the N-E portion of the sondage.
Filled by US 5 and 8; cuts US 2.

US 7 Small hole in the N-E portion of the sondage.
Filled by US 5 and 8; cuts US 2.

US 8 Large rocks (maximum length 80 cm) which may have fallen from the sides of the chamber positioned in the northern portion of the sondage.
Covered by US 1 and 5; fills US 6 and 7; covers US 2.

US 9 Dark grey lens, slightly carbonaceous visible inside US 2.

US 10 Carbonaceous horizontal lens visible inside US 2.

US 11 Pale grey layer not investigated at the base of structure US 4.
Covered by US 3 and 4.

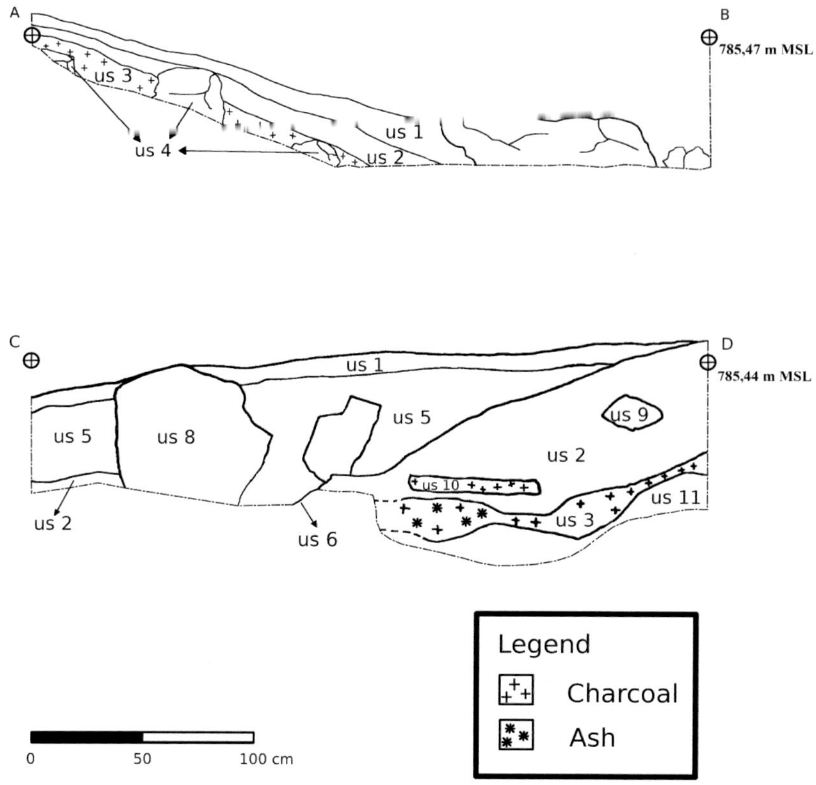

Figure 11: Chamber 1, 1999 sondage: sections A-B and C-D (see Figures 10 and 13).

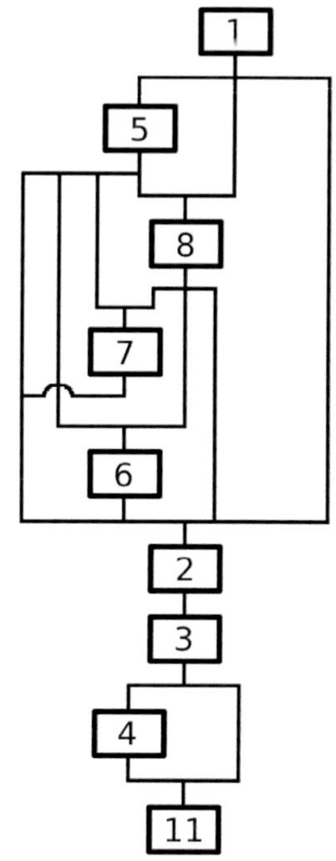

Figure 12: Chamber 1, 1999 sondage: Harris matrix.

Inspections between 2016 and 2018

Between 2016 and 2020 one of the authors of this volume (M.B.), in the course of explorations intended to recover measurements, discovered and reported new illegal sondages carried out inside Chamber 3, Zone 2 and inside Chamber 1. These were mostly small sondages 50 cm in depth and circa 40 cm in width. The largest sondage was opened at the entrance to Chamber 1 a quadrangular excavation measuring 180x130 cm by 60 cm in depth.[4] Fortunately, that sondage involved in large part the refilled ground with sterile earth made at the end of the excavation in 1999. Even so, particularly at its south-eastern edges, numerous artefacts seem to have been removed from a highly carbonaceous layer probably identifiable as US 3. We know the probable nature of the finds because numerous large fragments of pottery were recovered on the edge of the excavation and taken to the Civic Museum of Rovereto[5] and here published.[6] These artefacts come without doubt from the squares A1, A2, B1 and B2 (see **Figure 13**) and, it is extremely likely, from US 3, as stated.

Inside Chamber 3, however, half way along the passage leading to the deep gully known as Chamber 4, another illegal sondage was identified which had emptied a natural, rocky cavity at the base of a boulder. The cavity has a sub-rectangular shape approximately one metre by two and circa 30 cm. deep. In it, a carbonaceous layer rich in ash and fauna has been excavated but only the mixed up soil left behind could be analysed. From this ground a piece of baked clay was also recovered: sub-circular in shape, clearly manipulated, it will be dealt with in more depth in

[4] The edges of the illegal sondage in Chamber 1 are shown with a continuous line in **Figure 13**.
[5] Reported to the Ufficio Beni Archeologici, Province of Trento.
[6] See finds n. 207–209, 211, 213, 216–221, 225–226.

Figure 13: Chamber 1: cave plan with placement of 1974 and 1999 sondages (black dot-dashed line) and of the recent illegal excavation (red dashed line). The virtual grid created before the excavation is represented with black dashed lines.

later chapters. This was one of the few parts in Chamber 3 still with an anthropic heap of earth over its bed of natural limestone debris. Whereas at other points one walks directly on the bare rock of the landslide boulders beneath, since the continuous dripping of water from the vault at the points of greatest incline probably makes the natural sediments caused by the flaking limestone slide towards the sinkhole in Chamber 4.

During the survey of 2018, thanks to the collaboration with the Cave Group E. Roner CAI SAT Rovereto and in particular with Michele Zandonati, a three-dimensional survey using laser instrumentation[7] was carried out. This survey confirmed the validity of the plans and sections already published during the 1980s[8] (**Figure 3**) and above all the formulation of the hypothesis that the cavity housing the grave inside Chamber 3 (Zone 1) could be a sort of low corridor that originally led into Chamber 1. From the 3D survey, in fact, it can be noted that, completely emptying the cavity of Tomb 1 and then continuing to the south for a little over a metre, one should be able to emerge in the northernmost part of Chamber 1.[9] If it were like this, Zone 1 inside Chamber 3 would have been much more accessible and, consequently, the deposition of the inhumed and connected burial rituals would certainly have been performed in more favourable environmental conditions than those of today. In this regard, it should be noted that the only human bone found in Chamber 1 comes from the very bottom of the chamber, not far from the possible direct access to Chamber 3.

[7] Hardware used: Disto X2; Software: Blender; algorithm of integration elaborated by Michele Zandonati of Gruppo Grotte E. Roner CAI SAT Rovereto.

[8] Chiocchetti 1985.

[9] Detail that can also be observed, although in two dimensions, from section A-B in **Figure 3**.

3 – The Material Culture

The Castel Corno Caves have yielded a great number of artefacts during both the excavation and the washing and sifting phases. Greater part of the most minute material was recovered at the earth washing station just outside the caves. Some was also discovered in the laboratory, in checking the already sifted material.

Many of these finds, as will be seen later, can be attributed to an initial phase of the Bronze Age (between the end of 3rd and beginning 2nd millennium BC).

Compiling a total of the artefacts recovered from the site between 1969 and today, now deposited at the Civic Museum of Rovereto, enables us to list 4716 potsherds, 1763 flints, eight of other types of stone finds, two of metal, eight of fired clay, 825 fragments of baked clay and 17 of animal raw material (bone, antler and shell).

The pottery

In total, as stated, 4716 potsherds have been catalogued. This includes all the material from the excavation campaigns of 1998–1999 and a minimal part from preceding excavations (between 1969 and 1987). Out of the total number of potsherds 1116 identifiable fragments and 3600 unidentifiable can be counted; the overall weight of the latter is about 43.528 kg.

As regards the finds' specific place of origin, approximately 49% were discovered in Chamber 1, 29% in Chamber 3, 10% in Chamber 2 and lastly 12% were found outside the caves. It is evident that a disproportionate quantity of material was found in Chamber 1 compared with that coming from other chambers or external areas. This depends in the first place on the better access to that chamber in comparison with the others and, therefore, on the fact that it was possible to carry out a more ample and systematic excavation there. Secondly it is to be considered that, in the same way, this chamber was more accessible in antiquity too, compared with the other three, and so probably much more frequented, as will be seen in the subsequent chapters.

As to the fabric quality and the surface treatment, the sample appears fairly heterogeneous. The statistical population taken into consideration in this volume consists of 258 fragments. Given the general uniformity of the density and dimension of the inclusions, the pottery was subdivided into just three large fabric classes: 'fine', 'medium' and 'rough'.[1] Of these 85% have a medium fabric, 9% a fine fabric and 6% coarse.

Most of the pottery (59.8%) has a regular surface, that is uniform and without evident roughness. As regards the surface treatment, pottery which has undergone only smoothing (both inside and outside) predominates, altogether 71% of the total, followed by 9.7% which has a burnished surface and by 9.3% with a coarse surface (untreated).[2] The remaining 10% are to be subdivided into various combinations of treatment, distinguishing between inner and outer surfaces.

Of particular interest is the presence of dark-burnished pottery, typical especially of small and medium sized globular or biconical mugs, common in the tradition of the Polada culture.[3]

[1] On the basis of the schematization proposed in the Munsell Soil Color Charts 1994 it was decided to define 'fine' the fabric having up to 1% density of inclusions, 'medium' that between 2% and 5%, 'rough' that type of fabric with a percentage of inclusions between 5% and 7% (finds with a percentage of inclusions above 7% are not documented).

[2] For the definition of the various surface treatments see Forte 2019.

[3] Dal Ri and Tecchiati 1996; Leonardi *et al.* 2015, p. 285.

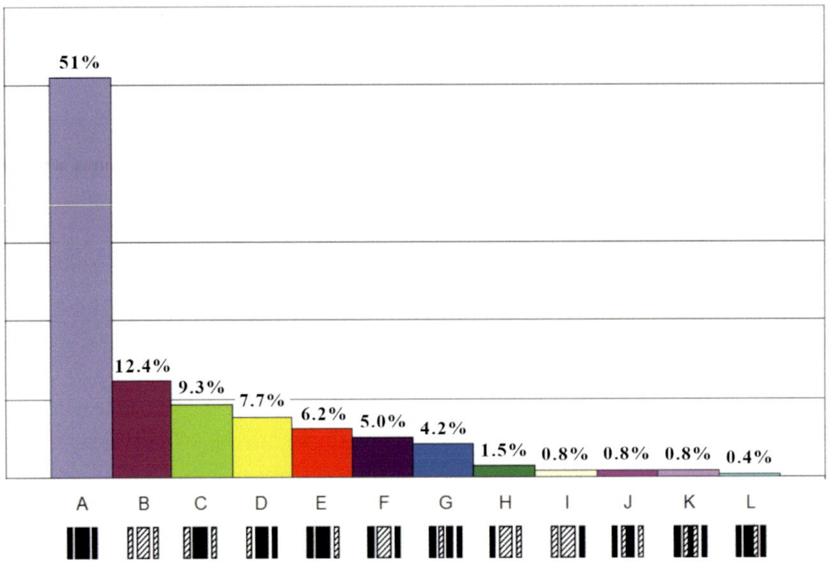

Figure 14: Correlation between surfaces and fabrics color. There are 12 different kinds of fabric recorded in the site. In the drawings below the outer surface is the one to the left. (Image from Regola 2005).

Since the pottery examined presents a vast range of colours with many different tones (even on just one small surface of a single pottery fragment), it is difficult to use objective chromatic references like the Munsell Soil Color Charts. In the study phase it was therefore decided to put all the colours together in two large, generic categories: light and dark.[4] Analysing possible colour comparisons, there emerged a clear prevalence of fragments traceable to type A (**Figure 14**), thus characterized by dark surfaces (inner and outer) with a dark core, probably indicating having been fired in a reducing context (closed or covered), that is devoid of oxygen. The percentage of pottery with a light core and surface (type B) is notably less. All the other combinations are represented percentage-wise in a fairly homogeneous way. Particularly interesting are the types G-J-K-L in which can be noted a reddening of the fabric colour in the zone defined as *margin*, that is in proximity to one or both of the outer surfaces, which on the contrary are very dark. In this case perhaps it could be surmised that a sudden intake of oxygen took place, followed by its decisive reduction in the final stage of firing (opening and closing of the fire pit?).

Forms, accessories and typology

All the ceramic artefacts were found fragmented. However, compared with material brought to light in contemporary adjacent settlements,[5] the pottery of Castel Corno can be distinguished both for its lower fragmentation index and the excellent preservation of the surfaces, even if in some cases they were coated by a patina of calcium carbonate. The quality of conservation of these surfaces is determined by the particular context of their deposition: a cave, in which the stability of temperature and humidity and protection from atmospheric agents are guaranteed. The average size of the fragments, however, is due to the fact that these cavities were probably seldom frequented, consequently little affected by being trodden on.

Among the fragments selected, analyzed, drawn and published here, most plentiful are the many medium and large size vessels, which include jars, ollas and dolia (53%),[6] followed by beakers (15%), mugs (15%) and lastly bowls (7%).

[4] Considered light are the following tones: reddish, light brown, light grey, yellowish; all other colours are defined dark.
[5] As for example in the settlements of the Pizzini at Castellano (Battisti 2001) and at Dosso Alto at Borgo Sacco (Trinco 2020).
[6] For the vessel class definitions used in this volume see appendix 'Vessel classes', at the end of the volume.

The shapes of the medium and large size vessels vary from truncated-cone shaped profiles to more or less ovoid shaped profiles then coming finally to the ollas, with their strongly convex walls. Their dimensions vary notably, from 16 cm in diameter at the mouth (**38**) up to a maximum of 54 cm (**21**). The rims are generally straight with a rounded or flat edge; everted or inverted rims are less frequent. Some of these rims have been decorated with fingertip or stick impressions (**5, 196**). The same identical forms are documented for the medium-small vessels which fall into the category of beakers or small jars. Many have horizontal applied cordons on the walls and other applied elements such as lug handles and knob handles. Dolia, jars and beakers with similar forms and decorations are very common and transversally present in the Early and Middle Bronze Age in northern Italy. For a regional comparison we can cite as an example the pile dwelling site at Fiavé, especially for the great typological variety documented, due not only to the considerable number of vessels found, but even for their completeness.[7]

Also documented are plastic decorations, much more complex than those so far described: segments of applied cordons both horizontal (e.g. **40, 41**) and vertical (e.g. **47**) and intricate patterns with an interlacing of horizontal, vertical, twisting or zig-zag cordons (e.g. **143**). Similar decorations are documented at Pizzini di Castellano[8] and at Dosso Alto di Borgo Sacco,[9] in the area of Vallagarina, and for example at Lasino, [10] Ledro[11] and Fiavé[12] in south-western Trentino.

Some jars have pierced holes in a horizontal row under the rim, often accompanied by horizontal applied cordons (**125–129**). This typology, whose general function is the subject of debate,[13] is attested to in numerous contemporary sites, within and outside the region, characteristic of the Polada culture *stricto sensu* or the horizon which follows it in the EBA II[14] (e.g. Fiavé,[15] Pizzini di Castellano,[16] Dosso Alto,[17] Ledro,[18] Monte Covolo,[19] Lasino,[20] Lucone di Polpenazze,[21] Lavagnone,[22] Montesei di Serso,[23] Riparo Gaban[24] and Ledro[25]). The lug handles in many cases are attached directly on the cordons. The most represented forms are: horned lug handles (e.g. **9,106**), sub-triangular lug handles (e.g. **7, 113**) and truncated-cone shaped knob handles (e.g. **28, 111**). Also present are vertical lug handles under the rim (e.g. **43, 46**). The jars in most cases are characterized by their smoothed or coarse irregular surfaces and a medium or coarse fabric, whereas burnished surfaces and fine fabrics are completely missing. The percentage incidence of jars and dolia of various sizes (54%) and the poor quality of their craftsmanship is in line with a daily usage compatible with widely employed consumer goods.

The most valued vessels are constituted by the mugs. Of 38 fragments illustrated here, eight have a globular body, three a biconical body and for a further 27 it has not been possible to reconstruct the profile. The diameter at the mouth varies between 6 and 18 cm, including the category of the bigger mugs, also definable as small ollas. Of particular importance are the 9 mugs of a notably small size (a maximum diameter under 8 cm). Shapes of comparable sizes have

[7] See for example the pile dwelling site of Fiavé (Perini 1994).
[8] Battisti 2001, plate 14:1, plate 31:1.
[9] Marzatico 1987, p. 60:307, 515; p. 67:524; p. 69:275; p. 71:245; p. 72:328; see also Trinco 2020, plate 16:3; plate 18:4; plate 24:4.
[10] Tecchiati 1991, plate 32:1.
[11] Rageth 1974, plate 78:8, plate 86:1.
[12] Perini 1994, plate 64:882.
[13] Kashina and Petrova 2019; Tews 2016; Camps and Rostan 1982.
[14] According to the chronology proposed in de Marinis 1999: EBA IA (2200–2000 BC), EBA IB (2000–1900 BC), EBA IC (1900–1800 BC), EBA II 1800–1650 BC).
[15] Perini 1994, plate 32:320, plate 34:467, plate 31:433, plate 38:538.
[16] Battisti 2001, plate 19:5.
[17] Marzatico 1987, fig. 10:465, 470, 526, fig. 13:336, 342, 447; Trinco 2020, plate 13:4, Tav.19:1.
[18] Rageth 1974, plates 76, 77, 78.
[19] Barfield 1974, fig. 5.
[20] Tecchiati 1991, plate 30:6–8, plate 58.
[21] Bocchio 1988, plate IX:4.
[22] Rapi 2007, figs 31, 32.
[23] Perini 1973a, plate II.
[24] Pedrotti 1981, plate 48:3.
[25] Rageth 1974, plates 87–88.

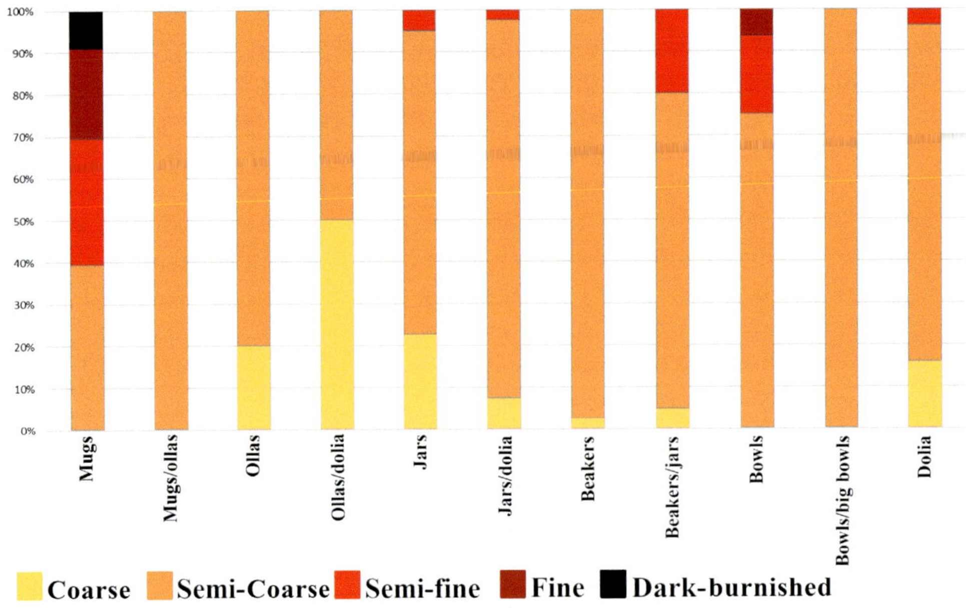

Figure 15: Correlation between vessel and quality classes.

also been found in other contemporary regional sites (e.g. Fiavé,[26] Pizzini di Castellano,[27] Dosso Alto[28]).

One of these mugs has an elbow handle with a short axe-shaped appendage slightly raised above the rim (**84**), comparable with shapes found in the site, is datable in the EBA in general[29] but mainly in the EBA II (e.g. Fiavé,[30] Lavagnone[31]). The handles with axe-shaped appendage in reality already appear in the oldest phases of the EBA[32] but become more widespread in successive centuries.

Lastly attention should be drawn to a small globular mug, well preserved in comparison with other specimens, with a slightly everted rim and strap handle (**Figure 16**). The profile is only slightly sinuous and the bottom is wide and flat (**60**). The vessel finds parallels relatively similar in sites of EBA at Pizzini,[33] Ledro,[34] Barche di Solferino,[35] Lucone di Polpenazze,[36]

Figure 16: Mug from Chamber 1, US 5 (number 84 in the plates).

[26] Perini 1994, plate 8:124, 142;
[27] Battisti 2001, plate 3:9.
[28] Marzatico 1987, fig. 12:292; Trinco 2020, plate 15:2.
[29] Tecchiati 1991, p. 53:1 and p. 37:7.
[30] Perini 1994, plate 50:743, plate 57:816.
[31] de Marinis 2000, fig. 55:8, fig. 56:6, 8.
[32] Leonardi *et al.* 2015, p. 2090 fig. 6a; Rapi 2007, fig. 21:43, 49, 51.
[33] Battisti 2001, plate 27:3.
[34] Rageth 1974, plate 30:6.
[35] Fasani 1984, p. 493:1.
[36] Bocchio 1988, plate V:9; Guerreschi 1981, plate XVI:329.

Cattaragna[37] and Canar.[38] Its shape also falls within the typological classification 'bo6a' of the pottery of Nössing.[39] Nevertheless, based on a comparison with mugs closer to our specimen in shape, identifiable among the grave goods of the cemetery of Haid[40] and in the phase EBA AI of Lavagnone,[41] we might think of ascribing this artefact to an initial phase of the EBA. Most of the mugs found in the site of Castel Corno Caves are of superior craftsmanship with fabric and surface treatment of an excellent quality (**Figure 15**).

Recognisable among the material are 18 potsherds belonging to various sized and shaped bowls, having walls with a more or less convex profile, which come under the most common artefact classes in the region in the EBA (e.g. Fiavé,[42] Ledro[43]). One bowl has an applied cordon which curves several times at 90° partially framing a vertical lug handle near the rim (**223**). Although pertinent comparisons have not been found, we underline the fact that the plastic decorations which bend at a right angle are present in other sites, in layers dating back to the EBA, for example in the sites of Fiavé[44] and Canàr.[45]

Particularly interesting is a bowl featuring three vertical lug handles, two of which are horizontally pierced (**77**), whose profile can be compared with vessels coming from Lavagnone[46] and the nearby site at Colombo di Mori.[47] In the layers of EBA IC of Lavagnone was found a truncated-cone shaped vessel of shallow depth with a vertical lug handle horizontally pierced in every way similar to those of the vessel of Castel Corno.[48] Nonetheless the specimen discovered here does not have comparisons in terms of shape and its functional interpretation remains in doubt. The presence of holes in the vertical lug handles and the particular context of its finding could lead to its being seen as a sort of lamp that could have been suspended from cords. In view of the small size of the vessel, functionally however it would be difficult to imagine a live flame a short distance from the cords suspending it. Given the ritual nature of the site, the hypothesis of a different function could be made linked to the emanation of essences and therefore its possible use imagined as a censer, although no evident traces of burning have been found inside.

Among the fragments of beakers whose profile it is possible to reconstruct there is documentation of truncated-cone (e.g. **42, 204**) and cylindrical shapes (e.g. **40, 43, 47, 48, 50**), while the closed shapes with slightly convex walls (**39, 51, 118**) are rarer. At a decorative level the beakers are characterized by various forms of plastic decoration often intersecting: horizontal and vertical cordons (e.g. **44, 47**), vertical lug handles (e.g. **43, 118**) and knob handles (e.g. **40, 42**). The horizontal lug handles are present only on the larger beakers, comparable in size to a small jar (e.g. **115, 116, 117**). Similar forms are documented in various coeval sites at a regional level (e.g. Fiavé, Lasino,[49] Ledro,[50] Dosso Alto di Borgo Sacco[51]). In some cases, handled beakers (**51, 161, 206**) are also documented. One of these, with a closed shape and an elbow handle attached on a horizzontal cordon (**51**), can be compared with vessels from Dosso Alto di Borgo Sacco,[52] Lasino[53] and Cattaragna.[54]

[37] Aspes 1972, plate II:4.
[38] Bellintani, 1987, plate 1:1.
[39] Tecchiati, in preparation.
[40] Reitberger 2008, e.g. p. 104 Tomb 65.
[41] Rapi 2007, p. 147, fig. 18 No.1.
[42] Perini 1994, plates 13–14.
[43] Rageth 1974, plate 69.
[44] Perini 1994, plate 38:532, plate 66:916, 923.
[45] de Marinis *et al.* 2015, p. 284, fig. 3: 5,7.
[46] Perini 1988, plate 3:8; de Marinis 2000, p. 104, fig. 44:1.
[47] Anzelini *et al.* 1972; p. 37:65.
[48] Rapi 2007, p. 157, fig. 23:80.
[49] Tecchiati 1991.
[50] Rageth 1974.
[51] Marzatico 1987.
[52] Marzatico 1987, fig. 13:361.
[53] Tecchiati 1991, plate 52:2.
[54] Aspes 1972, plate V:1.

The least represented shape is that of the ollas, with just 12 recognisable fragments: these are large biconical vessels with rounded carination. The diameter at the mouth varies from circa 20 cm to 30 cm. Some have straight rims on a distinct neck (**88, 92, 94**), others everted rims which ideally continue the vessel's sinuous profile (**90, 93**). As for shape and size they can be compared with ollas from sites within the region (e.g. Dosso Alto,[55] Colombo di Mori,[56] Ledro,[57] Fiavé[58]) and outside the region (e.g. Lavagnone[59]). Documented are horizontal applied cordons (**90, 112, 113**), lug handles placed on the widest part of the vessel (**97**), on the upper body of the same (**112, 113**) or near the rim (**98**). In the case of a very large olla (or dolium) there is an elbow handle with a short-horned appendage (**160**) attached on two horizontal cordons. Given its size it is probable that there was another similar handle on the opposite side thus making it an ovoid amphora which can be compared, for example, with layer 'D' of Lucone di Polpenazze,[60] Barche di Solferino[61] and the horizon of Lavagnone 3.[62]

As regards the decorative aspect we would underline the total absence of incised decorations, which are, however, present in the nearby coeval site of Pizzini di Castellano[63] and in the EBA layers of Dosso Alto.[64]

On the other hand, the plastic decorations are plentiful, some of them quite rare in the Italian panorama of the EBA. Three short parallel vertical cordons joined above, applied to decorate a big beaker with a slightly ovoid body (**34**), for example, constitute a particular case which can be compared, though only vaguely similar, with the series of three vertical cordons present in the last phase of the EBA at Lavagnone,[65] at Fiavé[66] and at Montesei di Serso.[67] In the examples cited, however, the horizontal cordon continues along the whole perimeter of the vessel while in the case of Castel Corno it constitutes just a short connecting bridge between the three vertical cordons.

Another, apparently unpublished, type of plastic decoration is distinguished by a short wavy cordon (tracing a sort of 'omega') positioned immediately below a small knob attached on a horizontal cordon. This typology is documented on two fragments of jars certainly not belonging to the same vessel (**130, 131**). The decoration, which in both cases is placed just below the rim, finds approximate comparison in the EBA II layers of the site of the Montesei di Serso,[68] in the site of Polada[69] and also at Colombo di Mori,[70] even if they have a zig-zag pattern (a sort of 'W') and not a wavy pattern. Similar decorations are found on some vessels belonging to the Austrian culture of Wieselburg.[71] An elaboration of the same pattern, where the small knob above is linked to the wavy cordon, is found at the nearby site of Pizzini di Castellano.[72]

Particularly interesting is the base sherd of a probably large bowl with a plastic decoration consisting of a cross inscribed in a circle which also serves as a foot (**246**). It is, in fact, a typology absent in the province of Trento and quite rare in general. It is sporadically present in some sites

[55] Marzatico 1987, fig. 11.
[56] Anzelini *et al.* 1972, p. 35:159.
[57] Rageth 1974, plate 71:3.
[58] Perini 1994, plate 78:1102, plate 19:290, plate 20:303.
[59] Rapi 2007, figs 35–36.
[60] Bocchio 1988, plate VII:3; Perini 1988, plate III:10.
[61] Fasani 1984, p. 496:11.
[62] Perini 1988 plate III:10; Rapi 2020, p. 54 fig. 50, plate 34:251.
[63] Battisti 2001, plate 30:3 and 6, plate 31:4–6, plate 40:3.
[64] Marzatico 1987, fig. 9:509 and 15; Trinco 2020, plate 16:1, plate 18:2, plate 22:2.
[65] Cazzanelli 2007, p. 205, fig. 7:78.
[66] Perini 1994, plate 82:1169.
[67] Perini 1972, fig. 8:98.
[68] Perini 1972, fig. 8:100.
[69] Barich 1971, p. 133 fig. 24:8.
[70] Unpublished find (Civic Museum of Rovereto, inv. PRM04947).
[71] Hetzer 1949, p. 118:6; Leeb 1987, p. 238 b, p. 248.
[72] Battisti 2001, plate 11:1.

outside the province: in the province of Bolzano (Elvas[73]), the Veneto (Rocca di Rivoli[74]), Lombardy (Barche di Solferino,[75] Milzanello[76] and Ostiano[77]), Emilia Romagna (Casalecchio di Reno[78]) and in Austria (Bernhardsthal[79]). In some of these localities only highly fragmented potsherds are present, accordingly correlated only hypothetically to the artefact in question by the authors of this volume. Given the extreme rarity of the typology and the excellent quality of the surface treatment it is thought that this vessel must have been a particularly precious object. Moreover, the iconographic pattern of the cross inscribed in a circle, also defined as a 'wheel', recalls solar symbology.[80]

As regards the decorations connected to the handle appendages we indicate a sherd with a short double-button appendage (**167**) which finds comparisons at Dosso Alto,[81] Lasino,[82] Ledro,[83] Fiavé[84] and at Riparo Gaban,[85] and another similar typology but with umbonate buttons (**168**), documented, besides being in many coeval sites of the Vallagarina, also at Fiavé,[86] Ledro[87] and Lasino.[88]

Among the decorations we also enumerate some rims with fingertip impressions (**5**, **199**), which have parallels in the region in the pile dwelling sites of Ledro[89] and Fiavé,[90] as well as at Lasino[91] and at Pizzini di Castellano.[92]

Pottery technology

In studying the potsherds found in the Castel Corno Caves unfortunately it has not always been possible to collect enough elements for defining a complete and comprehensive picture of the pottery chaîne opératoire. The presence of inclusions, whether they were added as temper, or naturally present in the clay, is represented by fragments of limestone and to a lesser degree silicate. The fabric in many cases is characterized by the presence of iron oxide, which give the pottery a typically reddish colour. With regard to the methods of production only the use of the manual technique known as 'colombine'[93] is well documented. Some fractures in fact have been observed exactly at the point where one strip of the wall overlaps another.

We can propose the hypothesis that the pottery was produced without using a kiln but by firing in a pit in the ground. The vessel surfaces' colouring in fact is often not uniform, typical of variable temperatures and rapid, sudden inflows of oxygen.

A more accurate analysis of the pottery fragments has enabled the different type of section to be distinguished on the basis of the existing relationship between the core colour, the margins and the inner and outer surfaces, in order to be able to reconstruct the various methods used in firing the clay (**Figure 14**). Studies made on the colouring of the fabric have shown that uniformity in the colour of the core, the margins and the surfaces is an indicator of constant firing conditions,

[73] Farina 2016, plate 27:5 (probably drawn upside down in this thesis).
[74] Barfield 1976a, fig. 40:311a.
[75] Morandi *et al.* 1996, pp. 374–375.
[76] Cattaneo Cassano 1996, p. 365:3.
[77] Pia 1987, fig. 15:317.
[78] Steffè 1984, plate 4:7; Dal Santo et al. 2014, p. 217, Fig.10, n. 23.
[79] Neugebauer 1979, fig. 5:15.
[80] Morandi *et al.* 1996, pp. 372–374.
[81] Marzatico 1987, fig. 9:508.
[82] Tecchiati 1991, plate 31:2.
[83] Rageth 1974, plate 40.
[84] Perini 1994, plate 9:149; plate 49:726.
[85] Pedrotti 1982, plate 38:1.
[86] Perini 1994, plate 6:105, plate 9:148.
[87] Rageth 1974, plate 41:6–7.
[88] Tecchiati 1991, plate 65:4.
[89] Rageth 1974, plate 78:15.
[90] Perini 1994, plate 34:468, plate 44:646.
[91] Tecchiati 1991, plate 62:1.
[92] Battisti 2001, plate 2:4, plate 16:1, plate 20:1.
[93] Gradual overlapping of strips of clay joined together with simple manual pressure.

whereas the presence of grey or black parts, depending on the cases, is due to the possible presence inside the fabric of organic material not consumed in firing or by firing in a reducing atmosphere.[94] Observing the section of potsherds there can be noted lighter layers alternating with darker layers at times in rapid succession, an index therefore of diversified firing conditions, when phases of intake of air and drawing well are followed by phases totally without oxygen, consequently absorbing carbon black and vice versa. Experimental trials carried out by one of the authors of this volume (M.B.) produced similar results firing the vessels in a hole in the ground and covering the fire pit with clods of earth in the final phases of firing.

Studying carefully the points of fracture it can be surmised that the cordons and other accessory elements in general were all usually applied before firing, creating beforehand, in the case of lug handles and handles, large holes in the walls and clay pivots on the elements to be added.[95]

The connection between the typology of the vessel type (in the cases in which it has been possible to establish it with certainty) and the quality of its manufacture, related to both the fabric and surface treatment, reflects quite rigid criteria. As can be seen from the graph (**Figure 15**) jars, ollas and dolia are the coarser vessels, while the mugs and bowls are more refined.[96]

Fired and baked clay

We can number many fired-clay finds including hundreds of baked clay fragments, a loom weight, five spindle whorls and a fragment of tuyère. Of the five spindle whorls which came to light, four are fragmentary and only one is whole (**259–263**); all are of discoid shape. One of these has a decoration consisting of a series of engraved points along the outside edge (**263**), which can be compared with artefacts from Ledro[97] and Pizzini di Castellano.[98] The diameter varies from a minimum of 3 cm (**260**) to a maximum of 4.6 cm (**259**). For shape and size the spindle whorls found at Castel Corno can be compared with many EBA sites in the region (Pizzini,[99] Ledro,[100] Lasino,[101] Dosso Alto[102]) but the discoid spindle whorl is an element of little diagnostic use chronologically, in that its shape scarcely changes between the IV and II millenniums BC.[103]

In the burial zone (Chamber 3, Zone 1) a fragment of a sub-cylindrical loom weight (**264**) and a fragment of a truncated cone shape tuyère (**265**) were found. The loom weight is comparable, for typology and size, with other specimens found in the region[104] in Bronze Age sites, but in this case too morphology has no great diagnostic value at a chrono-typological level. The tuyère can be compared with finds in the region (Acquaviva di Besenello,[105] Vela Valbusa,[106] Ledro,[107] Riparo Gaban[108], Tof de la Val[109]) and neighbouring areas (Barche di Solferino,[110] Lavagnone[111] and Lucone di Polpenazze[112]). The use of clay tuyères spread over a vast area covering most of Europe between the end of the Copper Age and the EBA.[113] However the major concentrations of finds demarcate an area

[94] Mannoni and Giannichedda 1996.
[95] Example of traces of applied element applied are visible on fragment 97.
[96] The class of quality is here considered as a synthesis in which the surface treatment and the fabric quality are condensed.
[97] Raget 1974, plate 92:25.
[98] Battisti 2001, plate 38:5.
[99] Battisti 2001, plate 2:2, plate 3:3.
[100] Bazzanella and Mayr 2009; Raget 1974, plate 92.
[101] Tecchiati 1991, plate 31:6, plate 34:7.
[102] Marzatico 1987, fig. 13:272.
[103] Baioni *et al.* 2003, pp. 100–110; Marzatico 1997, pp. 137–138; Bazzanella *et al.* 2003.
[104] Raget 1974, plate 93:1; Perini 1994, plate 47:15; Battisti 2001, plate 32:1.
[105] Pedrotti 2001b, p. 212.
[106] Fasani 1990, fig. 8:3.
[107] Rageth 1974, plate 90:8, plate 91:11–16.
[108] Pedrotti 1982, plate 44:6.
[109] Perini 1973b, p. 249.
[110] Fasani 1984. p. 497:11.
[111] de Marinis 2000, fig. 88.
[112] Guerreschi 1981, p. 77:476.
[113] Lachenal *et al.* 2010, pp. 555–556.

which includes the zone of Lake Garda (involving the regions of Lombardia, Veneto and Trentino Alto Adige) and central-eastern Europe.[114] Other studies have already shown[115] that several factors contribute to a strong connection between these two geographical realities. This connection is also testified to by, for example, the area of prevalence and the concentration of enigmatic tablets, superimposable on that of the clay tuyères and the commonality of similar artefact classes of metal tools. This connection seems to have already found its roots by at least the second half of the III millennium BC, a period characterized by the Bell Beaker horizon.

In all the sectors investigated, 825 reddish-orange baked clay fragments were recovered. Of the best preserved, 54 have a flat, smooth face often covered by a whitish-grey patina with carbonaceous halos (**Figure 17b-c**). With an average thickness of about 2 cm, some of these finds also show vegetal and small stone impressions on the side opposite to the flat face. They are probably fragments of baked clay platforms, typical for example of clay hearths discovered in inhabited areas, inside domestic structures.[116] Since all the baked clay finds come from within the caves it is possible to postulate their use as being cultic, particularly when related to the burials area (Chamber 3). A similar function has been proposed for a baked clay platform found at the site of Lasino (locality Riparo del Santuario) in the same arbitrary level (spit K) and not far from the area where the human remains came from, ascribable to a secondary burial. In this case too several baked clay fragments were found, with a reddish-orange fabric and flat, light grey face with blackish halos (**Figure 17a**).[117]

Figure 17: Baked clay platform fragments (a: from Riparo del Santuario (Lasino), b and c: from the Chamber 3 of Castel Corno).

The baked clay fragments found on the site of Castel Corno Caves and at Lasino lend themselves to a similar functional interpretation (clay hearths) also because of the lack of traces of vegetal matter,[118] typical of the plaster on wattle walls and very common on purely settlement sites. Among the hundreds of baked clay finds from the nearby site of Pizzini di Castellano, for example, approximately 60 fragments have been identified with different types of impressions clearly ascribable to vegetal structural elements of varied sizes and therefore identifiable as plaster fragments.[119] Unlike the

[114] Roden 1988.
[115] de Marinis and Valzolgher 2013, p. 552; Marzatico and Tecchiati 2002, p. 46.
[116] Several examples of clay hearth or cooking plates in prehistoric and protohistoric sites are well documented in Peinetti *et al.* 2019. See also Bassetti and Degasperi 2002 for a microscopic analysis of some similar baked clay specimens from the site of Lavagnone.
[117] Tecchiati 1991, pp. 130, 131, 134–135.
[118] Tecchiati 1991, p. 135.
[119] Battisti 2001, pp. 56–58.

domestic fireplaces, the rare presence of blackened traces in comparison with the ashy-grey ones[120] leads to the hypothesis that the fires were perhaps only occasionally lit, brief and of a limited size - a method quite plausible considering that the caves, although partially aired, did not permit an adequate replacement of oxygen during combustion.

The theory of the use of clay during cultic practices linked to the lighting of small fires is also supported by the abundance of carbon fragments and carbon lenses within the caves and evident post-depositional traces of combustion presented by the skull found in Tomb 1 (**Figure 24**). The percentage distribution of the baked clay finds within the various stratigraphic units shows a particular concentration in the US 8, the layer covering the mound in Tomb 1.

Some of these fragments of baked clay platforms show traces of vegetal interweaving on the downward-facing side (opposite the flat face). Given the evident perpendicularity of the twist (**Figure 18**), traces due to the presence of plant remains mixed into the fabric can probably be excluded. What could however be cautiously hypothesised is the presence of mats spread on the damp, muddy ground of the caves in preparing the worship areas or maybe to cover the bodies.[121]

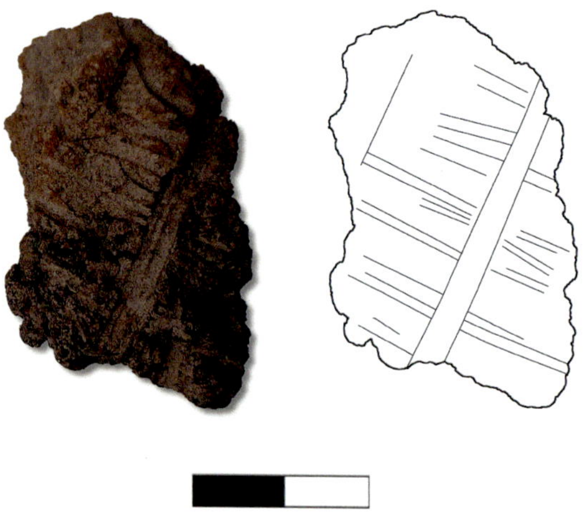

Figure 18: Baked clay platform fragment with traces of vegetal interweaving.

Figure 19: Shapeless baked clay lump with traces of handling.

In Chamber 3, lastly, among the remains of an archaeological deposit disturbed by looters, was found a shapeless baked clay lump weighing 270 grams with evident traces of handling (**Figure 19**). Considering the fragile consistency of the find, the baking was probably only partial and at a very low temperature. That object, both for its size (maximum length circa 10 cm) and state of conservation, would not have penetrated to such a depth by natural causes only and seems like a block of clay ready to be worked but then partially consolidated and altered by the heat of a small fire or at the edge of a main fire. Perhaps it is what remained of a larger block of clay brought into the caves to make the clay hearths already referred to.

[120] For experimental comparisons on the clay hearths see D'Oronzo 2019.

[121] A woven pattern surprisingly similar to those visible in **Figure 18** were found in a mat used to cover the body in a Scottish EBA burial at Langwell Farm (Lelong *et al.* 2014; Cooper *et al.* 2019).

Stone tools

The most well-documented stone tools are those in flint. The 1769 finds consisted of 1707 flint flakes, 59 tools and three cores. 505 finds, 28.5% of the total, show morphological and chromatic alterations due to fire. Apart from an arrowhead fragment, a sickle blade fragment and an end scraper fragment the other flints altered by heat are represented exclusively by flakes not apparently linked to any tool. Exposure to high temperatures has not only caused modifications at a morphological level, recognisable from the detachment of microfragments from the surface, but also considerable chromatic variations: many burned flints have a dark colouration tending to purple-grey tones. Their appearance would lead to the idea that they were subjected to temperatures close to 600 degrees.[122]

On the site a total of 59 tools (some fragmentary) were found, including: 18 sickle blades, seven retouched flakes, 14 blades, six arrowheads, seven end scrapers and seven side scrapers.

It is interesting to note that, although most finds (ceramic, flint and bone) were made inside the caves - where more consistent excavations took place - the highest concentration of flint tools (51%) was to be found on the outside (**Figure 20**).

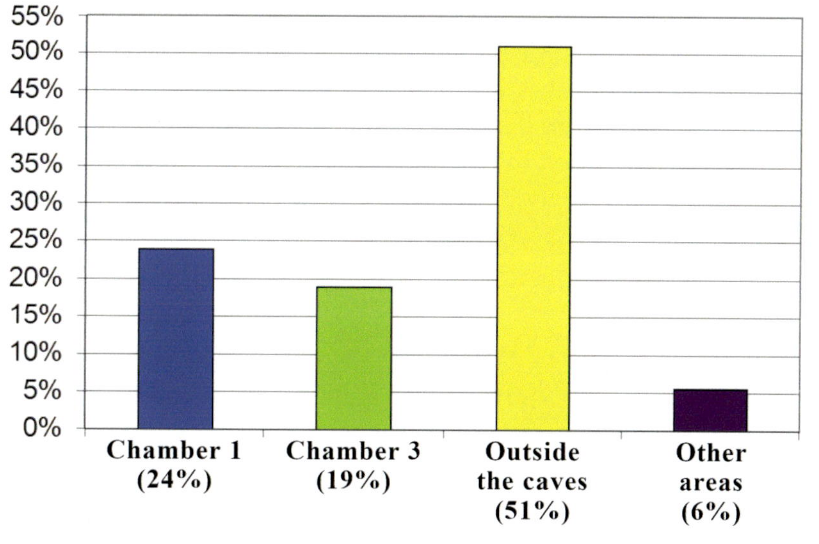

Figure 20: Place of discovery of flint tools (image modified from Regola 2005).

Of the sickle blades, 12 were whole and six fragmentary. More than half (11 out of 18) have edges with polished use-wear traces probably due to cutting cereals, although it is not to be excluded that the wear could have been caused by the cutting of other herbaceous plants.

In total the site has furnished three barbed arrowheads, two hollow-based and one with a short stem. Three of these come from the burial area, regrettably most come from mixed up layers. For one of these (**306**) we have a reliable stratigraphic reference in the basal layer of Tomb 1 (US 10), in direct contact with the buried bones. Despite the tomb being partly damaged by amateur non-stratigraphic excavations at the end of the '60s, we can postulate that the arrowhead may have been part of grave goods. This is an arrowhead with squared barbs reminiscent of forms widespread in the Late Copper Age considered characteristic of the Bell Beaker set. This artefact finds comparisons in the region on the site of Pigloner Kopf,[123] but other stratigraphic contexts, datable to the same horizon, rendering

[122] Cfr. Gurova *et al.* 2020.

[123] Oberrauch 2014, fig. 5:4.

similar finds can be identified in the areas of Verona and Brescia: Praelle di Novaglie,[124] Monte Covolo[125] and Ca' di Marco.[126] It should be noted however that these type of arrowhead seem to have remained partially in use also during the EBA I.[127] A small hollow-based triangular arrowhead (**305**) was found in the sondage effected in Chamber 1 (US 2). Outside the caves, along the path leading to the castle, were found two more arrowheads, one with barbs (**300**) and another with a short wide stem (**301**) recalling artefact classes common especially in the Copper Age.[128] In the same zone was also found a long flint blade of triangular section measuring almost 13 cm (**299**). Blades of such length have rarely been found in EBA contexts and are instead more common in a period from the Neolithic to the Copper Age.[129]

The site has also yelded some side-scrapers (e.g. **285–286**) and end-scrapers of a sub-rectangular or sub-circular shape (e.g. **292, 293, 295, 297**).

Among the hundreds of flint flakes brought to light, shades of red and reddish brown (10R, 2.5YR, 5YR and 7.5YR on the Munsell Soil Color Charts) dominate. Most of the production debris and rejects (over 60% of the total) is represented in fact by poorly workable stone types[130] of various shades of red, easily obtained locally from the Scaglia Rossa Formation, whereas over 60% of the finished tools were produced from flint with a medium/high degree of workability, ochre, olive, yellowish or greyish coloured and at least partly obtained from Scaglia Variegata and Biancone Formations (**Figure 21**). Low quality flint found on the spot must therefore have been highly exploited, but mainly for producing disposable tools (retouched flakes) and, perhaps, for use in the learning phases of the flint knapping techniques. The more sophisticated tools, on the other hand, would have been imported or made on the spot using big, high quality flint flakes, also imported, like those discovered on the site of Pizzini di Castellano.[131] This could explain the low quantity of production debris and rejects in ochre, grey, olive and yellowish coloured flint in relation to the substantial number of tools found (clearly evident in **Figure 21**).

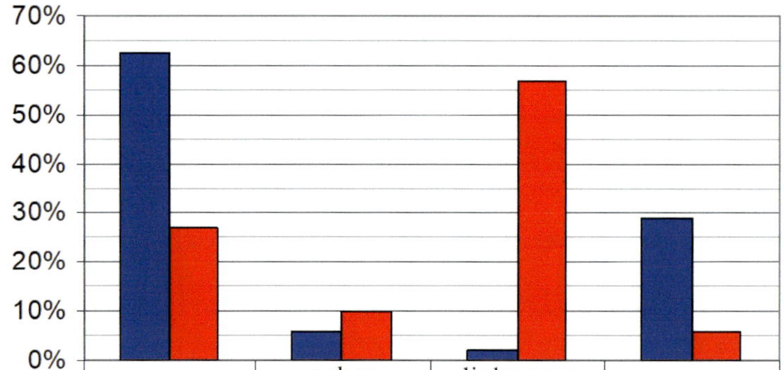

	Reddish brown	ocher greenish yellowish	light gray and grayish	color altered by heat
Chips	62.6%	6%	2%	29.4%
Tools	27%	10%	57%	6%

Figure 21: Colour of flint tools and chips.

124 Fasani 1980, fig. 6:22.
125 Barfield *et al.* 1995, fig. 61:10.
126 Tirabassi 2000, fig. 6:2.
127 Leonardi *et al.* 2015, p. 288.
128 Salzani 2014, p. 32, plate III; Tirabassi 2000, fig.8 n.34; Chiarenza 2013, p. 287 fig. 7:12; Battisti 2016, p. 704 and fig. 741:2.
129 Leonardi *et al.* 2015, p. 288; Bagolini 1980, fig.9; Perini 1987, plate IX; Lincetto and Valzolgher 1998, p. 28 plate VII:259; Marzatico 1987, p. 382.
130 For the definition of a scale of 'degree of workability' cfr. Barbieri *et al.* 2014.
131 Battisti 2001, plates 44, 45, 46.

Analogous situations, with two different sources of supply of raw materials of radically dissimilar quality, are also documented in other sites of the Copper Age and the EBA.[132] The possibility should not be excluded beforehand that rare local flint deposits of high quality were utilized, documented for example in the nearby Val di Gresta or on the ridge Stivo-Bondone,[133] but the production of tools on the spot beginning directly with blocks of raw materials, would have created a great deal of debris due to the knapping which should be sizable in percentage terms and therefore also have a certain visibility in the archeological records. Such production would probably also have left as evidence some small cores no longer usable. What is however significant is the fact that the only three cores found on the site belong to the local type of stone of poor quality and a reddish-brown colour (e.g. **296**).

Similar proportions in the relationship between the number of flakes and tools, in relation to the differing quality of the raw material, are identifiable in the nearby site of EBA of Pizzini di Castellano and on the site of Lasino, for which the same dynamic of double sourcing has been proposed (autochthonous/allochthonous).[134]

Artefacts made out of stone other than flint

Among the artefacts in non-flint stone, we can include a fragmentary parallelepiped block of sandstone with a wide central groove and semicircular section, a brassard (wrist-guard) in serpentinite from Chamber 1, a serpentinite burnisher and four necklace beads from the excavations in Chamber 3.

The sandstone tool (**308**) has commonly been interpreted as an arrowshaft smoother.[135] Similar artefacts proliferated in the Late Copper Age, probably due to the great cultural and social role which archery performed within the Bell Beaker phenomenon[136] and which remained in vogue up until the Late Bronze Age.[137] Besides their practical function, they seem to have acquired a particular symbolic value, having been found in ritual and funerary contexts.[138]

Very common in central Europe, similar artefacts to the one found in the layer nearest the surface of Chamber 1 of Castel Corno, have been found, within the regional area, in the pile dwelling site of of Ledro,[139] at Pizzini di Castellano[140] and at the Montesei di Serso.[141]

From the US 3, in the sondage carried out in the same chamber, originates a perforated stone tablet referable typologically to the family of wrist-guards (**309**). It is identifiable as type '2Wpp' according to the classification devised in the framework of the Leiden Beaker Project.[142] The code describes in this order: the presence of two holes for attaching, the hourglass shape and sub-rectangular section. The analyses carried out on the find led to the identification of the type of stone: serpentinite.[143] This artefact finds many comparisons both in Trentino (e.g. Pizzini di Castellano,[144] Colombo di Mori,[145] Fiavé,[146] Ledro,[147] San Bartolomeo di Ceole[148]) and in the surrounding regions (Barche di Solferino,[149]

[132] Leonardi *et al.* 2015, p. 287.
[133] Barbieri *et al.* 2014.
[134] Battisti 2001, p. 60–61; Tecchiati 1991, pp. 139–140
[135] Raghet, 1974, p. 189; Nicolas 2019.
[136] Fokkens *et al.* 2008, p. 123; Nicolas 2019.
[137] Casini 2005, p. 84.
[138] Nicolas 2019, p. 120; Verwers 1964.
[139] Rageth, 1974, plate 110:5,6,8.
[140] Battisti 2001, plate 61:5.
[141] Perini 1973a, fig. 7:63. Perini in reality interprets it as a fragment of a casting form comparing it with another artefact (n. 62) certainly related to metallurgic activity.
[142] Fokkens *et al.* 2008.
[143] The analyses were carried out by Fabrizio Bizzarini in the microscopy laboratory in the Museo Civico of Rovereto.
[144] Battisti 2004, p. 25.
[145] Anzelini *et al.* 1972, plate IV:17.
[146] Perini 1987, plate XXIV:409.
[147] Rageth 1974, plate 108:1–10.
[148] Marzatico 1997, p. 262, fig. 100; Marzatico 2013, p. 131, fig. 12b:36.
[149] Mezzena 1965; Fasani 1984, p. 499.

Cattaragna,[150] Lavagnone,[151] Lucone di Polpenazze[152]). Beyond north-eastern Italy this typology, which also falls into the type 'F' in the scheme devised by Sangmeister,[153] is also widespread in Germany, Holland, Spain and Portugal. As regards their functional interpretation, these objects resemble the modern, plastic forearm protections, or leather ones in an earlier period, used by archers to save the arm from the occasional impacts with the bow string, once the arrow has been shot. If, in general, the functional aspects of this kind of stone tools have been widely reduced by other authors,[154] in the case in question, the prevalently symbolic character, above and beyond the integrity of the artefact, its optimal state of preservation and the absence of use-wear traces is even more evident. The wrist guard in fact has only two holes, is of a very small size and has a sub-rectangular section: three characteristics which make it hardly functional. The stone wrist guards which also have functional characteristics and use-wear traces, next to the symbolic-ritual ones, seem to have had greater dimensions, a convex-concave or plano-convex cross-section and at least four holes for attaching.[155] Even if the general functionality of these objects is obviously inferior to that of the more slender and close-fitting wrist guards in leather, the hypothesis remains of their strong symbolic link with the world of archery which, as has already been shown, had taken on a role of great importance and prestige in European communities between the late 3rd and early 2nd millennium BC. At a chronological level this kind of artefact seems to have appeared in the Bell Beaker Age and stayed in use for the whole of the EBA with sporadic appearances also in the early Middle Bronze Age.[156]

Outside the caves a serpentinite pebble was found, a dark greenish-grey colour with evident use wear traces, interpretable as a burnisher (**266**). Similar objects already appeared in the Neolithic Age but endured until the Iron Age.[157] Of the same shape and size is a burnisher found on the nearby site of Pizzini di Castellano in a layer dating back to the EBA.[158] Morphologically similar burnishers have also been found in later contexts (e.g. in the MBA layers at Fiavé 5).[159] The morphology of the specimen of Castel Corno seems to belong to type 1 (triangular) of the smoothing pebbles found on the Bronze Age site at Lavagnone, a very common and widespread typology which finds comparison in contexts of highly diverse epochs.[160]

The four stone necklace beads, perhaps part of one or more grave goods in the burial area of Chamber 3, seem to be of calcite.[161] Two have an approximately sub-rectangular shape with very rounded edges (**323, 324**). Regarding the other two, of a much smaller size, one has a quadrangular section (**327**) and the other circular (**330**).

Necklace beads of a similar shape are found in various contexts dating from the Copper Age to the EBA (e.g. Riparo Valtenesi,[162] Corna Nibbia,[163] Velturno,[164] Scalucce di Molina,[165] Romagnano Loc,[166] La Vela di Val Busa,[167] Pizzini di Castellano,[168] Ledro[169], Arano,[170] Lavagnone[171]). These necklace beads seem

[150] Aspes 1972, plate IX:1–2.
[151] de Marinis 2000, p. 116 ; Casini, 2005, fig. 8:8–10.
[152] Simoni 1966, p. 43.
[153] Sangmeister 1974.
[154] Fokkens *et al.* 2008; Palumbo 2012; Turek 2015; Casini 2005, p. 83.
[155] Fokkens *et al.* 2008; Turek 2015.
[156] E.g. Perini 1987, plate XXIV:408–409.
[157] Casini 2005, pp. 94–96.
[158] Battisti 2001, plate 61:1.
[159] Perini 1987, plate XXIV:410.
[160] Casini 2005, pp. 93–96, figs 10–11.
[161] In this case no in-depth analysis of the stone-type was performed.
[162] Barfield 2007.
[163] Baioni 2017; Baioni 2004, fig. 7a.
[164] Dal Ri and Tecchiati 1995, p. 20 fig. 7:1; Bagolini *et al.* 1988, p. 342 fig. 4.
[165] Valzolgher and Lincetto 2002, pp. 174–177.
[166] Perini 1975, fig. 15.
[167] Fasani 1990, fig. 4.
[168] Battisti 2004, fig. 8.
[169] Rageth 1974, plate 92.
[170] Salzani 2014, pp. 72–73 plates V-VI.
[171] Casini 2005, fig. 9:21–30.

therefore to have an element of tradition, that is they carry forward into the EBA aspects of personal decoration already present in the Copper Age.

Shell, bone and antler artefacts

The shell, bone and antler artefacts found at Castel Corno are 17 in total. They include seven awls (**310, 312–316, 318–319**), a pin/needle (**317**), a spatula (**314**), a possible fragment of a handle (**311**) and seven shell necklace beads (**320–322, 325–326, 328–329**).

Among of the seven awls, one differs from the others in that it has a through hole at its base certainly made by the hand of man (**319**). In fact, it happens quite often that bone tools have through holes, as for example was also found in spatulas and fire striker handles of Fiavé,[172] probably for hanging on a belt, round the neck or on a wall. Among the many sites in the region yielding awls and spatulas similar in appearance to those illustrated here we cite only a few: Fiavé,[173] Ledro,[174] Pizzini di Castellano,[175] Dosso Alto di Borgo Sacco,[176] Lasino.[177] Of these artefacts we wish to point out an awl made from a bear fibula (**313**). One much longer awl, also made from a bear fibula, comes from the nearby EBA site of Colombo di Mori.[178]

It should however be noted that this type of artefact presents forms which remain almost invariable all through the millenniums from the Neolithic Age[179] to historical times.[180] Finds of this kind are difficult to date if come across outside their original context.[181]

A bone tool 5 cm long with a tapered distal part and pierced, enlarged proximal part (**317**), finds comparison, for example, with materials from Fiavé, [182] Ledro[183] and Lucone di Polpenazze.[184]

Similar artefacts are also widely scattered beyond the Alps[185] where they have often been found in a funeral context (mainly in female tombs).[186] The functional interpretation is still being debated between those who see these tools as needles for sewing[187] and those who on the other hand see them as pins, that is accessories to clothing,[188] at times compared with proto-fibulas (imagining they can be furnished with a cord).[189] The specimen found at Castel Corno falls into the category of the so-called 'Ringkopfnadel' found north of the Alps, for example in the cemetery of Haid.[190] Although the presence and particular position of these objects in the grave goods would seem to make the function of clothing accessory much more credible, here we wish to point also to the similarity with bone needles used for knitting, referring in particular to the technique of Nalbinding.[191]

172 Perini 1987, plate VI:51, plate VII:77.
173 Perini 1987, plate V:31; plate VIII:90.
174 Rageth 1974, plates 98–99.
175 Battisti 2001, plate 67:1–2.
176 Trinco 2020, plates 32–34.
177 Tecchiati 1997; Tecchiati 1991, plates 86–87.
178 Orsi 1882, plate IX:1.
179 See for example the site of the Rocca di Rivoli in Barfield 1976b, pp. 127–128.
180 See for example the nearby early medieval site of Saint Andrea Island at Loppio in Pezzato 2016, fig. 705:34–37.
181 E.g. Marzatico 1997, pp. 118–119.
182 Perini 1987, plate IV:1, plate VI:39.
183 Rageth, 1974, plate 95:4.
184 Aimar and Gregoriani 2000, plate IV:58.
185 For example, in the German necropolises of Haid, Mantching, Mintraching, Franzhausen (Reiter 2008, pp. 83–87).
186 Reitberger 2008, p. 63.
187 Bazzanella *et al.* 2003, p. 139; Peroni 1996, p. 140. Similar needles could be used not only for making various kinds of fabric but also for sewing skins or weaving fishing nets.
188 Perini 1987, p. 68. Perini however proposes that the shorter pins could also have functioned as needles.
189 Theory supported by the specific position of the artefacts inside the tomb and by experiments (Reiter 2008, p. 83).
190 Reitberger 2008, pp. 61–62, e.g. p. 255 plate II:4.
191 Nobelen 2016, pp. 26, 30; Kramer 2017, pp. 58–59; Olsen and Svanberg 2010; see also 'Nålebinding' on Wikipedia.

The only tool made from red deer antler was cut and burnished and has a small through hole (**311**). The artefact is fragmentary and finds comparisons, for example, in the material at the pile dwelling site of Fiavé[192] where they have been interpreted as flint fire striker handles.[193]

As regards the shell artefacts we can count a good seven pierced necklace beads. Two different types can be distinguished: large sub-rectangular and sub-triangular beads which can be over 2 cm at their maximum (size) (**320–322**) and small discoid beads with a diameter between six and eight millimetres (**325–326, 328–329**). The finest bead's thickness approaches one millimetre. The beads are all whole except for the sub-rectangular and sub-triangular ones. Similar artefacts have been found in the nearby sites of Colombo (EBA)[194] and Bersaglio at Mori (Copper Age and EBA)[195] but also in the sites of Romagnano Loch (EBA),[196] Nogarole di Mezzolombardo (Copper Age and EBA),[197] Rocca Lonato (EBA and Middle Bronze Age),[198] in the Copper Age cemetery of Remedello di Sotto[199] and between the grave goods of the Swiss site of Conthey en Sensine (EBA I).[200]

For smaller, finer beads we find numerous and valid comparisons on the site datable in the EBA I of Vela Valbusa.[201]

Metals

No metal objects were found on the site of the Castel Corno Caves with the exception of a minute shapeless fragment from the US 2 of Chamber 1 and a piece of slag typical of copper reduction process activities (**331, Figure 22b**), from the older anthropic layer of Chamber 3 (US 10), inside the mound of Tomb 1.

It is difficult to establish the origin and significance of the small copper residue (or of a copper alloy), with it being less than a centimetre in size (**Figure 22a**).[202] For the slag, however, given its extreme proximity to the human bones in Chamber 3, it could be thought it was part of some grave goods or a funeral offering.[203]

Figure 22: Metal artefacts. a: small copper residue (or of a copper alloy), b: piece of smelting slag.

[192] Perini 1987, plate IV:7; plate V:36.
[193] Perini 1987, pp. 75–76.
[194] Artefacts conserved in the Civic Museum of Rovereto, inventory numbers: 3956, 3957.
[195] Avanzini *et al.* 1985, p. 34, fig.7:11–12.
[196] Perini 1971, p. 48 fig. 32:27, 34, 47.
[197] Mottes and Nicolis 2019, p. 207.
[198] Girod 2005, pp. 128–129 fig. 8.
[199] Mangani and Longhi 2008, pp. 129–130; Girod 2005, pp. 128–129 fig. 7.
[200] Borrello and Girod 2008, p. 113, fig. 5:C.
[201] Fasani, 1990, fig. 4. For a list of Bronze Age burial sites in northern Italy where shell necklace beads have been found see Bandera and Tecchiati 2020.
[202] It could also be just a casting residue (inv. PRM031133).
[203] See paragraph 4 for more details on the possible link between metallurgy and burials.

4 – The Burial Places

As was already mentioned in the first chapter, when the site was discovered in 1969, some human bones were found inside Chamber 3, which included a whole skull without its mandible, the only skull so far to emerge from this cave complex. In 1985 Marco Avanzini, during a site inspection, identified the remains of a tomb still in situ, even if partly disturbed. On that occasion he retrieved the remains of two mandibles of immature individuals. In 1998, during the excavations of the Civic Museum of Rovereto, among the bones in Tomb 1 a small mandible fragment was found that was part of one of the two mandibles recovered in 1985. It was also discovered that the other mandible found in the same year must certainly belong to the skull found in 1969. Thus, without any doubt, it was clear that all three inspections pertained to the same burial context. This had also become evident on comparing the description made by Dario Candioli, interviewed by one of the authors of this volume (U.T.), the precise graphic and photographic documentation carried out by Marco Avanzini and the stratigraphy that emerged during the excavation campaign in 1998.

Between 1969 and 1998, within Chamber 3, in the cavity defined 'Zone 1' (see **Figure 3**) a total of 190 human bones were found concentrated in two different areas, which in the excavation phase were preliminarily defined Tomb 1 and Tomb 2. The anthropological analysis of the human remains established that these bones belonged to at least six different individuals: three subadults (Individuals 2, 3 and 4), two adults (Individuals 5 and 6) and one perinatal (Individual 7).[1] The only human bone found outside this context consists of a vertebra of an adult individual (Individual 1) found in Chamber 1 during the excavations of 1974.

As regards Tomb 1 the records of the excavations in 1969 report numerous stones placed at the sides and over the graves which constituted a sort of small mound. Burial sites in rocky ravines bordered or covered by stones are widely documented in the region in contexts datable between the Copper Age and EBA (for example Romagnano Loc,[2] Mezzocorona-Borgonuovo,[3] Paludei di Volano,[4] Nogarole,[5] Orno,[6] Lasino,[7] Solteri,[8] Vela Valbusa,[9] Cosina di Stravino,[10] Nogaredo[11], Peri[12]), and in general over the whole of Italy and Western Europe where a similar tendency was to be found between the 4th and 3rd millenniums BC.[13] In the mountainous areas between eastern Lombardy, Trentino Alto Adige and western Veneto there seems to exist a general continuity in the manner and funerary ritual between the Copper Age and EBA which favours rock shelters, caves, landslides and ravines of various shapes and sizes in addition to clear evidence of manipulation of human remains.[14] The context of Castel Corno however differs from all the others due to the considerable depth and complexity of its cave system.

Inside Tomb 1 and Tomb 2 some intrusive artefacts were found, partly referable to chronologically later layers, which contaminated the primary assemblage caused by the partial disturbance of the context during the excavations in 1969. Even so, among the artefacts from the US 9 and 10 of Tomb 1 and US 18 of Tomb 2, the only ones in direct contact with the human bones, we can identify

[1] Mazzucchi *et al.* 2020.
[2] Perini 1971; Perini 1975; Capitanio 1973.
[3] Nicolis 2001.
[4] Bagolini *et al.* 1980; Corrain and Erspamer 1980.
[5] Bagolini *et al.* 1986; Mottes *et al.* 2019.
[6] Bonomi *et al.* 1986, pp. 184–186.
[7] Chiusole and Vettori 1972; Tecchiati 1991; Bonardi and Tecchiati 2005.
[8] Nicolis 2001, p. 352.
[9] Fasani 1990.
[10] Roberti 1913a.
[11] Roberti 1913b.
[12] Salzani *et al.* 2004; Lincetto and Valzolgher 2018; Valzolgher and Quarta 2009.
[13] Leonini and Sarti 2006.
[14] Mottes and Nicolis 2019, p. 194; Nicolis 2016, p. 136; Leonardi *et al.* 2015, p. 295.

some finds as perhaps being part of the original grave goods or grave offerings: they consist of an arrowhead with squared barbs (**306**), a smelting slag (**331**), four necklace beads (**321**, **326**, **327**, **330**), an end scraper (**292**) and two clay spindle whorls (**260**, **261**). To these we could add further 7 necklace beads (**320**, **322–325**, **328–329**) found in layers in close contact with the burial sites but partly disturbed by looters and the clay tuyère (**265**), discovered in the course of the 1969 excavations when the skull was also found.

The materials located in the tombs of Castel Corno do not deviate typologically from those found in other cultic and funerary contexts datable between the end of the Copper Age and EBA; for example, regarding grave goods, where present, it can be noted that in most cases, they are represented by few artefacts prevalently consisting of decorative objects.[15] Elements of necklace beads and pendants were also found, for example, at Romagnano Loc,[16] Vela Val Busa[17] and Solteri.[18]

While aware that 'the archaeologist excavates tombs and not funerals'[19] and also bearing in mind the degree of disturbance of the primary assemblage, some hypotheses have nonetheless been formulated on the type of rituals practised on this site, based mainly on statistical considerations, comparisons with similar sites and particularly on what emerged in that last excavation campaigns (1998–1999).

Even if, as has often been stated, the burial sites appear partly disturbed by looting, we wish to propose that this was not the only element to disturb the original burial contexts. The bones of the six individuals found inside Zone 1 (see **Figure 3**) were apparently distributed randomly between US 9, the layer covered by the mound of stones of Tomb 1, US 10, the layer on the floor of the grave (US 15) and thus in direct contact with the sterile layer beneath,[20] and finally US 18 (the so-called 'Tomb 2').

Many collective burials, apparently simultaneous, in reality hide a succession of distinct events which can be attributed to individual interments that ensued in the same place at different periods of time.[21] From the stratigraphic point of view alone it is almost impossible to be able to distinguish such operations from one another because of the disturbance which the original deposits underwent several times. In the context under consideration, it also appears evident (excluding the partial disturbance due to recent interventions) that US 9 and US 10 were already partially altered in ancient times, possibly because of funerary practices relative to the deposition or removal of human remains. The minimum number of individuals found among the accumulation of bones and artefacts called Tomb 2 and their estimated age are perfectly compatible and not superimposable with the data derived from the depositions found in Tomb 1. This seems to suggest the possibility that some of the human bones were moved and accumulated two metres away, towards the entrance to the cavity.[22] Even if the stratigraphic data do not allow to reliably reconstruct the chronological sequence of the burials, it is quite clear that the stratigraphic context investigated is the result of subsequent burials which involved the displacement of portions of the skeletons belonging to the previous burials. We could also hypothesize that the burial of Individual 2, datable to the last phase of use of the mound thanks to a recent radiocarbon dating (see further on), was probably not the last to be buried. In fact, most of his bones appear to have been moved to the so-called Tomb 2 (see **Figure 23**), perhaps to make room for a later burial.

---

15 Nicolis 2001, pp. 357.
16 Perini 1975, p. 301.
17 Fasani 1990, pp. 168–172.
18 Mottes 1996, p. 543:3.
19 Frisone 1994, p. 12.
20 See stratigraphy in **Figure 7**.
21 Nicolis 2016, p. 137.
22 Mazzucchi *et al.* 2020, pp. 9–10.

Seeing that there was only one skull with a minimum number of seven individuals and a low number of bones for some of these, it is thought that other types of intervention might have altered the formation of the stratigraphy, perhaps linked to ritual removals connected to the practice of a secondary burial and the cult of skulls. Similar rituals, widely documented in the region,[23] record a particular cultic manipulation linked to the funerary sphere which foresaw the periodic reopening of burial contexts and removal of portions of the skeleton, especially the long bones and the skull.[24] In many cases these bones were then put in another place. This kind of ritual was usually accompanied, also on an ethnographic basis, by funerary practices tending to represent physically the journey of the soul towards the afterlife. In this delicate moment of time when the dead person is transformed into an ancestor, the soul had to pass through various stages corresponding to specular stages of the social elaboration of mourning.[25] In other words the rituality with which the bones were extracted, manipulated and finally replaced reflected the process of progressive liberation of the soul from its mortal remains and its consequent distancing from the community of the living to which it might do harm.[26]

However ethnographic studies show that the motivation which can lead to the exhumation of some parts of the body of the dead and their successive manipulation (tanatometamorphosis) may be much more complex, diversified and elaborate and involve, for example, even long phases of exposition and cult of the bones extracted before the secondary burial[27] and so their temporary transformation into relics.[28] Thus the body of the deceased continues to perform an important social function even after death: human remains become potent symbols.[29]

	TOMB 1 US 9	TOMB 1 US 10	TOMB 1 US INDET. (1969 excavation)	TOTAL TOMB 1	TOMB 2	TOTAL BONES
Individual 2 (8–9 years)	6	10	1	17	34	51
Individual 3 (11 years)	19	8	5	32	5	37
Individual 4 (11 years)	2			2	1	3
Individual 5 (adult)	1	1		2		2
Individual 6 (adult)		1		1		1
Individual 7 (fetus)	1			1		1
Individuals 3 or 4	18	13		31	3	34
Individuals 5 or 6	7	10		17	13	30
Total bones	54	43		97	56	153

Figure 23: Distribution of human bones.

One archaeological record of such practices is to be found at the nearby archaeological site of Colombo di Mori: at the top of the slope which has produced evident traces of a settlement of the EBA, inside a small natural ravine, in 1881 Paolo Orsi discovered four skulls together with a few

[23] Nicolis 2001.
[24] Long bones and skulls were considered relics of primary importance (Reliquiae insignes) even in the Christian tradition (Favole 2003, p. 91)
[25] Favole 2003, p. 63.
[26] On beliefs about the danger represented by the spirits of the dead and the ways to protect oneself from them see Frazer 2016.
[27] Frazer 2016, pp. 108–109, 135 (ch. 5, 6).
[28] For details on the cult of relics and historical/ethnographic comparisons see Favole 2003.
[29] These themes are extensively covered in Favole 2003 and Remotti 2006.

other human remains.[30] Further evident traces of secondary burials have been found for example on the site of the Riparo del Santuario at Lasino, where a skull had been placed inside a big jar in a niche in a rock shelter,[31] on the site of Mezzocorona Dos de la Forca[32] and at Romagnano Loch.[33] The so-called 'cult of skulls' continued sporadically at least until the Middle Bronze Age, as seems confirmed for example by the tomb 2 at Calferi di Stenico (Trento)[34] and by the Bovolone cemetery (Verona).[35]

The least damaged skeleton, that of Individual 3,[36] reached us partially incomplete and with few anatomical connections, most probably caused by the excavations in 1969 and successive looting activities. Considering the presence of the skull complete with mandible and many other bones, a secondary burial can probably be excluded. At least for this individual we can therefore assume this to have been a primary burial, then disturbed perhaps only partially in antiquity, as already stated, to make room for a new burial. On the basis of the documentation of the excavation campaign in 1998, the reports of the excavation in 1969, the few remains which still have a partial anatomic connection and taphonomical considerations we can envisage that the youth must have been buried in a crouched position on his right side facing the south.

The skull has a conspicuous burn on the left parietal portion of the cranial vault, probably due to a small fire lit for ritual purposes after the decomposition of Individual 3. The heat cannot have been too intense or the bones would appear calcified and must have been well located in a limited area, otherwise it would have also burnt more parts of the skull. The general shape of the burn seems to suggest the skull was partly or totally buried when the fire was lit and that only a small part of it was relatively near the flames (darker mark in **Figure 24**).[37]

The fact that a fire lit in the cave after the deposition of Individual 3 left traces of burns in the left portion of the skull suggests, if we also consider the position of the pelvis and forearm bones in relation to the shape and size of the grave and the burial mound, that the young man was probably placed in a crouched position on his right side (**Figure 25**).

The lighting of fires inside Chamber 3 is well documented after all by the plentiful amount of charcoals, the numerous burned animal bones (60%), high percentage of flints altered by heat (29%) and by the baked clay platforms described in the previous chapter. Furthermore, in Chamber 1 and Chamber 3 numerous superimposed layers of ash and charcoals have been identified, linked perhaps to post-depositional cultic practices. In view of the imaginable difficulties of managing a fire inside these intricate caves (especially Chamber 3) it is possible that some fires were lit and left until they burnt out without direct, constant control. From the data available, however, it is difficult to understand fully the old smoke escape routes. In fact, some ducts now obstructed by earth and stones may have been free, or they could have been blocked by ducts now freed by speleologists.

In addition to the aforementioned site of Lasino (see Chapter 3), baked clay platforms in possible relationship with cultic practices are also documented in the site of Corna Nibbia (BS).[38] On the site of Solteri compact deposits of ash, charcoals and baked clay finds are documented, interpretable

[30] Orsi 1882.
[31] Chiusole and Vettori 1972; Tecchiati 1991, p. 190; Bonardi and Tecchiati 2005; Corrain and De Marchi 1980.
[32] Bagolini *et al.* 1991, p. 151.
[33] Perini 1971, p. 45.
[34] Nicolis 2001, p. 358.
[35] Salzani 2010, pp. 53, 121 (tomb n. 30).
[36] Biological sex assignment was performed using shotgun sequencing data and the method implemented in Skoglund *et al.* 2013 (https://doi.org/10.1016/j.jas.2013.07.004) Unpublished data, Institute for Mummy Studies-EURAC-Research (Bolzano), in the context of the project: 'Genomic diversity of prehistoric individuals from the Iceman's territory in the Eastern Italian Alps' granted by Provincia Autonoma di Bolzano – Alto Adige , bando di concorso 'Research Südtirol/Alto Adige' 2019.
[37] For more detailed considerations see Mazzucchi *et al.* 2020, pp. 15–16.
[38] Baioni 2004, p. 63.

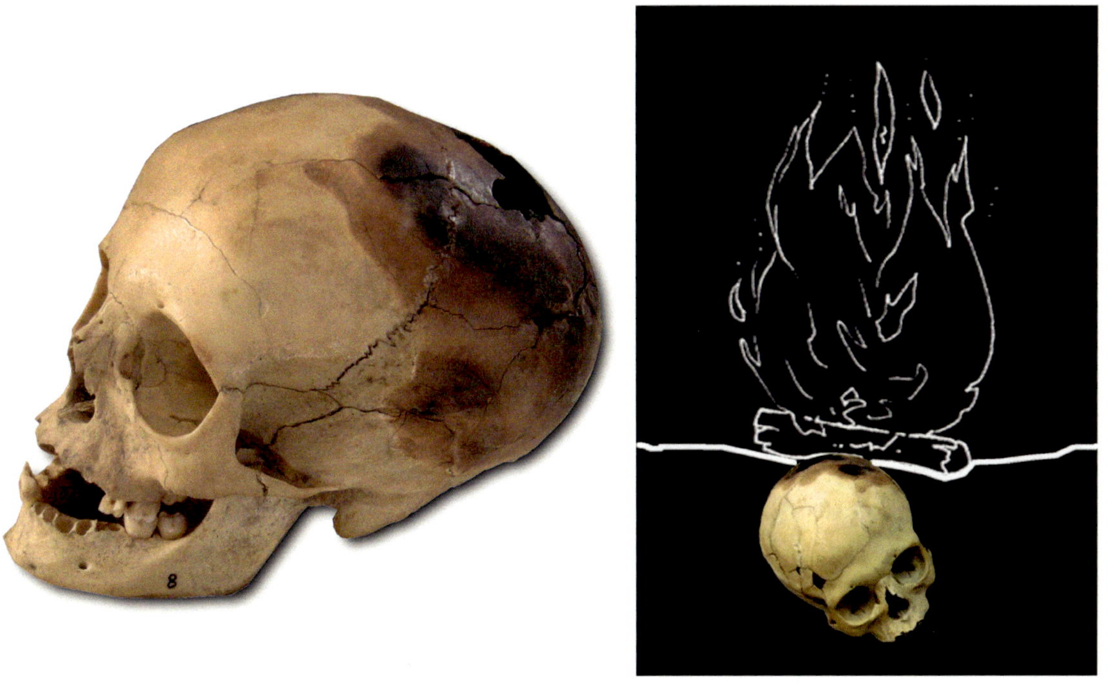

Figure 24: Individual 3's skull and hypothetical position of it at the time of burning.

as clay hearths.[39] At Riparo Nogarole 3 were also documented the remains of a combustion structure interpreted as a hearth destined for funerary rituals.[40] Whereas at Romagnano Loc, the finding of human bones altered by heat is not correlated to funerary rituals, but to successive metallurgical craft activities.[41]

If it is by now known that the lighting of fires in association with burials at times conceals a ritual intention,[42] an already common practice in the region in Neolithic times,[43] what is more difficult to establish is if and where a direct connection between metallurgy and funerary cults existed.[44] This connection, already implied in the Copper Age, for example on the site of Acquaviva di Besenello[45] and at the Riparo Marchi,[46] seems noticeable also in the EBA as seen at the previously mentioned sites of Romagnano Loc[47]

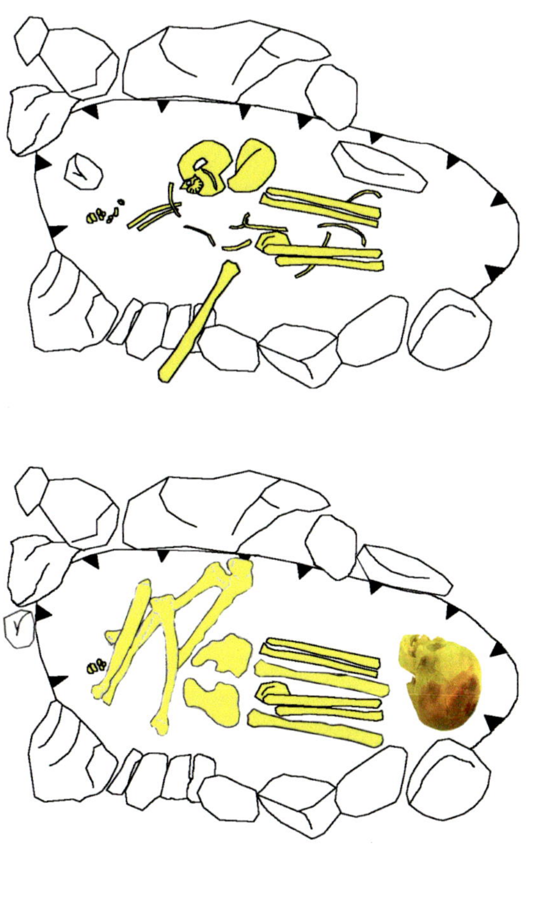

Figure 25: Reconstruction of the original position of individual 3's skeletal remains.

[39] Nicolis 2001, p. 352.
[40] Nicolis 2001, p. 349.
[41] Nicolis 2001, p. 340.
[42] Marzatico and Tecchiati 2002, p.49; Mottes and Nicolis 2019, pp. 201, 209; Leonini and Sarti 2006, p. 152; Nicolis 2016, pp. 112–113.
[43] Pedrotti 2001b, p.149.
[44] A possible ritual connection between metallurgy and funerary situations has been proposed in Mottes *et al.* 1999, pp. 84, 86 and in Bassetti *et al.* 2005, p. 39 (for central Italy see Pacciarelli and Sassatelli 1997, p. 16; Lucentini 1997, p. 38; D'Ercole 1997, p.57).
[45] Angelini *et al.*, 1980, pp. 67–69.
[46] Mottes and Nicolis 2019, pp. 196–197.
[47] Nicolis 2001, p. 340.

and Vela Val Busa.[48] In some of these cases it is however difficult to verify if such evidence was really linked to the cult and funerary rituals or if it derived from random use of the same space for different activities.[49] The problem therefore is to establish if it is simply a case of the promiscuous use of some particular geomorphological contexts constituted primarily of rock shelters.

As far as Castel Corno is concerned, the situation is relatively different from the ones just described: the rugged place, difficult to access, the lack of ventilation, the limited space and many other elements, lead to excluding the hypothesis that productive activities could be carried on inside. In this section of the valley of the River Adige moreover, no deposits of slag have been found, nor sites connected to metallurgical activities. So, it seems more logical to interpret the lighting of small fires and the presence of artefacts typical of metallurgical activity as actual ritual practices. Above all it is difficult to maintain that a single tuyère and, in particular, a one and only piece of slag, can prove that activity related to metallurgy was carried on. It is more likely that these elements were attributed a particular significance making them acquire strong symbolic connotations, as also documented in the ethnographic field.[50] Referring in particular to the find of the clay tuyère it seems appropriate at this point to cite a testimony precisely from this sector of studies: 'The Ogowe,[51] who have no knowledge of iron and, therefore, do not work with it, venerate the bellows of the blacksmiths of the neighbouring tribes'.[52]

The finding of smelting slag, isolated and far from areas of production, is not frequent but relevant enough to begin to ask questions about its likely symbolic significance. 12 slags were found next to the skeleton of a young man of about 5 years in the oldest mound of Gardolo (EBA I).[53] A single piece of slag comes from cut H on the site of Lasino,[54] a level with clear similarities to the Caves of Castel Corno, with their baked clay platforms and the remains of a secondary burial covered by a small mound of stones (see the preceding chapter). A handful of small smelting slag, probably originally contained in a vessel made of perishable material, was found in the settlement of the EBA at Pizzini di Castellano (Villalagarina, TN), where there was no sign of activity of metallurgical crafts in the locality or nearby. Some slag, an ingot, a tuyère and some polished porphyry pebbles come from the worship site of Volano San Rocco, on the other side of the valley.[55] Some small slags were also found at the monumental worship site at Velturno Tanzgasse (BZ), for which a symbolic interpretation linked to ritual activities has already been proposed[56] and from the worship sites at Anvoia and Ossimo-Pat in Val Camonica.[57] Broadening our out look to the European context, in some cemetery ascribable to the Bell Beaker horizon the sporadic presence of slag has been noted among elements of the grave goods.[58]

Regarding the state of health of the individuals buried in the Castel Corno Caves, recent anthropological analyses on the bones showed enamel hypoplasia and cribra orbitalia, tooth decay, tartar, wear and a dental situation with many growth anomalies, maybe of a hereditary nature and therefore an index of close familiarity between the individuals buried or endemic in the population. Furthermore, the degree of post-cranial bones fusion would be consistent with a younger individual compared to the dental age development. This difference could indicate a growth retardation.[59] Finally, in the vertebra of an adult individual from Chamber 1, evident traces of arthrosis were found.[60]

[48] Fasani, 1990.
[49] Nicolis 2016, p. 137; Nicolis, 2001, p. 356.
[50] In many cultures the bellows and other tools of the trade are venerated (Eliade 2018, p. 25).
[51] Gabon, Africa centrale.
[52] Eliade 2018, p. 25.
[53] Mottes *et al.* 2011, p. 521.
[54] Tecchiati 1995.
[55] Bassetti *et al.* 2005, p. 39.
[56] Dal Ri *et al.* 2004, p. 152.
[57] Fedele and Fossati 2012, p. 195; Poggiani Keller 2006, pp. 255–256.
[58] Peška 2016 p. 5; Pajuelo Pando and López Aldana 2016, p. 62.
[59] Mazzucchi *et al.* 2020, p. 14.
[60] Mazzucchi *et al.* 2020.

ORDER nr. D09/19	
Sample Name	Radiocarbon age
GCC5	**3946 (40)**
DSH code	AMS $\delta^{13}C$
DSH9256_GE	**-11 (1)**

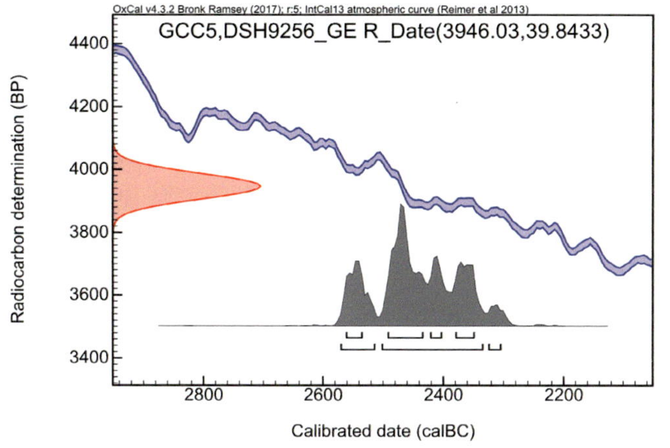

Sample name **GCC5**			Lab. CODE **DSH9256_GE**	
			1 sigma	
2561BC	-	**2536BC**	RelativeProbability	**17%**
2492BC	-	**2434BC**	RelativeProbability	**50%**
2421BC	-	**2404BC**	RelativeProbability	**13%**
2379BC	-	**2349BC**	RelativeProbability	**21%**
			2 sigma	
2570BC	-	**2514BC**	RelativeProbability	**19%**
2502BC	-	**2334BC**	RelativeProbability	**78%**
2324BC	-	**2305BC**	RelativeProbability	**3%**

Figure 26: Calibration made with the software Oxcal v.4.3.2 (Bronk Ramsey 2017) and IntCal13 atmospheric curve (Reimer *et al.* 2013).

In particular the cribra orbitalia was also discovered in individuals buried among the boulders of the landslide on the nearby site of Bersaglio di Mori[61] and in many other Copper and Bronze Age sites also outside Trentino Alto Adige region.[62] It has been documented how cribra orbitalia and porotic hyperostosis were in many cases caused by megaloblastic anemia and were generally quite widespread among ancient populations and, in an ethnographic terms, among communities living on a subsistence economy.[63] That seems to be caused by a decreased intake of nutritious substances (especially vitamin B_{12}) typical of periods of famine and which particularly affects the younger age group.[64] Such disorders could also be caused, or significantly worsened, by gastrointestinal parasite infections,[65] which noticeably increased from the Neolithic period onwards in agro-pastoral communities.[66] It should however be borne in mind that cribra orbitalia could also be the result of other pathologies such as scurvy, rickets, hemangiomas and traumatic injuries.[67]

As for the chronology of these burials a radiocarbon dating effected in 2019 by the laboratory AMS CIRCE-INNOVA in Naples[68] on a homerus found in Tomb 1 (sample n. GCC5) established that

[61] Avanzini *et al.* 1985, pp. 44–54.
[62] Pacciarelli and Teegen 1997, p. 33.
[63] Walker *et al.* 2009, p. 115.
[64] Walker *et al.* 2009, p. 112, fig. 3.
[65] Walker *et al.* 2009, p. 114–115.
[66] Ledger *et al.* 2019.
[67] Walker *et al.* 2009, p. 115.
[68] INNOVA SCaRL, Via Calabritto 20, 80121 Napoli, email: info@innova.campania.it; Terrasi *et al.* 2008.

Individual 3 lived at the end of the Copper Age. The outcome of the analysis (3946 -+ 40BP) and its calibration in fact places it between 2570 and 2305 BC (2 sigma, 95%), with an inner interval of greater probability (78%) between 2502 and 2334 BC (**Figure 26**) This result has since been recalibrated (and confirmed) thanks to the expertise of Erio Valzolgher, as between 2570–2300 BC (2 sigma, 95%).[69] On the other hand, a new dating carried out on the bone remains of Individual 2 gave a different result: 2276–2041 BC (2 sigma, 95%).[70]

In light of the resulting figures, we can suggest that all the burials analysed can be dated between the late Copper Age (at the time of the Bell Beaker horizon) and the initial phase of EBA. The artefacts dated in the later phases of EBA found near the human remains can be attributed to posthumous activity probably related to cultic practices possibly linked to ancestor worship (see Chapter 6).

[69] We thank Dr. Valzolgher for his consultancy. Notes from the Valzolgher report: 'The conventional radiocarbon age was converted into calendar years using the curve of calibration for terrestrial samples of the northern hemisphere IntCal13 (Reimer *et al.* 2013) and the software OxCal v4.3.2 (Bronk Ramsey 2009) [Interface build: 119; updated 23.09.2019]. The range of the data calibrated data, rounded to the decade, was calculated using the probability method (Stuiver and Reimer 1993).'

[70] Unpublished data, Institute for Mummy Studies-EURAC-Research (Bolzano), in the context of the project: 'Genomic diversity of prehistoric individuals from the Iceman's territory in the Eastern Italian Alps' granted by Provincia Autonoma di Bolzano – Alto Adige, bando di concorso 'Research Südtirol/Alto Adige 2019'.

5 – Paleoenvironmental and Economic Aspects

Many useful pointers emerged from the Castel Corno Caves excavations for the reconstruction of the surrounding natural environment and the site economy. The thorough sifting and flotation of the earth taken from inside the caves during the excavations in 1998 and 1999 led to the collection of abundant bone and botanical remains even of minute dimensions.

The analysis of the fauna,[1] together with that of the plant remains,[2] enables us to reconstruct, at least hypothetically, the type of ecosystem to be found outside the caves between the Late Copper Age and EBA.

Archaeozoology

A first brief archaeozoological study was completed and published in 1988.[3] It concerned a few dozen bone remains recovered during the survey by the Rovereto Civic Museum in 1987,[4] an investigation particularly concerned with the area of the castle and which led to the production of various publications and an exhibition.[5] Most of the bones were the remains of cattle *(Bos Taurus)*, followed by sheep and goats (*Ovis aries/Capra hircus*) and a few pigs (*Sus domesticus*) slaughtered at a young age. Given the high percentage of artefacts attributed to the Medieval Age in the material found on the surface around the castle, it would seem fair to assume that this group of faunal finds represents settlement phases relative to life in the castle (12th to 17th centuries AD).[6]

Regarding research in the area of the caves, the archaeozoological analysis of the bone remains was only carried out on finds from within their interior.[7] The sondages not stratigraphically excavated, carried out externally in the 1980s[8] by amateurs, are in fact characterized by a selective collection of bone remains which gave precedence to the artefacts rather than the simple skeletal remains. This new study involved 7904 animal bone finds of which 95% were found to be domestic species. Most of these remains were attributed to sheep and goats (49%), followed by pigs (27%) and then cattle (19%). As has already been shown for the EBA site of Pizzini di Castellano,[9] the high percentage of goats compared to the average for the period should be noted.[10]

Considering the sample analysed as a whole and thus including all the phases when the site was utilized, from the first burials in the Late Copper Age up to last occupation in the EBA, and keeping in mind that the latter contributed in a decidedly more relevant manner to the formation of the archaeological deposit, it appears plausible to use for comparison the framework well defined elsewhere[11] that takes into consideration an appropriate number of sites in north eastern Italy dated at the beginning of the Bronze Age. From this comparison it emerges that the percentage ratio between the domestic animals found at Castel Corno falls fully into the so-called 'Gruppo 3', to which the nearby sites of Colombo di Mori and of Pizzini di Castellano also belong. The contexts inserted into this group have a predominance of sheep and goats, a significant amount of pigs

[1] Analysis made by Alex Fontana (Fontana 2007) and published in Fontana *et al.* 2010.
[2] Carpological analysis made by Barbara Proserpio (University of Studies Milano, ARCO Cooperativa di Ricerche Archeobiologiche soc. coop. Laboratorio di Archeobiologia dei Musei Civici di Como); Anthracological analysis made by the dendrochronology section of Rovereto Civic Museum and, in particular, by Stefano Marconi, using the microscopes of Laboratorio 'B. Bagolini' courtesy of the Department of Letters and Philosophy University of Trento (Marconi *et al.*, in press).
[3] Avanzini 1988.
[4] See Chapter 1.
[5] Pasquali 1991.
[6] Maurina 2006, pp. 26–37.
[7] Fontana 2007; Fontana *et al.* 2010.
[8] See Chapter 1.
[9] Battisti and Marconi 2004, p. 48.
[10] Fontana *et al.* 2010, p. 46.
[11] Battisti and Marconi 2004.

followed by cattle. What stands out is the affinity with the fauna found at the settlement of Pizzini di Castellano, only two kilometres away as the crow flies.

Separating the fauna of the older layers in contact with the tombs (Chamber 3, US 9 and 10) from the rest of the determined bones, the only number that appears to vary much is the increased percentage of cattle which, from 10% in the older layers, rises to 21% in the contexts attributable with certainty to the EBA. This increase is mostly at the expense of the pigs which, beginning at 39% in the US 9 and 10, diminish to 22% in the other contexts. It should be noted however that, taking into consideration all the fauna found inside Chamber 3, the deepest and hardest to reach from the outside, the same difference is found, that is an increased percentage of pigs, compared with the other chambers. This would lead to the conclusion that the reason for this difference is not due to changes in the composition of the domestic fauna occurring between the end of the Copper Age and the beginning of the Bronze Age but rather to an explicit selection, perhaps concerning the modalities of worship.

Whatever the case, whether inside Chamber 3 or in the other places, even if the percentages vary in quite a relevant manner, the composition of the domestic fauna always remains within the parameters which characterize the afore mentioned Group 3 (predominance of sheep and goats, followed by pigs and cattle).

If to these figures we juxtapose the unusual concentration of sheep and goat perinatal individuals in Chamber 3, the discovery of the single bone of a dog showing signs of being butchered among the finds in Tomb 1 and the high percentage of burnt bones, there emerges the concrete possibility that all this evidence, anomalous among the areas investigated so far, indicates particular cultic practices linked to the burials.[12]

These practices are also suspected in other places of worship in the region: the presence of faunal remains in the funerary spaces at Riparo del Santuario,[13] at Cosina di Stravino, at Volano-San Rocco, at Solteri di Trento and at Riparo Nogarole 3 was interpreted as evidence of funeral banquets consumed near the tombs or as sacrificial offerings for the deceased.[14]

The wild fauna, in line with the trends of the period, only represents 3% of the total sample. Among these (in order of importance) red deer, wild boar, roe deer, hare, marten, bear, several species of small mammals and birds and, possibly, the wildcat have been documented.[15]

Various remains of shells typical of slow-moving aquatic environments were found too,[16] probably collected in the valley floor on the banks of the River Adige which at the time had a widely meandering form,[17] its water flowing at a much slower speed.[18] Together with some wild goose remains,[19] they provide some indication of how the resources of the valley floor were also used by these mountain communities.

Archaeobotany

Thanks to the sifting and flotation of the earth taken from the caves, many charcoal pieces and many carpological remains were sampled. The analyses so far carried out relate to the layers in direct

[12] As already proposed in Fontana *et al.* 2010.
[13] Riedel and Tecchiati, 1992.
[14] Nicolis 2001, p. 357.
[15] Fontana *et al.* 2010, pp. 52–58.
[16] Fontana *et al.* 2010, pp. 59–60.
[17] Angelucci 2016.
[18] During the 19th century AD, a drastic straightening of the alpine section of the River Adige took place: many meanders were filled in and the course of the river largely aligned also to facilitate the building of bridges and the railway to the detriment of the river navigation (Gorfer 1992, pp. 217, 247–248).
[19] Fontana *et al.* 2010, pp. 61.

contact with the human bones of Tomb 1, precisely in US 9 and 10. Considering the manipulation which already took place in ancient times and the partial contemporary disturbance we have had to attribute the charred remains to a very wide chronological time span from the end of the Copper Age until the beginning of the Bronze Age.

Among the species of origin of the charcoal analysed so far, the oak and ash stand out; to a lesser extent beech and maple, more sporadically hazel, cornelian cherry, poplar, elm and Scots pine were found (see **Figure 27**).[20] Considering the minute dimensions of the vegetal material collected, consisting primarily of branches rather than tree trunks, given the heterogeneous nature of the sample and the probable percentage distribution of species which prefigures a typical forest ecosystem of a sub-mountainous zone, we can realistically propose that a particular selection of species was not made during collection and the firewood was not brought from a great distance from the site or at least a height very different from that of the caves (800 masl). It would have been a typical ash and oak mixed forest that, given the altitude and the association, could probably have consisted of mainly downy oak.

	NR	
Quercus sp.	38	44.2%
Fraxinus sp.	19	22.1%
Fagus sylvatica L.	13	15.1%
Acer campestre L.	9	10.5%
Corylus avellana L.	2	2.3%
Ulmus sp.	2	2.3%
Populus sp.	1	1.2%
Pinus Sylvestris L.	1	1.2%
Cornus mas L. *cfr. Cornus sanguinea* L.	1	1.2%
TOTAL	**86**	

Figure 27: Determination of tree species of US 9 and 10 (Chamber 3).
Indeterminable remains have not been considered in this table.

If the statistical sample obtained is compared with the present composition of the woodland surrounding the archaeological site, strong similarities can be seen mainly from the presence of oak, ash, beech and maple, but also hazel, cornelian cherry and elm. Some species present today do not however figure among the charcoal analysed; for instance, the absence of hornbeam (*Ostrya carpinifolia*) is particularly notable, a tree generally quite common at this altitude.[21]

In the period of the burials (2500–2300 BC) we should be at the beginning of the climatic phase known as sub-boreal, characterized by a progressive drop in temperature.[22] The beech, for example, present only sporadically in the Atlantic period, was extremely widespread at the beginning of the sub-boreal.[23]

Given the similarity with the species present today in the same area, it could be cautiously proposed that the average temperature of the time, although dropping, was not so different from that of today, which instead is clearly rising rapidly.[24] It should be stressed, however, that the sub-boreal in northern Italy is characterized by a succession of phases alternately arid and humid, with a

[20] Analyses in course of elaboration by Stefano Marconi (Dendrochronology and Anthracology Laboratory of the Rovereto Civic Museum Foundation) to be published in the next edition of the Annali del Museo Civico di Rovereto; Marconi *et al.* (in press).
[21] The present floristic information is taken from the database of the botanic section of the Fondazione Museo Civico di Rovereto (personal communication of Alessio Bertoldi and Giulia Tomasi and from: Festi and Prosser 1991).
[22] Orombelli and Ravazzi 1996; Bertoldi 1968.
[23] Bertoldi 1968, p. 144.
[24] For a general picture of the temperature trend from the last glaciations to today see McMichael 2012.

general trend towards greater humidity in the EBA.[25] Moreover radically varied phenomena seem to manifest themselves in relatively contiguous geographical areas[26] which is why it is difficult to rely on a unique paleoclimatic model for large areas.[27]

It is interesting to note how, even though at a much lower altitude, also in the layers datable between the end of the Copper Age and the EBA in the Gaban rock shelter site at Trento, a high percentage of oak (54%) and ash (9%) were found, although perhaps, in this case, this presence could also be influenced by the presence of wood structural elements close to the shelter.[28] Since this shelter is situated near the valley floor, obviously the presence of beech has not been documented in this case, whereas at Castel Corno it represents the third species in order of importance; but cornelian cherry and hazel are present here too, the latter's proliferation probably conditioned by anthropic needs and activities.[29] The anthracological analyses conducted on levels dated in the Late Copper Age at the site of worship at Velturno (BZ), situated at a similar altitude to the site which is the subject of this volume, found oak clearly prevalent over other species (72%).[30]

The carpological analyses carried out on the samples derived from the flotation, permit the determination of 2235 vegetal remains, 60% of which consisted of cereals, followed by 37% fruit, 3% legumes peas and grass pea and other vegetal species like flax.[31] The cereals documented, in order of importance, are as follows: *Triticum monococcum*, *Triticum dicoccum*, *Hordeum vulgare*, *Triticum aestivum/durum*, *Triticum spelta* and *Triticum timopheevi* (see **Figure 28**).

Of the fruit trees the cornelian cherry predominates followed by the grapevine, hazel, oak, pear, blackthorn and apple (see **Figure 29**).

Comparing these figures with those of other sites of a similar period in the region, an affinity can be seen with the percentage distribution observed on the site near the Adige valley floor at Gaban rock shelter (TN), for the cereals rather than the fruit, but also for the percentage of the various cereal species. There is a net difference where the fruit are concerned since at the latter site there is a prevalence of vines compared to the cornelian cherry fruits.[32]

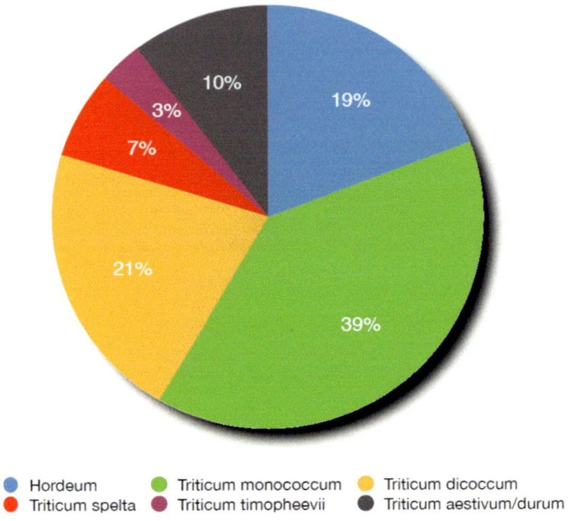

Figure 28: Determination of cereal plants of US 9 and 10 (Chamber 3).

Cornus mas	88.7%
Vitis vinifera (and cfr *vitis vinifera*)	4.4%
Quercus sp. (and cfr *quercus* sp.)	3.2%
Corylus avellana	2.9%
cfr. *Pyrus* sp.	0.4%
Prunus spinosa	0.3%
Malus sp.	0.1%

Figure 29: Determination of fruit remains of US 9 and 10 (Chamber 3). Indeterminate remains have not been considered in this table.

[25] Leonardi *et al.* 2015, p. 296.
[26] Leonardi *et al.* 2015, p. 297.
[27] Dörfler 2015, p. 330.
[28] Nisbet 1984, p. 305.
[29] Nisbet 1984, pp. 301–302.
[30] Castiglioni and Tecchiati 2005, p. 516, tab. 3.
[31] Analyses made by Barbara Proserpio (Università degli studi di Milano, ARCO Cooperativa di Ricerche Archeobiol ogiche soc.coop. Laboratorio di Archeobiologia dei Musei Civici di Como) to be published in the next edition of the Annali del Museo Civico di Rovereto: Marconi *et al.* (in press).
[32] Nisbet 1984.

Compared to the site of Riparo del Santuario at Lasino[33] in the Castel Corno Caves site a greater percentage of fruit is found with respect to cereals with a lesser presence of barley (38% of the total cereals at Lasino and only 19% at Castel Corno). This could indicate a greater inclination to cultivate cereals at Lasino probably due to its geomorphological situation with broad flat spaces a short distance from the site. Conversely, the steep wooded slopes interspersed with the small isolated valleys characteristic of the landscape around the Castel Corno site probably made forest management more worthwhile, perhaps via coppicing, thus benefitting the expansion of small fruit trees.

The carpological study also led to observation of the state of conservation of the remains analysed. It seems reasonable to suppose that the plants were subjected to slow combustion, perhaps controlled and thus intentional, which prevented the burning of the offerings (in several cases even the fruit pulp was preserved).[34]

Reconstruction of the environment

Cross checking the archaeozoological and archaeobotanical data available, it is hypothetically possible to reconstruct the surrounding natural environment and the exploitation of the resources it offers by the human group located. The botanic data tend to show a quite varied ecosystem in which natural and purely rural aspects of an agropastoral kind coexist. The significant percentage of pigs, shared by other contemporary sites in this part of the Adige valley, is in tune with the anthracological evidence, which suggests an environment suitable for breeding them, especially in reference to the presence of beech and oak trees.

The traditional farming of pigs, before modern times, had these domestic animals grazing in wooded areas rich in acorns and beech nuts.[35] This practice has already been hypothesised, for the sites of the EBA at Colombo di Mori and of Pizzini di Castellano.[36]

The low incidence of cornelian cherry among the burnt wood remains contrasts with the abundance of cornelian cherries fruits documented among the carpological remains. Given the prominence this fruit seems to have enjoyed during the Copper and Bronze Ages, probably also used to produce alcoholic beverages from its fermentation,[37] it is likely that the cornelian cherry trees were cared for and protected and so not generally used for firewood. The abundance of cornelian cherry fruits remains in US 9 and 10 of Tomb 1, 644 charred remains constituting 85% of all the fruit found,[38] seems to emphasize the importance this fruit must have had in worship practices. An anthropic management of the mixed oak forest creating the proliferation of fruit trees like the cornelian cherry has already been proposed by various authors, a process which seems to have begun in the Copper Age and was already being tried in an early form in the Neolithic Age.[39] The presence of cornelian cherries fruits and hazelnuts has also been documented, in the region, in the sites of Velturno,[40] Riparo Gaban,[41] Lasino[42] and Ledro,[43] contexts that extend from the Late Copper Age to the EBA.

The numerous remains of cereals found in the burial mound in Chamber 3, together with polished use-wear traces on sickle blades found both in Chambers 1 and 2 and in the outside area, would

[33] Costantini *et al.* 2003.
[34] Marconi *et al.* (in press).
[35] Sebesta 1996, pp. 189–196.
[36] Bonardi *et al.* 2002, p. 97; Battisti and Marconi 2004, p. 49.
[37] Colledge 2007, p. 398; Battaglia 1943, p. 26.
[38] Including indeterminate remains. See Marconi *et al.* (in press).
[39] Nisbet 1984, p. 302; Pals and Voorrips 1981, p. 40; Rottoli 2001, p. 16; Tecchiati *et al.* 2013, p. 47–48.
[40] Castiglioni and Tecchiati 2005, pp. 521–524.
[41] Nisbet 1984.
[42] Costantini *et al.* 2003.
[43] Battaglia 1943, pp. 12, 26, 27.

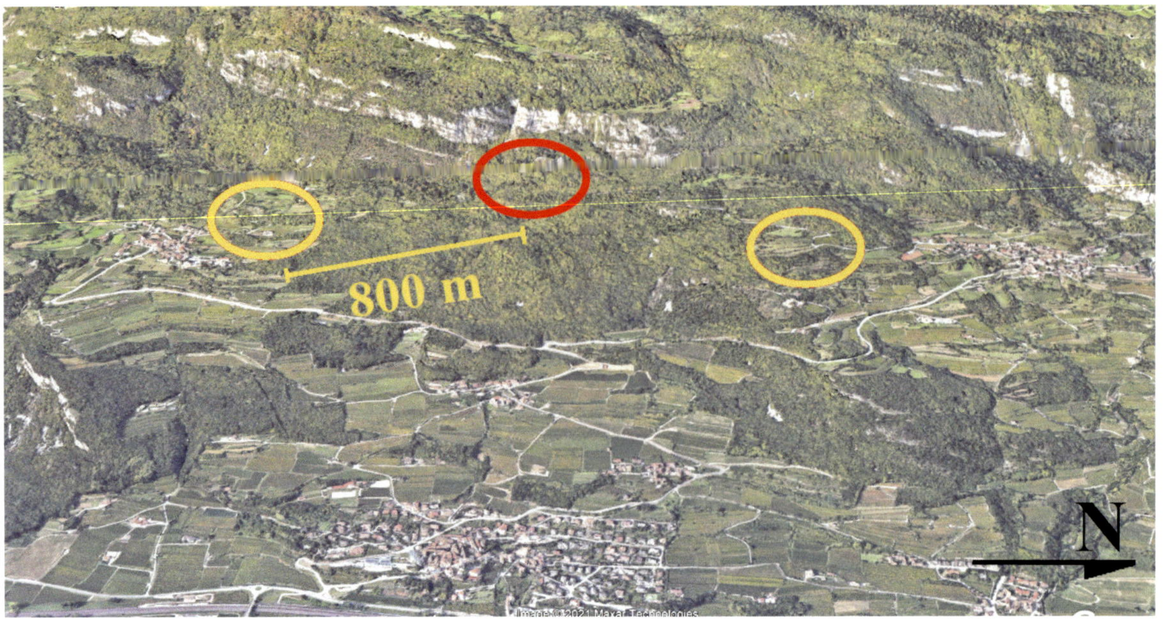

Figure 30: Localization of hypothetical flat cultivable fields near the site (red circle: site location; yellow circle: flat fields location - image taken from Google Earth).

suggest the existence of spaces dedicated to their cultivation in places not too far from the site. Given the steepness and ruggedness of the slopes and the surrounding terraces, partly determined by the landslide which created the caves, it is possible there were small cultivated plots perhaps inside the hollows to the west of the rocky 'corna' (horns) on which the castle was later built. Nevertheless, seeing the limited space, we could picture the use of wider terraces near the present day village of Lenzima, to the south, or near today's village of Patone, to the north. In either case the nearest flat spaces would have been about 800 metres away as the crow flies (see **Figure 30**), less than one-hour walking distance.

Regarding the extent of the area of anthropogenic impact around the settlements, it should be noted that studies carried out on the agropastoral economies of other contemporary sites tend to propose that, between Late Copper Age and EBA, the anthropic impact on the ecosystems only had an important effect on a limited area close to the place of residence.[44] However, considering that the geomorphological context in which the site of Castel Corno Caves is inserted is radically different from those that characterize the typical pile-dwelling environments, the type of land management could consequently be very different. For example, it cannot be excluded that, given the scattered and widespread type of population that seems to characterize this stretch of the Adige Valley, especially during the EBA, each community was organized in such a way as to control and exploit its territory in a widespread way, and not centralized on a particular settlement (see chapter 6). It is intended that, in other words, the same community that managed the pastures, the fruit trees and the place of worship in the Castel Corno area could at the same time cultivate its cereal fields a few kilometres away, giving rise to small detached settlement structures united in one fractional but well-organized network.

In conclusion we can picture a very varied environment. Next to the deciduous woodland near the settlement, probably kept for pig grazing, there would have been zones where some forest management was practised with a sizable amount of cornelian cherry plus other fruit trees like vines, pears, apples and blackthorn. Areas reserved for sheep and goats and cattle pasture were perhaps higher up, on the wide terraces of Nagustello (1000–1200 masl), near Bordala (1200 masl) or, even higher, on Mount Stivo (up to 2000 masl). This would require relocation of some kilometres

[44] Leonardi *et al.* 2015, p. 294.

to skirt the cliffs of the site and climb to the pastures with the livestock. In the area of Passo Bordala and the summit of Mount Stivo three flint arrowheads were found datable between Late Copper Age and EBA,[45] giving rise to the theory that these high lands were used for pasture.[46]

The shepherds, far from their settlement and therefore also from its food resources, probably occasionally hunted. Furthermore, it cannot be excluded that these tools could also be used as weapons to resolve issues and tensions relating to the use of high pastures by different communities.

Finally, perhaps there could have been some fields cultivated with cereals not far away, on the flatter terraces of the present day Lenzima and Patone.

[45] Battisti and Cavalieri 2019.
[46] Battisti and Cavalieri (in press).

6 – General Discussion and Conclusions

The archaeological site of Castel Corno Caves, despite many stratigraphic associations having been lost as a result of digging by looters and with the non-stratigraphic excavations carried out by local amateurs at the end of the 60s and beginning of the 70s of last century, has produced a considerable quantity of useful data for understanding living conditions and other cultural and socio-economic aspects related to the human group settled there; this study involved comparisons extended to a wide geographical chessboard. This was made possible, as already described in the earlier chapters, thanks to the excavation campaigns of the Rovereto Civic Museum conducted in 1998 and 1999 and to the detailed study of all the collected finds and all the textual, graphic and photographic documentation archived from 1969 to today.[1] All these data indicate that the area of the caves and the castle were frequented from between the Copper Age and EBA.

It seems permissible to imagine, principally on the basis of the pottery typology, an intense occupation of the site during EBA II (see Chapter 3), and an apparently less intense occupation during EBA I, however confirmed by radiocarbon dating (see Chapter 4). The contexts disturbed by looting in Chamber 3, as a matter of fact, did not permit a clear reading of the stratigraphy which made a precise chronological scan of each stage of use difficult. The least damaged layers (US 9 and 10) produced both material datable to both the end of the Copper Age and the Early Bronze Age (see **Figure 31**).

Some of these artefacts can be dated with certainty to an advanced phase of EBA (EBA II, see Chapter 3) but it cannot be excluded, as already stated, that some types of ceramic forms attributable to a broader chronological spectrum, are maybe the result of a EBA I frequentation.

It should however be pointed out that most of the EBA pottery comes from the top layer (US 13) which is the product of remixing due to the non-stratigraphic excavations which took place in

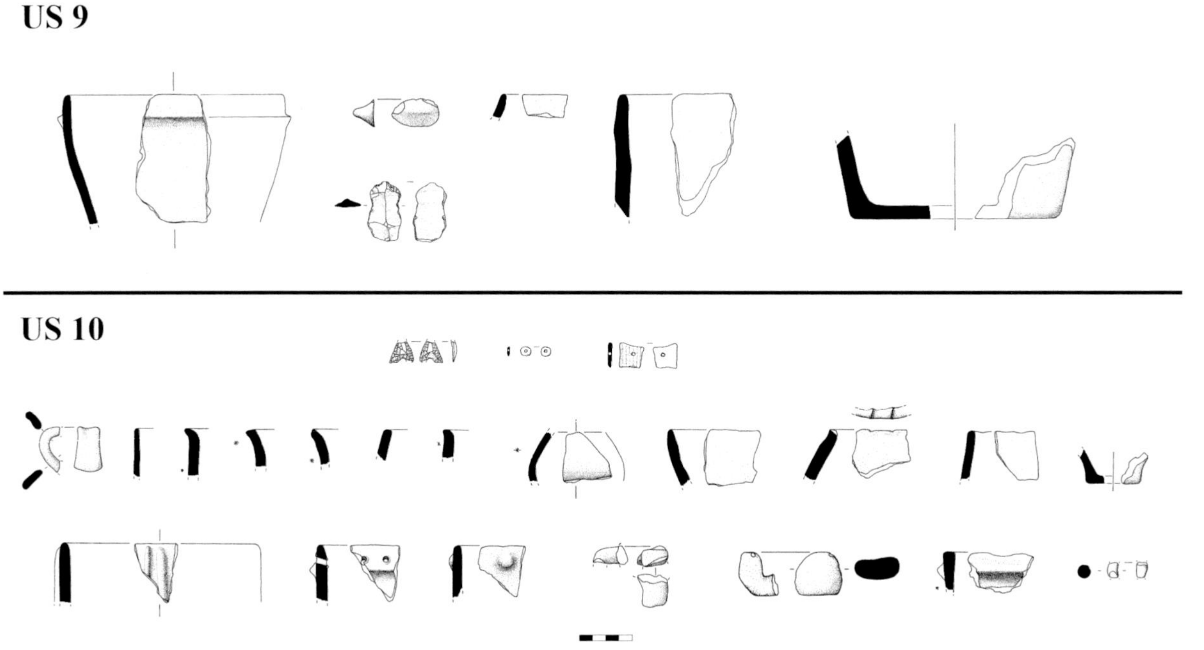

Figure 31: Vessel potsherds from US 9 and 10 (Chamber 3).

[1] Decisive, in this sense, was the degree thesis work of Elena Regola who organized all the previous material and paper documentation, present in the museum, referring to the site (Regola 2005).

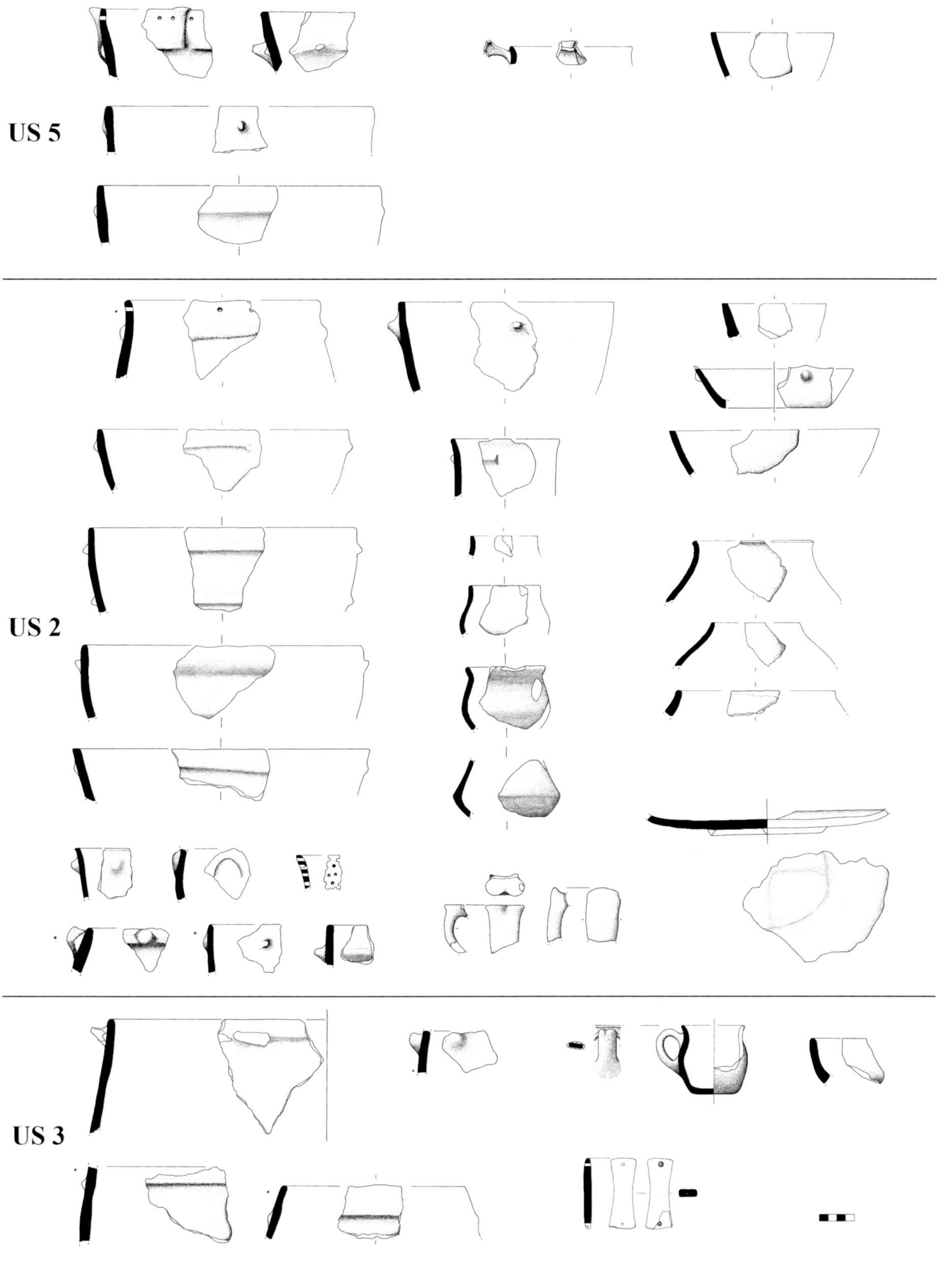

Figure 32: Vessel potsherds from Chamber 1 in order of excavation: US 5, 2 and 3.

the decades before the campaigns of the Rovereto Civic Museum. It is thus impossible to be able to reconstruct the form and dimensions of the hypothetical occupation layers datable to the EBA inside this chamber, which must have been situated between the so-called Zone 2 and the mound of Tomb 1. It is also impossible to understand whether those activities damaged the layers of Tomb 1 or the mishandling was all the result of the first excavations in 1969.

The undamaged stratigraphic situation that emerged in 1999 inside Chamber 1 allows us however to assume an EBA I date for US 3, the deepest layer investigated in that sector (see Chapter 3 and **Figure 32**).

Settlement, cemetery or place of worship?

One of the theories sustained in the past described a landslide happening at two different moments with a consequent intermediate phase in which the area between the boulders from the first landslide was occupied for settlement and cultic purposes. The stratigraphy thus formed would then have been covered and crushed by a second landslide.[2] This would explain the fact that the stratigraphic succession, in some points (for example inside Chamber 3), completely filled (to roof level) the empty spaces between the stacked boulders. In the light of new studies and numerous inspections carried out in recent years this hypothesis should probably be discarded in view of some geological and stratigraphic factors. If we were to take into consideration the hypothesis that the boulder that forms the vault of Chamber 3 and the rest of the landslide over it, fell subsequently, the impact would have been very significant. Given the vertical profile that mount Biaena has in this area, in fact, the landslide would not have slid along a slope, but dropped vertically, accumulating great kinetic energy. With these volumes (sub-quadrangular boulders sometimes over 10 metres wide), the boulders underneath would at the least have been fractured or partly crumbled. Any archaeological stratigraphy would have undergone significant trauma, clearly visible to the naked eye or more probably have totally disappeared, scattered among the rocky debris. As always happens in the case of large landslides, the impact of a fall like that would have been of sufficient violence to generate a thick layer of crumbled stone between the boulders making up the roof and the walls of the caves. This intermediate layer does not exist at Castel Corno and the boulders are in close contact one against the other without any apparent impact trauma. Furthermore, from a visual analysis, walls, floor and roof of Chamber 3 seem, with all probability, to belong to a single large boulder whose cracks, caused by the impact, would have formed empty spaces within itself, which were then frequented during the EBA. Finally, most of the layers which fill Zone 1 (see **Figure 7**) would seem to be of natural origin: anthropic soil that flooded into the caves so as to totally fill the southern portion of the cavity defined as Zone 1 (see **Figure 3**).[3] Excluding these earliest hypotheses, apart from the interpretative difficulties connected to the poor conservation of the original sites, the general interpretation of this cave complex as a place of worship and burial has never since been put in doubt. The evidence of burials found inside Chamber 3 were discovered covered by layers full of charcoal and baked clay fragments related to small baked clay platforms: a context which, even if partially damaged, can with every likelihood be attributed to the funerary and cultic sphere. The high percentage of burned flints and bones is also an index to keep in mind for reconstructing the usage patterns of the site. A comparison with the nearby sites of Pizzini di Castellano and Dosso Alto di Borgo Sacco, Bronze Age contexts purely dwelling places is, in this sense, enlightening. The burned flints in these settlements constitute, in fact, 11–12% of the total[4] while at Castel Corno they come to 28.5%. For burned bones the difference is even more marked: in fact, we find very low percentages at Pizzini (0.3%) and at Dosso Alto

[2] Tecchiati 2005; Avanzini 1985.
[3] Part of these geological and pedological considerations have been taken from the personal communications of the geologists Michela Canali (Earth Science Section of the Rovereto Civic Museum Foundation), Marco Avanzini and Michele Bassetti, on the occasion of three different inspections inside the caves.
[4] For the Pizzini di Castellano see Battisti 2001; for the site of Dosso Alto see Trinco 2020.

(7.3%),[5] while very high rates for Castel Corno, where 60% of the fauna has been altered by heat.[6] Comparing these percentages with those documented for a place of worship in the Copper Age at Pigloner Kopf (Pfatten, BZ),[7] we note an even more extreme situation: 91.7%f the bones here show alterations due to fire in varying degrees.

It is however to be noted that the stratigraphic contexts that have arisen inside the caves must have had diversified origins and modes of formation. For Chamber 3, for instance, we can document both anthropic activities linked to burials and worship practices, as well as natural formations probably of colluvial origins. Considering the trend and composition of the visible layers in section A-B of Chamber 3 (see **Figure 7**) it is in fact likely that US 1, 2, 3, 4, 5, 6 and 7 were of colluvial origin and, layer after layer, they gradually filled the southern portion of the cavity defined as Zone 1, the antrum for the tombs. In this regard it should be mentioned that all these layers were strongly inclined. According to the data collected during the explorations of 1969, at the entrance to the cavity housing the tombs (Zone 1) the rock vault was about 50 cm from the floor. Around 150 cm inside the cavity the earth already began to touch the rock vault, with a gradient of 33%. This situation should reflect the original conditions, before any kind of excavation activities, not apparent to the first explorers in 1969.[8] It seems plausible therefore to imagine that the layers that cover the burial mound were deposited from south to north giving rise to this incline. The theory already formulated (see Chapter 2) of a possible ancient direct access connecting Chamber 1 to Chamber 3 could offer a better explanation for this accrual, probably of colluvial origin: the layers would have slid from Chamber 1 towards Chamber 3 one after another until they completely blocked the narrow passage. The fact that these layers are of colluvial origin would be proved not only by their composition and inclination but also by their visible trend in section (see **Figure 7**). The slight central depression would in fact suggest the formation of a small riverbed caused by water flowing from south to north.

In the current state of the research, we would however exclude the idea of an occupied settlement within the cave complex examined. Considering the extreme conditions which characterise a large part of the caves explored (difficult access, reduced dimensions of the space inside, very high humidity, total absence of natural light, etc.) we can with certainty exclude such a use for Chambers 2, 3 and 4. Chamber 1, on the other hand, could possibly have been used as an occasional shelter, having partial natural illumination, easy access and ampler space. Nevertheless, the internal excavations in 1974 and 1999 did not lead to the identification of any clear evidence in that sense. Chamber 1 seems to have been made use of principally as an antechamber for the burial and worship zones. However there also remains the possibility, already proposed in Chapter 3, that at least part of the deposits found near the Chamber 1 entrance, could be due to anthropic rubbish disposal or colluvial accumulations coming from external settlement contexts. The abundance of animal bone remains, for example, could have a similar origin considering that the distribution percentage of each species found in Chamber 1 differs from that documented inside Chamber 3, linked more probably to ritual offerings than to random discards of external origin.

It has to be remembered that until now only a small portion of the stratigraphic context formed inside Chamber 1 has been investigated, a superficial portion datable to the EBA. The finding of an adult vertebra in the floor of this chamber in Sondage 2 in 1974, for example, opens the possibility that this spacious location was also used, at least in part, for burial purposes.

If up to the 21st century BC these caves seem to have been used as a burial site, the subsequent occupation in the more advanced phases of EBA could possibly fit well with its posited ritual

[5] Personal communication of Stefano Marconi (data taken from the database of the Zooarchaeology Section of the Rovereto Civic Museum Foundation).
[6] Fontana *et al.* 2010, p. 62.
[7] Oberrauch 2014.
[8] Communication of the discoverer, sig. Dario Candioli, interviewed by one of the authors of this volume (U.T.).

nature, in the framework of a cult oriented towards their ancestors. Ancestor worship, its various manifestations being well documented at an ethnographic level,[9] seems to have found fertile soil all over Europe at least from the Copper Age: a phenomenon often linked to megalithism (not just in the strictly European panorama).[10] Megalithism and the related ancestor worship seems to be attested for example, in the mound of the site of Gardolo (TN). Even if in this case the succession of events is shifted forward by some centuries (from the EBA to the Late Bronze Age), in Gardolo the same situation observed in the Castel Corno Caves seems to have occurred: a burial and cultic area which, over the centuries, abandoned its initial function to become an important place of memory probably dedicated to ancestor worship.[11]

Although a phase of low frequentation took place during the EBA I, as has already been assumed, it is likely that the successive use for cult purposes during the EBA II could still be connected, directly or indirectly,[12] to the more ancient burial practices documented in Chamber 3 and dated between the Late Copper Age and EBA I. The reuse of ancient monuments or burial sites is often directly connected to the construction of a social memory, identity of the community and descent.[13] Even after a long gap the reclaiming of these places can be interpreted as an 'attempt to construct a tradition'.[14] In some cases the ancestors' burial site may not only act as a door to the world of the hereafter, but also as a spiritual centre through which the dead exercise their power over the living.[15]

At this point it seems opportune to suggest a further general reflection of an essentially anthropological nature regarding the connection between the geomorphological and environmental characteristics of the site and its use for burial and worship purposes. This cave complex, formed by the random stacking of the enormous boulders of the landslide, generated an intricate maze of chambers, pits, corridors, gullies, ravines and crevices not always easily passable. Considering the numerous interconnections between the caves, some impossible to navigate, with air currents generated from within, warm in winter and cool in summer, to the eyes of the communities settled here this site would certainly have appeared a very special place. The spiritual value these places must have possessed in the Copper Age is confirmed by the previously mentioned worship site at Pigloner Kopf, geomorphologically very similar to Castel Corno although of different geological origin.[16] For that matter, in all cultures worldwide the chthonic depths have always had a strong link with the spiritual sphere, both in death and rebirth, thus amounting to places of creation and regeneration.[17] Furthermore, a particular place like this one might also suggest more than a generic search for contact with the 'earthly mother', perhaps common to other burials in rock shelters widespread in the region between the end of the III and beginning of the II millennium BC (see Chapter 4); given the unusual geomorphological characteristics and the depth of these caves, this site may have represented, for the local communities, a sort of 'omphalos', i.e. the creator and regenerator centre of their world, beginning and end of all things and so a direct link with the realm of the dead.[18]

Although the studies so far carried out have mostly concerned the interior of the caves and therefore the cult aspects, the evidence of settlement occupation of the site is not irrelevant. The majority of the artefact classes most commonly found in settlement contexts were discovered outside the caves. For example, 72% (13 out of 18) of the sickle blades, which in many cases show polished use-

[9] Steadman *et al.*1996.
[10] Genov 2016; Aswani and Kumar 2018.
[11] Gardolo - GARM 2: Mottes and Nicolis 2019, p. 212; Mottes *et al.* 2011.
[12] Direct: in the oral tradition the symbolic value of the site was preserved; indirect: the chance find of ancient human bone remains could have been the origin of a new form of cult in the same place.
[13] Holst 2013.
[14] Holst 2013, p. 112.
[15] Holst 2013, p. 115.
[16] Oberrauch 2014; among other things there are documented on this site phenomena related to air currents similar to those of Castel Corno.
[17] Eliade 2001, pp. 221–229, ch. 86–88.
[18] Eliade 2001, pp. 210–212 ch. 81, pp. 340–344 ch. 143.

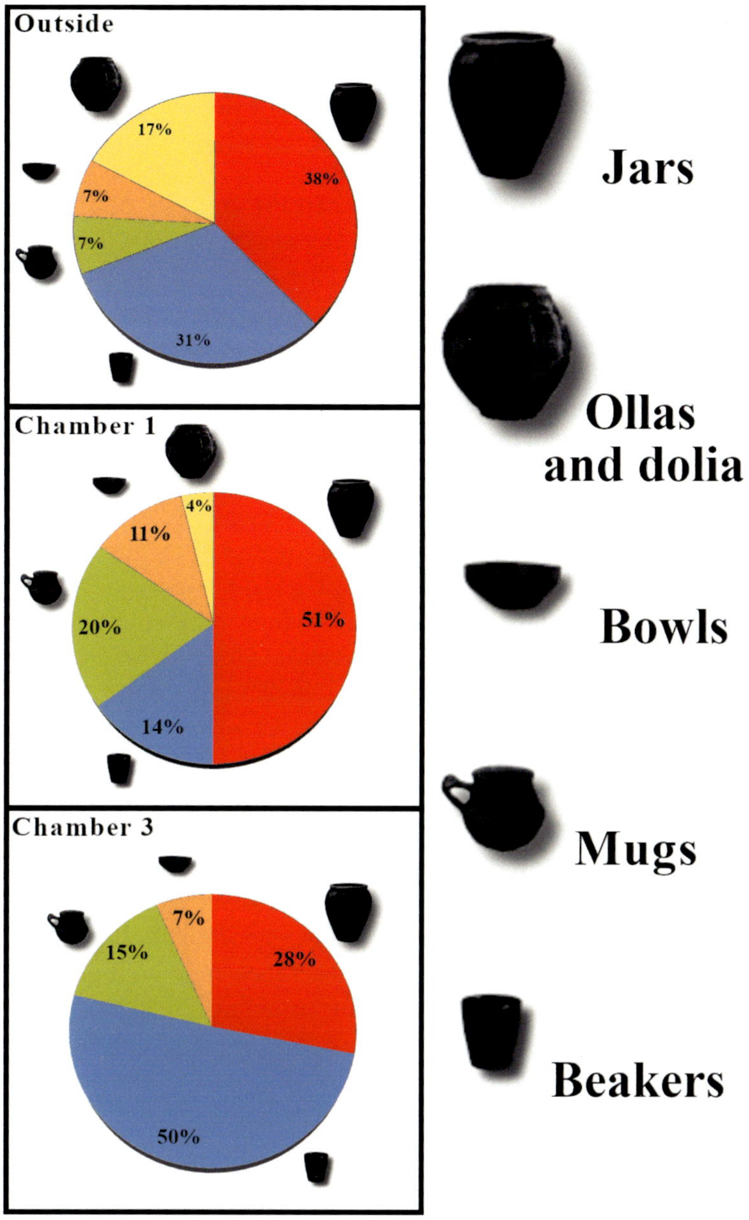

Figure 33: Distribution of the vessel classes in the site.

wear traces were found during sondages made between the 1970s and 80s outside the caves (see Chapter 1). Among these, ten were found in a flat area in the open exactly over Chamber 1. This area can be described as a sort of wide corridor bounded by two vertical, parallel rock walls roughly three metres high which create a protected plateau of about 53 square metres (3.5 m × 15 m) right on the top of the landslide accumulation which produced the cave complex being investigated. From the same area come numerous potsherds, three end scrapers, a side scraper, a burnisher and a retouched flint flake (see Chapter 1 and Plates 34–36), whereas three sickle blades come from the immediate vicinity of the castle. A further four, from the excavations in 1999, were found at the entrance of Chamber 1. As the access to this chamber slopes steeply inwards, this could support the hypothesis already proposed regarding the occasional presence of artefacts thrown out or perhaps naturally floated into this chamber from the settled area above. A single sickle blade has come from Chamber 2, where outside elements could easily have infiltrated through the direct, steeply inclined connection with the area above the caves (see the entrances in **Figure 3**). No sickle blades were found in the deeper chambers where the burials took place.

As regards the distribution of the different pottery types some differences can be noted between outside the caves, Chamber 1 and Chamber 3 (**Figure 33**). It is striking, for example, that the number of ollas diminishes progressively as one enters the caves and that inside Chamber 3 half the determinable potsherds consist of beakers.

In consideration of these reflections and after a careful analysis of the typology and spatial distribution of the finds in the whole area around the castle and the caves, we can presume the first occupation as being in the Late Copper Age. This involved the area near the ruins of the medieval castle (see Chapter 3), perhaps for settlement, and the cave complex as a place of burial. During the EBA the settled area seems to have moved directly over the caves perhaps making use of the sides of the landslide boulders as structural elements for the dwellings.[19]

Reconstruction of the chronological stages of the frequentation of the site and the manner of occupation has been affected by the limitation of the area investigated through regular stratigraphic excavations. Even if the use of the caves as places of burial seems to have been limited to the Late Copper Age and to the beginning of the EBA, it cannot be excluded, for example, that throughout the EBA they had continued to bury their dead using other caves. The area of the landslide with its great blocks piled up so as to form ravines, crevices and caves of various shapes and sizes, full of earth, is well spread out round the castle. Most of these caves are difficult to find being and covered with vegetation, but other small cavities are quite visible and accessible, at times unfortunately showing signs of looting. Basically, we wish to emphasize that the validity of the conclusions reached in this study is limited to the areas investigated. Starting from the data so far acquired we have tried to propose a general framework related to the phases and manner in which the whole area of Castel Corno was frequented, while aware of the fact that new research could modify this interpretation. Still open, for example, is the question whether the settlement was seasonal. Even though the site is situated at an altitude compatible with the establishment of a permanent settlement, other aspects related to the geomorphology and sun exposure level point in the opposite direction. The absence of flat terraces wide enough for cultivating cereals, the general harshness of the place and the continuous small landslips, still active today, would discourage the foundation of a permanent settlement. The EBA settlement of Pizzini di Castellano, not far from the site in question and only 100 m lower down (700 masl), enjoys excellent sun exposure, a milder climate and wide, flat terraces a very short distance from the site.[20] From this point of view the difference between the two sites is quite considerable.[21] Lacking further data on the settlement areas of the Castel Corno site, the research is, for the moment, postponed to the future, leaving the question open, envisaging the not entirely remote hypothesis of a seasonal use for pastoral purposes, a place half way up the mountain which could also serve as a base camp for making access to higher areas easier. In this case the traces of wear on the sickle blades might perhaps indicate reuse of tools already employed to cut cereals in the valley for mountain mowing,[22] or the wear could have been caused by wild grasses containing, in the same way as cereals, enough silicon to result in the classic polishing of the surfaces of the flint blade.

Settlement in Vallagarina between the Copper and Early Bronze Ages

In this stretch of the Adige valley not many sites can be dated to the Copper Age. The fact that much of the evidence consists of decontextualized occasional finds makes it quite difficult to reliably reconstruct the human settlement and the way the land was used. Suffice it to say that the only site in Vallagarina datable in the Late Copper Age which has a stratigraphic documentation is precisely that of the Castel Corno Caves. Having such incomplete documentation, it is even

[19] This refers to a natural corridor form positioned exactly above the caves, where numerous finds were made.
[20] Battisti 1999, 2001, 2003 and 2004.
[21] To compare the sun exposure level and acclivity of the slopes of the two sites see 'Carta delle esposizioni' and 'Carta delle pendenze' on the cartography site of the Provincia Autonoma di Trento (https://webgis.provincia.tn.it/) at the following coordinates WGS84: Castel Corno Caves - Lat. 45.88816, Long. 10.99073; Pizzini di Castellano - Lat. 45.92151, Long. 11.01267.
[22] In reference to possible seasonality of the settlement see Chapter 6.

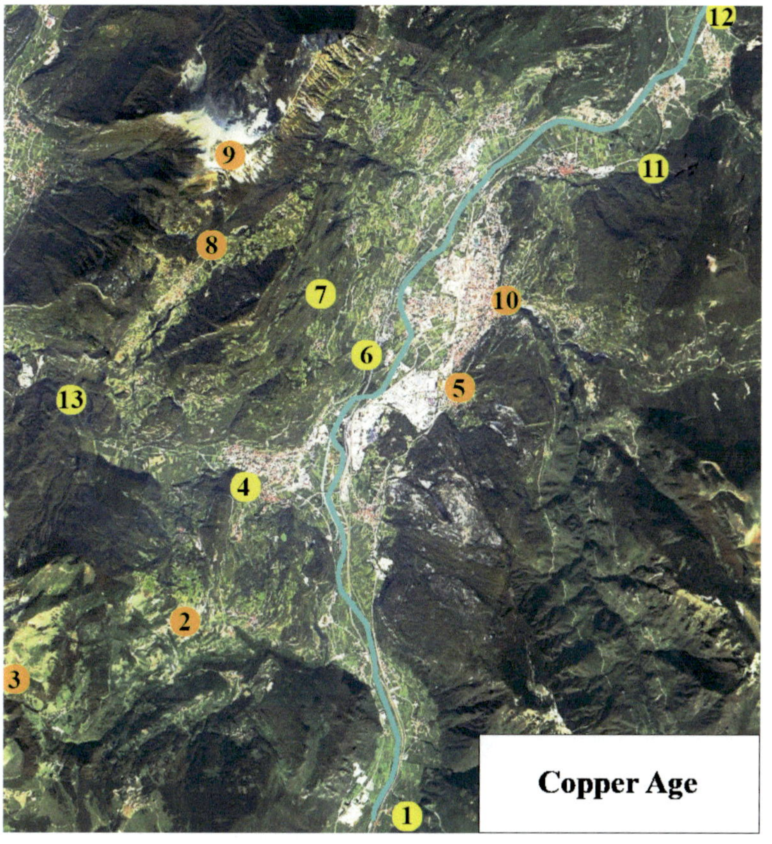

Figure 34: Distribution map of Copper Age finds (orange) and sites (yellow). 1. Le Corone, 2. Vico e Bojom, 3. M. Altissimo, 4. Bersaglio, 5. Lizzana, 6. La Torretta e Dos Pipel, 7. Grotte di Castel Corno, 8. Passo Bordala, 9. M. Stivo, 10. Balteri e Laste Rosse, 11. Paludei, 12. Acquaviva, 13. S. Andrea Island.

more difficult to try to expand the analysis in order to identify single chronological phases within the Copper Age.

At the current state of research, the distribution of sites (see **Figure 34**) appears compatible with the sparse settlement documented in the same area for the Neolithic Age,[23] except for the evidence attested in the high mountains (e.g. mount Stivo and mount Altissimo),[24] whose frequentation for pastoral purposes seems to start from the Copper Age also in other Alpine areas.[25]

At the site of Isera La Torretta, a settlement situated on a terrace a short distance from the valley floor and not far from the Castel Corno Caves, continuous settlement from the Neolithic to the Late Copper Age can be noted.[26] In general, however, during the Copper Age, at least as far as the Adige valley is concerned, a certain break could be perceived with respect to the preceding settlement:[27] the dynamics of settlement seem to change, even if for the moment only at an embryonic level. The Copper Age seems to be, therefore, a period of significant changes bringing new cultural, settlement and socio-economic assets, a phenomenon already seen in the neighbouring regions affected by the subsequent development of the Polada Culture.[28] In Vallagarina the dynamics of settlement changed in a clear and radical way during the EBA (2200–1650 BC). There was a proliferation of sites both at mid altitude and in the valley floor

[23] Tecchiati 1996a; Pedrotti 2001a.
[24] Battisti and Cavalieri 2019.
[25] Battisti and Cavalieri (in press).
[26] de Marinis and Pedrotti 1997, p. 259.
[27] de Marinis and Pedrotti 1997, p. 250, tab. 1.
[28] Rapi 2013, p. 526.

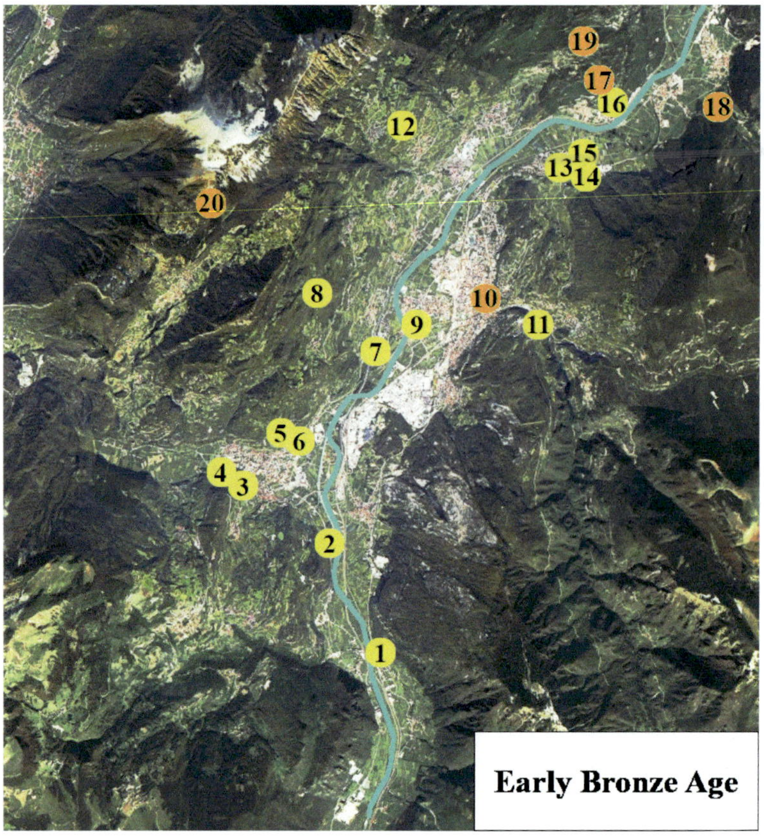

Figure 35: Distribution map of Early Bronze Age finds (orange) and sites (yellow). 1. Serravalle, 2. Castel Tierno e Montecatini, 3/4. Bersaglio e Colombo, 5. Monte Albano, 6. Molina, 7. Castel Pradaglia, 8. Grotte di Castel Corno, 9. Dosso Alto, 10. Rovereto city centre, 11. San Colombano, 12. Pizzini di Castellano, 13/14/15. Le Ville, San Rocco e Dos Destor, 16. Monte Corona, 17. Dos Alt (Nomi), 18. Castel Beseno, 19. Corona di Sachiel, 20. Becchetta.

(see **Figure 35**).[29] The area around today's town of Mori, in particular, has produced the largest amount of archaeological evidence, probably because it was a focal point of great importance for the control of the routes that connected the Adige valley to the Lake Garda area. Given the limited size of the contexts so far investigated it seems reasonable to hypothesise a dispersed settlement made up of numerous small inhabited areas distributed at various altitudes. An interconnected network controlled and exploited the various mountain ecosystems: from the cultivated fields and Adige waterway of the valley floor, to the woods of the lower mountains and, probably, also the pastures higher up.

On the other hand the theory that the apparent proliferation of these sites is due to a certain instability of the settlements which reduced their duration and caused their frequent and successive relocation, formulated for the area south of Lake Garda,[30] is disproved, at a local level, by the timeline that can be reconstructed on the basis of the material culture of sites like the Colombo di Mori,[31] Pizzini di Castellano,[32] Dosso Alto di Borgo Sacco[33] and the Castel Corno Caves. The artefacts seem to show in fact long term use of sites that lasted through several phases of the EBA. The picture that emerges would therefore seem better suited to the synchronicity of a coordinated system of numerous small settlements and isolated rural structures, a fragmented

[29] It should be emphasized that, while about 80% of the EBA evidence emerged in Vallagarina and represented in **Figure 35** refer to real archaeological sites, half of the evidence illustrated in **Figure 34** (Copper Age) are instead the result of occasional finds outside context. The number of archaeological sites documented in the EBA is therefore almost three times the amount of those of the Copper Age.

[30] Cazzanelli 2007, p. 187.

[31] Orsi 1882.

[32] Battisti 2001.

[33] Trinco 2020.

type of settlement also documented in South Tyrol.[34] As already noted elsewhere,[35] it is thus argued that the small communities living in the area of the Vallagarina were all interconnected forming a sort of economic macro-system which made an integrated use of the various resources, from those of the valley floor to those on the mountain sides.

The cultural context

The burial sites of the Castel Corno Caves are part of a highly complex panorama. The choice of place and generic manner of burial is in line with the widespread customs already described in the alpine basin of Adige and neighbouring regions between the Copper Age and the EBA. As regards the European panorama two great cultural areas can be distinguished: the Corded Ware culture, widespread in Central-Eastern Europe, and the Bell Beaker, widespread throughout most of Europe, with its influence documented in this region too.[36] Although pottery types approaching those of the Bell Beaker do not appear among the artefacts found in contact with the bones of the burial sites, the presence of an arrowhead with squared barbs has already been noted, as often occurs in contexts associated with Bell Beaker burials.[37] In view of the absence of other typical elements of grave goods it can be stated that the tombs of Castel Corno are not Bell Beaker burials strictly speaking, but can be referred to what, in a chronological and cultural sense, is commonly defined Bell Beaker horizon.

In later contexts though, inside Chamber 1, elements emerged which seem to give continuity to some aspects of the Bell beaker tradition. We refer to the artefacts already described connected to the world of archery : the brassard (wrist guard) and arrowshaft smoothers, artefacts very common among the grave goods of Bell Beaker burials.[38] The continuity of some elements introduced in the Bell Beaker period is moreover demonstrated by other archaeological sites in the valley and dated in the EBA, as at Pizzini di Castellano[39] and Colombo di Mori,[40] in which are found small stick-type pendants (or Montgomery type buttons) and brassard (wrist guards).

The young male individual (Individual 3), probably placed in a right-sided crouched position with the head facing south (see Chapter 4), would not reflect, on the other hand, the typical North-South orientation of the Bell Beaker horizon, in which males were generally placed in a left-sided crouched position with the head facing east. However, it is necessary to consider that it is not a Bell Beaker burial in the strict sense, but a deposition that can be generically framed within its horizon. Although the orientation and position of Individual 3 seem to reflect the burial modalities characteristic of the Corded Ware Culture,[41] this similarity is more probably ascribable to a simple coincidence, also taking into account the fact that such a burial must surely have been affected by physical limitations imposed by the specific context: given the complexity of this web of caves and the limited space of movement, the orientation of the body could have been random or due perhaps to a local funeral code.

In the regional panorama, however, there did not seem to be a clear cultural code defining the orientation and methods of burial on the basis of gender between the Copper Age and EBA.[42] But since much of the evidence has come from old excavations and occasional finds not well documented or referable to secondary burials or manipulated primary burials, it is rather difficult

[34] Dal Ri and Tecchiati, 1996, p.532.
[35] Battisti 2010.
[36] Mottes and Nicolis 1998.
[37] Straham 1998, p. 28; Clément 2020, Ch. 2.1.
[38] Clément 2020.
[39] Battisti 2001.
[40] Artefacts preserved at the Museo Civico di Rovereto (inventory numbers: PRM003951, PRM003954).
[41] For the Bell Beaker and Corded Ware burials orientation see Straham 1998, p. 37, fig. 9; Turek and Černý 2001, p. 604; de Marinis and Valzolgher 2013, p. 551, fig. 3 and p. 552.
[42] Mottes and Nicolis 2019, pp. 197–199; de Marinis and Valzolgher 2013, p. 545.

Figure 36: Facial reconstruction of Individual 3 created by Viviana Conti. The 3D model of the skull was created with 3DF Zephyr (Education 5.016) and Pixologic Zbrush (2021). Facial features were estimated considering skeletal details of the skull and using juvenile tissue depths data from Wilkinson 2004 and Gibelli *et al.* 2016 as guidelines. The final composite image was produced in Adobe Photoshop (2021). (This is an artist impression).

in the current state of the research to formulate likely hypotheses on such a limited statistical sample.

Finally, considering the anthropological reflections already expressed, we could cautiously advance the hypothesis that, in a site like this one, the orientation of the bodies did not have great importance compared with the greater spiritual relevance of the context itself. It means that, while the orientation of the bodies in an open space was probably in relation to the movement of the stars, this may not be so relevant in such a closed, deep context as the one in question. Furthermore, given the great spiritual value this labyrinth of caves probably had, the bodies' orientation could have had a secondary role. From a topological point of view, we could therefore hypothesise that to specific attention towards horizontal orientation in open settings, in our case, a vertical orientation would be introduced. In other words, these tombs already have an intrinsic orientation: downwards, towards a chthonic afterlife.

Besides the orientation, as regards the generic burial methods, the evidence that emerged in the Castel Corno Caves could also be related to the long tradition of cave or shelter burials of the Civate Group, known in northern Italy between the Copper Age and the EBA,[43] which also denotes frequent use of the practice of secondary burials.

As regards the subsequent period of occupation, as stated there is evidence of a possible presence in the phase little documented until now related to EBA I. Most of the artefacts however date from EBA II and find precise comparisons at the regional level in the horizons of Fiavé 3,[44] Pizzini 3[45] and the settlement at Ledro.[46] The artefacts found would however seem to prove that this second phase of occupation covers the whole of the EBA, fitting well, as far as the pottery types are concerned, into the Polada Culture, widespread between the end of the 3rd millennium and first half of the 2nd millennium BC in North-Eastern Italy. Some typological aspects recall the Barche di Solferino horizon (EBA II) while others, e.g. the elbow handles with double button appendage, are involved also in a local reinterpretation of the classic Polada.[47]

In conclusion, the site of the Castel Corno Caves will enrich the documentation relative to the typology of the places chosen as sites for worship and burial in Alpine and Pre-Alpine areas. This model, which has been abundantly illustrated, is also reflected in the limited area of the Vallagarina, where, between the Copper Age and the EBA, all the sacred sites (both burial and worship places) are located in rock shelters or caves (e.g. Colombo di Mori, Bersaglio di Mori, Castel Corno and Volano-San Rocco).

The material culture analysed here also shows that the settlement at Castel Corno, besides being well integrated in the purely regional cultural framework, was also influenced by cultural flows from the Po valley and beyond the Alps (see chapter 3) that moved in both directions along the Adige valley, a watercourse which must have represented a favoured transit route. In that sense the presence of settlements is significant at Castel Pradaglia and Dosso Alto di Borgo Sacco, places in the immediate vicinity of the Adige controlling the narrowest point of the whole navigable stretch of the river (from Bronzolo right up to its mouth in the Adriatic). In the same spot a rigid control of river traffic and crossings during Medieval times is historically well documented.[48]

---

[43] Roncoroni 2013, p. 405–406.

[44] Perini 1994.

[45] Battsti 2001.

[46] Raghet 1974.

[47] Perini 2000, p. 301–304. That happens in line with the generally observed process which sees a gradual loss of homogeneity of the typically Poladian types to the benefit of diversified local varieties (Cazzanelli 2007, p.187; Bermond Montanari *et al.* 1996, p.62).

[48] Battisti 2015, p. 13; Trinco 2020; Andreazza 1989.

Catalogue of Finds

The criteria described in the appendix were used to define the ceramic types and the quality of the fabric and surface treatment. For the determination of the colours, since the chromatic range of the ceramics is often not homogeneous even in a single potsherd, it was not considered appropriate to use the Munsell Soil Color Charts[1] as a reference, which were instead used to describe the colours of the flints.

The scale of the artefacts can be deduced from the scale placed at the bottom of each plate. An asterisk indicates that the inclination of the artefact is not certain.

The catalogue entries were written by Elena Regola and Maurizio Battisti.

The drawings were made by Elena Regola, Elena Zeni, Virginia Trinco, Barbara Rauss, Maurizio Battisti and Viviana Conti. Layout and graphic revision by Maurizio Battisti and Viviana Conti.

[1] Munsell Soil Color Charts 2000.

Catalogue Entries

1 (Inv. PRM002250)
Location and stratigraphy: outside the caves, on top of the landslide.
Excavation: Pasquali, 1975.
Description: two joining sherds of a truncated cone shape vessel with straight rim and two horizontal cordons.
Surfaces: irregular and coarse; ext. reddish, int. Reddish brown.
Fabric: medium; blackish gray.
Quality class: coarse.
Vessel class: jars.

2 (Inv. PRM002313)
Location and stratigraphy: Chamber 2.
Excavation: Gruppo Grotte E. Roner (hereafter referred to as GGR), 1972.
Description: slightly inverted rim sherd of an open form vessel with a small conical knob.
Surfaces: irregular and smoothed; ext. reddish, int. blackish.
Fabric: medium; black.
Quality class: semi-coarse.
Vessel class: jars.

3 (Inv. PRM021732)
Location and stratigraphy: Chamber 1, US 3, square A3-B3.
Excavation: Museo Civico di Rovereto (hereafter referred to as MCR).
Description: rounded rim sherd on inward-sloping wall with a horizontal cordon.
Surfaces: irregular and smoothed; blackish brown.
Fabric: medium; black.
Quality class: semi-coarse.
Vessel class: jars.

4 (Inv. PRM000220)
Location and stratigraphy: Chamber 3, Zone 1.
Excavation: Candioli, 1969.
Description: straight rim sherd on inward-sloping wall with a horizontal cordon.
Surfaces: irregular and smoothed; ext. reddish, int. brown.
Fabric: medium; black.
Quality class: semi-coarse.
Vessel class: jars.

5 (Inv. PRM002316)
Location and stratigraphy: Chamber 2.
Excavation: GGR, 1972.
Description: straight rim sherd decorated with fingertip on slightly convex wall with a horizontal cordon.
Surfaces: irregular and smoothed; ext. reddish, int. brown.
Fabric: medium; black.
Quality class: semi-coarse.
Vessel class: jars.

6 (Inv. PRM002226)
Location and stratigraphy: outside the caves, on top of the landslide.
Excavation: Pasquali, 1975.
Description: straight rim sherd on outward-sloping wall slightly convex wall with a horizontal cordon.
Surfaces: irregular and smoothed; ext. brown, int. blackish.
Fabric: medium; blackish.
Quality class: semi-coarse.
Vessel class: dolia.

7 (Inv. PRM002356)
Location and stratigraphy: Chamber 1, Sondage 2, spit 0÷30 cm.
Excavation: Centro Studi Lagarini (hereafter referred to as CSL), 1974.
Description: straight rim sherd of an open form vessel with a horizontal and triangular lug handles and a horizontal cordon.
Surfaces: irregular and smoothed; reddish brown
Fabric: medium; blackish.
Quality class: semi-coarse.
Vessel class: Jars/dolia.

8 (Inv. PRM002299)
Location and stratigraphy: Unknown.
Excavation: CSL, 1970.
Description: straight thinned rim sherd with a horizontal cordon.
Surfaces: irregular and smoothed; reddish brown
Fabric: medium; greyish brown
Quality class: semi-coarse.
Vessel class: dolia.

9 (Inv. PRM002358)
Location and stratigraphy: Chamber 1, Sondage 2, spit 0÷30 cm.
Excavation: CSL, 1974.
Description: straight rim sherd with a small horned lug handle and a horizontal cordon.
Surfaces: irregular and coarse; reddish.
Fabric: medium; grey.

Quality class: coarse.
Vessel class: jars/dolia.

10 (Inv. PRM015696)
Location and stratigraphy: Chamber 1, US 3, Square A3-B3
Excavation: MCR, 1999.
Description: straight rim sherd on slightly inward-sloping wall with a fragmentary lug handle set on a horizontal cordon.
Surfaces: irregular and smoothed; blackish brown.
Fabric: medium; greyish.
Quality class: semi-coarse.
Vessel class: dolia.

11 (Inv. PRM015697)
Location and stratigraphy: Chamber 1, US 2, Square B2
Excavation: MCR, 1999.
Description: straight rim sherd with cord decoration.
Surfaces: irregular and smoothed; blackish brown.
Fabric: medium; greyish.
Quality class: semi-coarse.
Vessel class: dolia.

12 (Inv. PRM015808)
Location and stratigraphy: Chamber 1, US 2, Square B2
Excavation: MCR, 1999.
Description: straight rim sherd with a horizontal cordon.
Surfaces: ext. regular and smoothed, int. regular coarse; ext. brown, int. reddish.
Fabric: medium; light grey.
Quality class: semi-coarse.
Vessel class: Jars/dolia.

13 (Inv. PRM015773)
Location and stratigraphy: Chamber 1, US 2, Square A2
Excavation: MCR, 1999.
Description: wall sherd with a horizontal cordon.
Surfaces: regular and smoothed; reddish.
Fabric: medium; greyish.
Quality class: semi-coarse.
Vessel class: dolia.

14 (Inv. PRM015782)
Location and stratigraphy: Chamber 1, US 2, Square A2-B2.
Excavation: MCR, 1999.
Description: straight rim sherd with a horizontal cordon.
Surfaces: ext. regular and smoothed; int. irregular coarse; ext. reddish, int. blackish grey.
Fabric: medium; reddish and blackish.
Quality class: semi-coarse.
Vessel class: Jars.

15 (Inv. PRM021687)
Location and stratigraphy: Chamber 1, US 3, Square A3-B3.
Excavation: MCR, 1999.
Description: wall sherd with a horizontal cordon.
Surfaces: irregular and smoothed; ext. reddish, int. brown.
Fabric: medium; black.
Quality class: semi-coarse.
Vessel class: Jars/dolia.

16 (Inv. PRM015812)
Location and stratigraphy: Chamber 1, US 2, Square B3.
Excavation: MCR, 1999.
Description: three joining straight rim sherds with a horizontal cordon.
Surfaces: irregular and smoothed; ext. brown, int. reddish brown.
Fabric: medium; greyish.
Quality class: semi-coarse.
Vessel class: dolia.

17 (Inv. PRM015813)
Location and stratigraphy: Chamber 1, US 2, Square B2.
Excavation: MCR, 1999.
Description: straight rim sherd on slightly convex wall with two parallel horizontal cordons.
Surfaces: ext. irregular and smoothed, int. regular and smoothed; ext. brown, int. dark grey.
Fabric: coarse; dark grey.
Quality class: coarse.
Vessel class: jars.

18 (Inv. PRM015814)
Location and stratigraphy: Chamber 1, US 2, Square B2.
Excavation: MCR, 1999.
Description: straight rim sherd on slightly convex wall with a horizontal cordon.
Surfaces: regular and smoothed; reddish brown.
Fabric: medium; blackish.
Quality class: semi-coarse.
Vessel class: jars/dolia.

19 (Inv. PRM020883)
Location and stratigraphy: Chamber 1, US 0.
Excavation: MCR, 1999.
Description: rim sherd of an open form vessel with a triangular lug handle set on a horizontal cordon.
Surfaces: irregular and smoothed; ext. reddish, int. blackish.
Fabric: coarse; blackish.
Quality class: coarse.
Vessel class: jars.

20 (Inv. PRM020856)
Location and stratigraphy: Chamber 1, US 0.
Excavation: MCR, 1999.

Description: straight rim sherd with a small horned lug handle set on a horizontal cordon.
Surfaces: irregular and smoothed; ext. blackish brown, int. reddish brown.
Fabric: medium; blackish brown.
Quality class: semi-coarse.
Vessel class: jars/dolia.

21 (Inv. PRM021512)
Location and stratigraphy: Chamber 1, US 5, Square C2.
Excavation: MCR, 1999.
Description: straight rim sherd with a horizontal cordon.
Surfaces: irregular and smoothed; reddish brown.
Fabric: medium; blackish brown.
Quality class: semi-coarse.
Vessel class: dolia.

22 (Inv. PRM021522)
Location and stratigraphy: Chamber 1, US 5, Square C3.
Excavation: MCR, 1999.
Description: straight thickened rim sherd with a small knob.
Surfaces: irregular and smoothed; blackish brown.
Fabric: medium; brown.
Quality class: semi-coarse.
Vessel class: jars/dolia.

23 (Inv. PRM021537)
Location and stratigraphy: Chamber 1, US 2, Square A2-B2.
Excavation: MCR, 1999.
Description: straight rim sherd on slightly conchamber wall with a horizontal cordon and pierced holes in a horizontal row.
Surfaces: irregular and smoothed; ext. reddish brown, int. reddish.
Fabric: medium; brown.
Quality class: semi-coarse.
Vessel class: jars.

24 (Inv. PRM021538)
Location and stratigraphy: Chamber 1, US 2, Square A2-B2.
Excavation: MCR, 1999.
Description: slightly everted rim sherd with a horizontal cordon.
Surfaces: irregular and smoothed; reddish brown.
Fabric: medium; grey.
Quality class: semi-coarse.
Vessel class: jars/dolia.

25 (Inv. PRM021556)
Location and stratigraphy: Chamber 1, US 2, Square A2-B2.
Excavation: MCR, 1999.
Description: three joining straight rim sherds of an open form vessel with a horizontal cordon.
Surfaces: irregular and smoothed; ext. reddish brown, int. blackish.
Fabric: medium; reddish.
Quality class: semi-coarse.
Vessel class: bowls.

26 (Inv. PRM021567)
Location and stratigraphy: Chamber 1, US 2, Square A3-B3.
Excavation: MCR, 1999.
Description: inverted rim sherd with a horizontal cordon.
Surfaces: irregular and smoothed; ext. brown, int. reddish.
Fabric: medium; blackish.
Quality class: semi-coarse.
Vessel class: jars/dolia.

27 (Inv. PRM015764)
Location and stratigraphy: access corridor to Chamber 1 (surface cleaning).
Excavation: MCR, 1998.
Description: rim sherd on outward-sloping wall.
Surfaces: irregular and smoothed; ext. brown, int. reddish.
Fabric: medium; blackish.
Quality class: semi-coarse.
Vessel class: jars/dolia.

28 (Inv. PRM021570)
Location and stratigraphy: Chamber 1, US 2
Excavation: MCR, 1999.
Description: rim sherd on slightly convex wall with a truncated cone shape knob.
Surfaces: irregular and smoothed; blackish brown.
Fabric: medium; reddish.
Quality class: semi-coarse.
Vessel class: jars.

29 (Inv. PRM021712)
Location and stratigraphy: Chamber 1, US 0.
Excavation: MCR, 1999.
Description: rim sherd of an open form vessel.
Surfaces: irregular and smoothed; brown.
Fabric: medium; reddish.
Quality class: semi-coarse.
Vessel class: bowls.

30 (Inv. PRM021741)
Location and stratigraphy: Chamber 1, US 2, Square B2.
Excavation: MCR, 1999.
Description: rim sherd of an open form vessel.
Surfaces: irregular and smoothed; ext. reddish, int. brown.
Fabric: medium; brown.

Quality class: semi-coarse.
Vessel class: jars.

31 (Inv. PRM0000210)
Location and stratigraphy: Chamber 3, Zone 1.
Excavation: Candioli, 1969.
Description: rim sherd on a slightly incurving wall.
Surfaces: regular and burnished; ext. blackish, int. brown.
Fabric: medium; grey.
Quality class: semi-fine.
Vessel class: jars.

32 (Inv. PRM0021755)
Location and stratigraphy: Chamber 1, US 0.
Excavation: MCR, 1999.
Description: straight rim sherd of a open form vessel with a horizontal cordon.
Surfaces: irregular and smoothed; ext. black, int. brown.
Fabric: medium; brown.
Quality class: semi-coarse.
Vessel class: jars/dolia.

33 (Inv. PRM0002231)
Location and stratigraphy: outside the caves, on top of the landslide.
Excavation: Pasquali, 1975.
Description: rim sherd of a open form vessel.
Surfaces: regular and coarse; reddish.
Fabric: medium; greenish grey.
Quality class: semi-coarse.
Vessel class: jars/dolia.

34 (Inv. PRM0002353)
Location and stratigraphy: Chamber 1, Sondage 1.
Excavation: CSL, 1974.
Description: straight rim sherd of an probable ovoid vessel with three small parallel vertical cordons.
Surfaces: regular and burnished; blackish brown.
Fabric: medium; grey.
Quality class: semi-fine.
Vessel class: beakers/jars.

35 (Inv. PRM0000208)
Location and stratigraphy: Chamber 3, Zone 1.
Excavation: Candioli, 1969.
Description: thinned rim sherd on a inward-sloping wall with a horizontal cordon.
Surfaces: regular and smoothed; dark grey.
Fabric: medium; blackish brown.
Quality class: semi-coarse.
Vessel class: beakers/jars.

36 (Inv. PRM0000233)
Location and stratigraphy: Chamber 3, Zone 1.
Excavation: Candioli, 1969.
Description: rim sherd on a slightly convex wall with a horizontal cordon.
Surfaces: irregular and smoothed; reddish brown.
Fabric: medium; blackish grey.
Quality class: semi-coarse.
Vessel class: jars/dolia.

37 (Inv. PRM015777)
Location and stratigraphy: Chamber 1, US 2, Square B2.
Excavation: MCR, 1999.
Description: rim sherd of an open form vessel with a horizontal cordon.
Surfaces: regular and smoothed; reddish brown.
Fabric: medium; dark grey.
Quality class: semi-coarse.
Vessel class: bowls/large bowls.

38 (Inv. PRM015740)
Location and stratigraphy: Chamber 3, Zone 1, Tomb 1, US 9.
Excavation: MCR, 1998.
Description: straight rim sherd of a truncated cone shape vessel with a slightly convex wall and a horizontal cordon.
Surfaces: regular and smoothed; reddish brown.
Fabric: medium; blackish, reddish near the outer surface.
Quality class: semi-coarse.
Vessel class: beakers/jars.

39 (Inv. PRM002244)
Location and stratigraphy: outside the caves, on top of the landslide.
Excavation: Pasquali, 1975.
Description: slightly everted rim sherd on an incurving wall with a cord decoration.
Surfaces: regular and smoothed; ext. brown, int. black.
Fabric: fine; grey.
Quality class: semi-fine.
Vessel class: beakers.

40 (Inv. PRM002354)
Location and stratigraphy: Chamber 1, Sondage 1.
Excavation: CSL, 1974.
Description: straight rim sherd with a horizontal cordon ending in a circular knob.
Surfaces: regular and burnished; ext. blackish brown, int. reddish brown.
Fabric: medium; grey.
Quality class: semi-coarse.
Vessel class: beakers.

41 (Inv. PRM002350)
Location and stratigraphy: Chamber 1, Sondage 1, spit 0÷65 cm.
Excavation: CSL, 1974.

Description: straight rim sherd on a slightly convex wall with two parallel horizontal cordons.
Surfaces: regular and smoothed; ext. yellowish brown, int. blackish.
Fabric: medium; black.
Quality class: semi-coarse.
Vessel class: beakers.

42 (Inv. PRM020859)
Location and stratigraphy: Chamber 1, US 0.
Excavation: MCR, 1999.
Description: straight rim sherd on a slightly convex wall with two small conical knobs set side by side on a horizontal cordon.
Surfaces: irregular and smoothed; brown.
Fabric: medium; black.
Quality class: semi-coarse.
Vessel class: beakers.

43 (Inv. PRM015762)
Location and stratigraphy: Chamber 3.
Excavation: MCR, 1998.
Description: straight rim sherd with a vertical lug handle set on a horizontal cordon.
Surfaces: irregular and smoothed; reddish.
Fabric: medium; greyish.
Quality class: semi-coarse.
Vessel class: beakers.

44 (Inv. PRM002281)
Location and stratigraphy: Chamber 2.
Excavation: CSL, 1970.
Description: thinned rim sherd on a inward-sloping wall with a horizontal cordon.
Surfaces: regular and smoothed; blackish brown.
Fabric: medium; brown.
Quality class: semi-coarse.
Vessel class: beakers.

45 (Inv. PRM000219)
Location and stratigraphy: Chamber 3, Zone 1.
Excavation: Candioli, 1969.
Description: straight rim sherd on a inward-sloping wall with a horizontal cordon.
Surfaces: irregular and smoothed; ext. reddish and brown, int. reddish.
Fabric: medium; brown.
Quality class: semi-coarse.
Vessel class: beakers.

46 (Inv. PRM002310)
Location and stratigraphy: Chamber 2.
Excavation: GGR, 1972.
Description: rim sherd of a truncated cone shape vessel with a vertical lug handle.
Surfaces: irregular and smoothed; ext. reddish, int. greyish brown.
Fabric: medium; brown.
Quality class: semi-coarse.
Vessel class: beakers/jars.

47 (Inv. PRM015732)
Location and stratigraphy: Chamber 3, Zone 1, Tomb 1, US 10.
Excavation: MCR, 1998.
Description: straight rim sherd with two parallel vertical cordon.
Surfaces: irregular and smoothed; ext. reddish brown, int. blackish.
Fabric: medium; greyish.
Quality class: semi-coarse.
Vessel class: beakers.

48 (Inv. PRM015811)
Location and stratigraphy: Chamber 1, US 2, Suare A2-B2.
Excavation: MCR, 1999.
Description: everted rim sherd on vertical wall with a horizontal cordon.
Surfaces: regular and smoothed; dark grey.
Fabric: medium; dark grey, reddish near the outer surface.
Quality class: semi-coarse.
Vessel class: beakers.

49 (Inv. PRM015735)
Location and stratigraphy: access corridor to Chamber 1 (surface cleaning).
Excavation: MCR, 1998.
Description: two joining rim sherds on a slightly convex wall.
Surfaces: irregular and smoothed; greyish brown.
Fabric: medium; black.
Quality class: semi-coarse.
Vessel class: beakers.

50 (Inv. PRM015755)
Location and stratigraphy: access corridor to Chamber 1 (surface cleaning).
Excavation: MCR, 1998.
Description: slightly everted rim sherd on a vertical wall.
Surfaces: irregular and smoothed; reddish.
Fabric: medium; reddish.
Quality class: semi-coarse.
Vessel class: beakers.

51 (Inv. PRM002308)
Location and stratigraphy: unknown.
Excavation: Avanzini, 1986.
Description: four joining sherds of a vessel with convex walls, inverted rim and an elbow handle set on a horizontal cordon.

Surfaces: irregular and smoothed; ext. blackish brown, int. blackish.
Fabric: medium; black.
Quality class: semi-coarse.
Vessel class: beakers.

52 (Inv. PRM015772)
Location and stratigraphy: Chamber 1, US 2, Square A2.
Excavation: MCR, 1999.
Description: wall sherd of a biconical vessel with rounded carination.
Surfaces: regular and burnished; black.
Fabric: fine; black, reddish near the outer surface.
Quality class: dark-burnished.
Vessel class: mugs.

53 (Inv. PRM020846)
Location and stratigraphy: Chamber 1, US 0.
Excavation: MCR, 1999.
Description: everted rim sherd of a close form vessel (biconical or globular mug)
Surfaces: regular and burnished; grey.
Fabric: fine; grey.
Quality class: fine.
Vessel class: mugs.

54 (Inv. PRM020954)
Location and stratigraphy: Chamber 1, US 0.
Excavation: MCR, 1999.
Description: straight distinct rim sherd of a close form vessel (biconical or globular mug).
Surfaces: regular and burnished; dark brown.
Fabric: medium; dark brown.
Quality class: semi-fine.
Vessel class: mugs.

55 (Inv. PRM002341)
Location and stratigraphy: outside the caves, northward, next to the path to the castle.
Excavation: Pasquali-Rauss, 1987.
Description: straight distinct rim sherd of a small close form vessel (biconical or globular mug) with a fragmentary handle (upper handle attachment).
Surfaces: irregular and smoothed; ext. reddish brown, int. brown.
Fabric: semi-coarse; brown.
Quality class: semi-coarse
Vessel class: mugs.

56 (Inv. PRM021558)
Location and stratigraphy: Chamber 1, US 2, Square A2-B2.
Excavation: MCR, 1999.
Description: straight rim sherd of a close form vessel (biconical or globular mug).
Surfaces: regular and burnished; black.
Fabric: fine; black.
Quality class: dark-burnished.
Vessel class: mugs.

57 (Inv. PRM021709)
Location and stratigraphy: Chamber 1, US 2, Square B2.
Excavation: MCR, 1999.
Description: straight rim sherd on an inward-sloping wall of a small close form vessel (biconical or globular mug).
Surfaces: regular and burnished; black.
Fabric: fine; greyish.
Quality class: fine.
Vessel class: mugs.

58 (Inv. PRM021539)
Location and stratigraphy: Chamber 1, US 2, Square B2.
Excavation: MCR, 1999.
Description: everted rim sherd of a close form vessel (biconical or globular mug).
Surfaces: regular and burnished; black.
Fabric: fine; reddish.
Quality class: fine.
Vessel class: mugs.

59 (Inv. PRM021754)
Location and stratigraphy: Chamber 1, US 0.
Excavation: MCR, 1999.
Description: straight distinct rim sherd of a small close form vessel (biconical or globular mug).
Surfaces: regular and burnished; ext. reddish brown, int. greyish.
Fabric: fine; black.
Quality class: fine.
Vessel class: mugs.

60 (Inv. PRM021994)
Location and stratigraphy: Chamber 1, US 3, Square B2.
Excavation: MCR, 1999.
Description: small fragmentary globular vessel with everted rim and a loop handle.
Surfaces: regular and smoothed; blackish brown.
Fabric: medium; blackish.
Quality class: semi-coarse.
Vessel class: mugs.

61 (Inv. PRM002293)
Location and stratigraphy: Chamber 2.
Excavation: GGR, 1972.
Description: straight rim sherd of a small globular vessel.
Surfaces: irregular and smoothed; reddish grey.
Fabric: medium; black.
Quality class: semi-coarse.
Vessel class: mugs.

62 (Inv. PRM015779)
Location and stratigraphy: Chamber 1, US 2, Square B2.

Excavation: MCR, 1999.
Description: small fragmentary globular vessel with everted rim.
Surfaces: regular and burnished; black and reddish.
Fabric: fine; black and reddish.
Quality class: semi-fine.
Vessel class: mugs.

63 (Inv. PRM002247)
Location and stratigraphy: outside the caves, on top of the landslide.
Excavation: Pasquali, 1975.
Description: straight rim sherd of a globular vessel with traces of handle attachment.
Surfaces: regular and burnished; ext. brown, int. greyish.
Fabric: medium; black.
Quality class: semi-fine.
Vessel class: mugs.

64 (Inv. PRM002318)
Location and stratigraphy: Chamber 2.
Excavation: GGR, 1972.
Description: four joining slightly everted rim sherds of a close form vessel with a fragmentary handle (upper and lower handle attachments).
Surfaces: irregular and smoothed; reddish brown.
Fabric: medium; black.
Quality class: semi-coarse.
Vessel class: mugs.

65 (Inv. PRM002312)
Location and stratigraphy: Chamber 2.
Excavation: GGR, 1972.
Description: small fragmentary biconical vessel with everted rim.
Surfaces: regular and smoothed; blackish.
Fabric: medium; black.
Quality class: semi-coarse.
Vessel class: mugs.

66 (Inv. PRM015784)
Location and stratigraphy: Chamber 1, US 2, Square B2.
Excavation: MCR, 1999.
Description: small fragmentary globular vessel with straight rim.
Surfaces: regular and burnished; blackish brown.
Fabric: fine; grey.
Quality class: fine.
Vessel class: mugs.

67 (Inv. PRM015748)
Location and stratigraphy: Chamber 3, Zone 1, Tomb 2 (US 18).
Excavation: MCR, 1998.
Description: distinct rim sherd of a small close form vessel.
Surfaces: irregular and burnished; black.
Fabric: fine; black.
Quality class: semi-fine.
Vessel class: mugs.

68 (Inv. PRM002315)
Location and stratigraphy: Chamber 2.
Excavation: GGR, 1972.
Description: fragmentary biconical vessel with straight rim.
Surfaces: regular and smoothed; grey.
Fabric: medium; blackish.
Quality class: semi-coarse.
Vessel class: mugs.

69 (Inv. PRM015752)
Location and stratigraphy: Chamber 3, Zone 1, Tomb 1, US 10.
Excavation: MCR, 1998.
Description: small fragmentary biconical vessel.
Surfaces: regular and burnished; black.
Fabric: medium; black.
Quality class: semi-fine.
Vessel class: mugs.

70 (Inv. PRM015806)
Location and stratigraphy: Chamber 1, US 2, Square B3.
Excavation: MCR, 1999.
Description: everted rim sherd of a small close form vessel (biconical or globular mug).
Surfaces: regular and burnished; black.
Fabric: medium; black.
Quality class: semi-fine.
Vessel class: mugs.

71 (Inv. PRM002285)
Location and stratigraphy: Chamber 2.
Excavation: CSL, 1970.
Description: distinct rim sherd of a close form vessel (biconical or globular mug).
Surfaces: regular and smoothed; yellowish.
Fabric: fine; yellowish.
Quality class: semi-fine.
Vessel class: mugs.

72 (Inv. PRM000206)
Location and stratigraphy: Chamber 3, Zone 1.
Excavation: Candioli, 1969.
Description: convex wall sherd of a small globular vessel with a fragmentary handle (handle attachment) and an incised horizontal line.
Surfaces: ext. regular and burnished, int. regular and smoothed; reddish.
Fabric: fine; reddish.
Quality class: semi-fine.
Vessel class: mugs.

73 (Inv. PRM002253)
Location and stratigraphy: outside the caves, on top of the landslide.
Excavation: Pasquali, 1975.
Description: two joining rim sherds on a convex wall.
Surfaces: irregular and burnished; black.
Fabric: medium; brown, reddish near the outer surface.
Quality class: semi-coarse.
Vessel class: bowls.

74 (Inv. PRM015701)
Location and stratigraphy: Chamber 3, Zone 1, US 13.
Excavation: MCR, 1998.
Description: inverted rim sherd.
Surfaces: irregular and smoothed; brown.
Fabric: medium; brown.
Quality class: semi-coarse.
Vessel class: bowls.

75 (Inv. PRM015761)
Location and stratigraphy: access corridor to Chamber 1 (surface cleaning).
Excavation: MCR, 1998.
Description: hemispherical bowl sherd with incised lines under the rim.
Surfaces: regular and smoothed; ext. reddish, int. greyish brown.
Fabric: medium; black.
Quality class: semi-coarse.
Vessel class: bowls.

76 (Inv. PRM021706)
Location and stratigraphy: access corridor to Chamber 1 (surface cleaning).
Excavation: MCR, 1998.
Description: rim sherd on a outward-sloping wall of a small open form vessel.
Surfaces: irregular and smoothed; reddish.
Fabric: medium; brown.
Quality class: semi-coarse.
Vessel class: beakers.

77 (Inv. PRM002302)
Location and stratigraphy: Chamber 3.
Excavation: CSL, 1974.
Description: fragmentary shallow vessel with slightly convex walls and three vertical lug handles, two of which pierced horizontally.
Surfaces: irregular and smoothed; reddish brown.
Fabric: medium; black.
Quality class: semi-coarse.
Vessel class: bowls.

78 (Inv. PRM002287)
Location and stratigraphy: Chamber 2.
Excavation: GGR, 1972.
Description: rim sherd on a convex wall.
Surfaces: regular and smoothed; reddish brown.
Fabric: medium; blackish.
Quality class: semi-coarse.
Vessel class: beakers or bowls.

79 (Inv. PRM021504)
Location and stratigraphy: Chamber 1, US 5.
Excavation: MCR, 1999.
Description: rim sherd of an open form vessel.
Surfaces: regular and burnished; blackish brown.
Fabric: fine; black.
Quality class: semi-fine.
Vessel class: bowls.

80 (Inv. PRM002288)
Location and stratigraphy: Chamber 1, US 5.
Excavation: MCR, 1998.
Description: slightly everted rim sherd on a convex wall.
Surfaces: irregular and smoothed; reddish.
Fabric: medium; reddish.
Quality class: semi-coarse.
Vessel class: beakers/jars.

81 (Inv. PRM015809)
Location and stratigraphy: Chamber 1, US 3, Square B2.
Excavation: MCR, 1999.
Description: rim sherd of a small open form vessel.
Surfaces: irregular and smoothed; light brown.
Fabric: medium; black.
Quality class: semi-coarse.
Vessel class: bowls.

82 (Inv. PRM021536)
Location and stratigraphy: Chamber 1, US 2, Square A2-B2.
Excavation: MCR, 1999.
Description: rim sherd on a slightly convex wall of an open form vessel.
Surfaces: regular and burnished; black.
Fabric: medium; black.
Quality class: semi-fine.
Vessel class: bowls.

83 (Inv. PRM015771)
Location and stratigraphy: Chamber 1, US 2, Square A2.
Excavation: MCR, 1999.
Description: fragmentary shallow vessel with a small knob near the rim, where the latter is slightly raised.
Surfaces: ext. irregular and burnished; int. irregular and smoothed; greyish.

Fabric: medium; brown, reddish near the outer surface.
Quality class: semi-coarse.
Vessel class: bowls.

84 (Inv. PRM021499)
Location and stratigraphy: Chamber 1, US 5.
Excavation: MCR, 1999.
Description: everted rim sherd with a fragmentary elbow handle with a short axe-shaped appendage slightly raised above the rim.
Surfaces: regular and burnished; black.
Fabric: fine; black.
Quality class: dark-burnished.
Vessel class: mugs.

85 (Inv. PRM002317)
Location and stratigraphy: Chamber 2.
Excavation: GGR, 1972.
Description: rim sherd on a conchamber wall of a probable large biconical or ovoid vessel.
Surfaces: regular and smoothed; ext. brown, int. reddish brown.
Fabric: medium; reddish.
Quality class: semi-coarse.
Vessel class: ollas.

86 (Inv. PRM000203)
Location and stratigraphy: Chamber 3, Zone 1.
Excavation: Candioli, 1969.
Description: straight rim sherd on an inward-sloping wall of a close form vessel.
Surfaces: regular and smoothed; ext. reddish, int. reddish brown.
Fabric: medium; black.
Quality class: semi-coarse.
Vessel class: mugs.

87 (Inv. PRM015765)
Location and stratigraphy: Chamber 3, Zone 1, Tomb 2 (US 18).
Excavation: MCR, 1998.
Description: two joining straight rim sherd on an inward-sloping wall of a close form vessel.
Surfaces: regular and smoothed; ext. black and reddish, int. brown.
Fabric: medium; black, reddish near the inner surface.
Quality class: semi-coarse.
Vessel class: mugs/ollas.

88 (Inv. PRM002347)
Location and stratigraphy: unknown.
Excavation: CSL, 1974.
Description: distinct rim sherd on an inward-sloping wall of a close form vessel.
Surfaces: regular and coarse; reddish brown.
Fabric: medium; black.
Quality class: coarse.
Vessel class: ollas.

89 (Inv. PRM021690)
Location and stratigraphy: Chamber 1, US 2, Square B3.
Excavation: MCR, 1999.
Description: rim sherd on an inward-slooping wall of a close form vessel.
Surfaces: regular and smoothed; reddish.
Fabric: medium; brown.
Quality class: semi-coarse.
Vessel class: mugs/ollas.

90 (Inv. PRM020881)
Location and stratigraphy: Chamber 1, US 0.
Excavation: MCR, 1999.
Description: everted rim sherd of a close form vessel with a horizontal cordon.
Surfaces: irregular and smoothed; reddish.
Fabric: medium; blackish.
Quality class: semi-coarse.
Vessel class: ollas.

91 (Inv. PRM002249)
Location and stratigraphy: outside the caves, on top of the landslide.
Excavation: Pasquali, 1975.
Description: rim sherd on a sinuous wall of a close form vessel.
Surfaces: regular and smoothed; ext. reddish brown, int. greyish.
Fabric: medium; greyish.
Quality class: semi-coarse.
Vessel class: beakers.

92 (Inv. PRM002232)
Location and stratigraphy: outside the caves, on top of the landslide.
Excavation: Pasquali, 1975.
Description: two joining distinct rim sherds on a, inward-sloping wall of a close form vessel.
Surfaces: regular and smoothed; blackish grey.
Fabric: medium; black, reddish near the outer surface.
Quality class: semi-coarse.
Vessel class: ollas.

93 (Inv. PRM002248)
Location and stratigraphy: outside the caves, on top of the landslide.
Excavation: Pasquali, 1975.
Description: ten joining sherds of a close form vessel (probably ovoid) with slightly everted rim.
Surfaces: regular and smoothed; ext. reddish, int. reddish grey.
Fabric: medium; light grey.

Quality class: semi-coarse.
Vessel class: ollas.

94 (Inv. PRM002325)
Location and stratigraphy: outside the caves.
Excavation: Pasquali-Rauss, 1983.
Description: distinct rim sherd on an inward-sloping wall of a close form vessel.
Surfaces: irregular and smoothed; reddish brown.
Fabric: medium; brown, black and reddish.
Quality class: semi-coarse.
Vessel class: ollas.

95 (Inv. PRM002355)
Location and stratigraphy: Chamber 1, Sondage 2, spit 0÷30 cm.
Excavation: CSL, 1974.
Description: everted rim sherd on an inward-sloping wall of a close form vessel.
Surfaces: irregular and smoothed; black.
Fabric: medium; black.
Quality class: semi-coarse.
Vessel class: mugs/ollas.

96 (Inv. PRM002291)
Location and stratigraphy: Chamber 2.
Excavation: GGR, 1972.
Description: everted rim sherd of a close form vessel.
Surfaces: regular and smoothed; ext. brown, int. yellowish brown.
Fabric: medium; black.
Quality class: semi-coarse.
Vessel class: mugs/ollas.

97 (Inv. PRM020814)
Location and stratigraphy: Chamber 1, US 2, Square B2.
Excavation: MCR, 1999.
Description: carinated wall sherd with a pierced circular hole and traces of a probable lug handle or knob attachment, originally attached with the use of a clay pivot.
Surfaces: irregular and smoothed; brown.
Fabric: medium; dark grey.
Quality class: semi-coarse.
Vessel class: ollas/dolia.

98 (Inv. PRM002346)
Location and stratigraphy: Chamber 1, Sondage 2, Spit 30÷40 cm.
Excavation: CSL, 1974.
Description: rim sherd on inward-sloping wall with a raised lug handle.
Surfaces: regular and smoothed; ext. black and reddish brown, int. blackish.
Fabric: medium; blackish.
Quality class: semi-coarse.
Vessel class: ollas.

99 (Inv. PRM015783)
Location and stratigraphy: Chamber 1, US 2, Square B2.
Excavation: MCR, 1999.
Description: rim sherd on an outward-sloping wall with a small truncated cone shape knob.
Surfaces: ext. regular and burnished, int. regular and smoothed; ext. brown, int. black.
Fabric: medium; dark grey, reddish near the outer surface.
Quality class: semi-coarse.
Vessel class: beakers/jars.

100 (Inv. PRM015803)
Location and stratigraphy: Chamber 1, US 5, Square B2.
Excavation: MCR, 1999.
Description: rim sherd on an outward-sloping wall with a triangular lug handle set on a horizontal cordon.
Surfaces: regular and smoothed; reddish brown.
Fabric: medium; reddish.
Quality class: semi-coarse.
Vessel class: jars.

101 (Inv. PRM015757)
Location and stratigraphy: access corridor to Chamber 1 (surface cleaning).
Excavation: MCR, 1998.
Description: rim sherd on a slightly convex wall with a small knob set on a horizontal cordon.
Surfaces: regular and smoothed; ext. reddish grey, int. brown.
Fabric: medium; black.
Quality class: semi-coarse.
Vessel class: beakers/jars.

102 (Inv. PRM015749)
Location and stratigraphy: Chamber 3, Zone 1, Tomb 2 (US 18).
Excavation: MCR, 1998.
Description: convex wall sherd with a small knob.
Surfaces: regular and smoothed; greyish brown.
Fabric: medium; greyish.
Quality class: semi-coarse.
Vessel class: beakers.

103 (Inv. PRM015743)
Location and stratigraphy: Chamber 3, Zone 1, Tomb 1, US 10.
Excavation: MCR, 1998.
Description: straight rim sherd with a small knob.
Surfaces: irregular and smoothed; blackish brown.
Fabric: medium; blackish.
Quality class: semi-coarse.
Vessel class: beakers.

104 (Inv. PRM021578)
Location and stratigraphy: Chamber 1, US 2, Square B3.

Excavation: MCR, 1999.
Description: straight rim sherd with a small knob.
Surfaces: irregular and smoothed; ext. reddish brown, int. black.
Fabric: medium; reddish.
Quality class: semi-coarse.
Vessel class: unknown.

105 (Inv. PRM015807)
Location and stratigraphy: Chamber 1, US 3, Square A3-B3.
Excavation: MCR, 1999.
Description: wall sherd with a knob.
Surfaces: regular and smoothed; ext. reddish brown, int. black.
Fabric: medium; black.
Quality class: semi-coarse.
Vessel class: unknown.

106 (Inv. PRM015785)
Location and stratigraphy: Chamber 1, US 0.
Excavation: MCR, 1999.
Description: straight rim sherd with a horned lug handle set on a horizontal cordon.
Surfaces: regular and smoothed; reddish.
Fabric: medium; dark grey.
Quality class: semi-coarse.
Vessel class: jars/dolia

107 (Inv. PRM020835)
Location and stratigraphy: Chamber 1, US 0.
Excavation: MCR, 1999.
Description: rim sherd on a slightly convex wall with a horned lug handle.
Surfaces: irregular and smoothed; ext. reddish, int. brown.
Fabric: medium; brown.
Quality class: semi-coarse.
Vessel class: bowls.

108 (Inv. PRM012710)
Location and stratigraphy: Chamber 1, Sondage 2, spit 30÷40.
Excavation: CSL, 1974.
Description: rim sherd of an open form vessel with a lug handle.
Surfaces: irregular and smoothed; ext. reddish brown, int. brown.
Fabric: medium; blackish.
Quality class: semi-coarse.
Vessel class: bowls.

109 (Inv. PRM015786)
Location and stratigraphy: Chamber 1, US 2, Square B2.
Excavation: MCR, 1999.
Description: straight rim sherd with a lug handle.
Surfaces: regular and smoothed; ext. blackis, int. reddish.
Fabric: medium; blackish.
Quality class: semi-coarse.
Vessel class: unknown.

110 (Inv. PRM021698)
Location and stratigraphy: Chamber 1, US 0.
Excavation: MCR, 1999.
Description: straight rim sherd with a small knob.
Surfaces: irregular and coarse; brown.
Fabric: medium; brown.
Quality class: semi-coarse.
Vessel class: unknown.

111 (Inv. PRM021579)
Location and stratigraphy: Chamber 1, US 2, Square B3.
Excavation: MCR, 1999.
Description: rim sherd with a knob set on a horizontal cordon.
Surfaces: irregular and coarse; reddish.
Fabric: medium; reddish.
Quality class: coarse.
Vessel class: unknown.

112 (Inv. PRM002222)
Location and stratigraphy: outside the caves, on top of the landslide.
Excavation: Pasquali, 1975.
Description: three joining inward-sloping wall sherds with a large lug handle on a horizontal cordon.
Surfaces: irregular and smoothed; reddish.
Fabric: medium; grey.
Quality class: coarse.
Vessel class: ollas.

113 (Inv. PRM002221)
Location and stratigraphy: outside the caves, on top of the landslide.
Excavation: Pasquali, 1975.
Description: inward-sloping wall sherd with a triangular lug handle on a horizontal cordon.
Surfaces: regular and smoothed; reddish.
Fabric: medium; blackhis.
Quality class: semi-coarse.
Vessel class: ollas.

114 (Inv. PRM015729)
Location and stratigraphy: Chamber 3, Zone 1, Tomb 1, US 10.
Excavation: MCR, 1998.
Description: lug handle sherd folded at right angles.
Surfaces: irregular and smoothed; brown.
Fabric: medium; brown.
Quality class: semi-coarse.
Vessel class: ollas.

115 (Inv. PRM002240)
Location and stratigraphy: outside the caves, on top of the landslide.
Excavation: Pasquali, 1975.
Description: wall sherd with a lug handle.
Surfaces: regular and smoothed; ext. brown, int. reddish brown.
Fabric: medium; black.
Quality class: semi-coarse.
Vessel class: beakers/jars.

116 (Inv. PRM002246)
Location and stratigraphy: outside the caves, on top of the landslide.
Excavation: Pasquali, 1975.
Description: wall sherd with a lug handle.
Surfaces: irregular and smoothed; ext. reddish brown, int. brown.
Fabric: medium; black.
Quality class: semi-coarse.
Vessel class: beakers/jars.

117 (Inv. PRM015768)
Location and stratigraphy: Chamber 1, US 0.
Excavation: MCR, 1999.
Description: wall sherd and a lug handle with a fingerprint.
Surfaces: irregular and coarse; reddish.
Fabric: medium; reddish.
Quality class: coarse.
Vessel class: beakers/jars.

118 (Inv. PRM015745)
Location and stratigraphy: Chamber 3, Zone 1, US 13.
Excavation: MCR, 1998.
Description: inverted rim sherd with a vertical lug handle.
Surfaces: irregular and coarse; ext. light brown, int. reddish brown.
Fabric: medium; blackish.
Quality class: semi-coarse.
Vessel class: beakers.

119 (Inv. PRM015730)
Location and stratigraphy: Chamber 3, Zone 1, Tomb 1, US 9.
Excavation: MCR, 1998.
Description: small lug handle sherd.
Surfaces: irregular and smoothed; reddish.
Fabric: medium; brown.
Quality class: semi-coarse.
Vessel class: unknown.

120 (Inv. PRM015789)
Location and stratigraphy: Chamber 1, US 2, Square B2.
Excavation: MCR, 1999.
Description: wall sherd with a fragmentary lug handle set on a horizontal cordon.
Surfaces: irregular and smoothed; ext. reddish brown, int. reddish.
Fabric: medium; dark brown.
Quality class: semi-coarse.
Vessel class: jars/dolia.

121 (Inv. PRM015802)
Location and stratigraphy: Chamber 1, US 0.
Excavation: MCR, 1999.
Description: wall sherd with a lug handle set on a horizontal cordon.
Surfaces: regular and smoothed; ext. reddish brown, int. reddish grey.
Fabric: medium; grey.
Quality class: semi-coarse.
Vessel class: jars/dolia.

122 (Inv. PRM021662)
Location and stratigraphy: Chamber 1, US 2, Square A3.
Excavation: MCR, 1999.
Description: slightly convex wall sherd with a small triangular lug handle.
Surfaces: regular and smoothed; ext. reddish, int. brown.
Fabric: medium; brown.
Quality class: semi-coarse.
Vessel class: beakers/jars.

123 (Inv. PRM020882)
Location and stratigraphy: Chamber 1, US 0.
Excavation: MCR, 1999.
Description: straight rim sherd on a slightly conchamber wall with two holes, one through and the other not. A vertical lug handle intersects a horizontal cordon.
Surfaces: irregular and smoothed; reddish.
Fabric: medium; reddish.
Quality class: semi-coarse.
Vessel class: dolia.

124 (Inv. PRM015770)
Location and stratigraphy: Chamber 1, US 2, Square A2.
Excavation: MCR, 1999.
Description: straight rim sherd with a pierced hole and a horizontal cordon with a fingerprint.
Surfaces: irregular and smoothed; ext. blackish brown, int. reddish.
Fabric: medium; reddish.
Quality class: semi-coarse.
Vessel class: jars/dolia.

125 (Inv. PRM002298)
Location and stratigraphy: unknown.
Excavation: CSL, 1970.

Description: straight rim sherd with two pierced holes and a horizontal cordon.
Surfaces: irregular and smoothed; reddish.
Fabric: medium; reddish grey.
Quality class: semi-coarse.
Vessel class: jars/dolia.

126 (Inv. PRM002245)
Location and stratigraphy: outside the caves, on top of the landslide.
Excavation: Pasquali, 1975.
Description: rim sherd on a inward-sloping wall with a horizontal cordon. Between the rim and the cordon stand two pierced holes and one non-through hole in a horizontal line.
Surfaces: irregular and smoothed; reddish.
Fabric: medium; reddish.
Quality class: semi-coarse.
Vessel class: jars/dolia.

127 (Inv. PRM020825)
Location and stratigraphy: Chamber 1, US 0 (at the end of the cavity).
Excavation: MCR, 1999.
Description: straight rim sherd on a slightly inward-sloping wall with two pierced holes and a horizontal cordon.
Surfaces: irregular and coarse; reddish.
Fabric: medium; dark grey.
Quality class: coarse.
Vessel class: jars.

128 (Inv. PRM015731)
Location and stratigraphy: Chamber 3, Zone 1, US 10.
Excavation: MCR, 1998.
Description: straight rim sherd with two pierced holes and a horizontal cordon.
Surfaces: irregular and coarse; reddish.
Fabric: medium; reddish.
Quality class: coarse.
Vessel class: jars or jars/dolia.

129 (Inv. PRM021521)
Location and stratigraphy: Chamber 1, US 5, Square C3.
Excavation: MCR, 1999.
Description: straight rim sherd on a slightly outward-sloping wall with three pierced holes in a horizontal line and cord decoration.
Surfaces: irregular and coarse; reddish brown.
Fabric: medium; black.
Quality class: coarse.
Vessel class: dolia.

130 (Inv. PRM000204)
Location and stratigraphy: Chamber 3, Zone 1.
Excavation: Candioli, 1969.
Description: straight rim sherd on a slightly convex wall with a small knob set on a horizontal cordon. Under the knob a short wavy cordon tracing a sort of 'omega'.
Surfaces: irregular and smoothed; reddish.
Fabric: medium; reddish.
Quality class: semi-coarse.
Vessel class: beakers/jars.

131 (Inv. PRM002351)
Location and stratigraphy: outside the caves, on top of the landslide.
Excavation: CSL, 1974.
Description: straight rim sherd on a slightly convex wall with a knob set on a horizontal cordon. Under the knob a short wavy cordon tracing a sort of 'omega'.
Surfaces: ext. irregular and smoothed, int. regular and burnished; reddish.
Fabric: medium; reddish.
Quality class: semi-fine.
Vessel class: jars.

132 (Inv. PRM021362)
Location and stratigraphy: Chamber 1, US 2, Square A2.
Excavation: MCR, 1999.
Description: slightly everted rim sherd with numerous pierced holes all over the wall.
Surfaces: irregular and smoothed; reddish.
Fabric: medium; reddish.
Quality class: semi-coarse.
Vessel class: probable strainer.

133 (Inv. PRM021533)
Location and stratigraphy: Chamber 1, US 2, Square A2-B2.
Excavation: MCR, 1999.
Description: convex wall sherd with cord decoration.
Surfaces: regular and smoothed; ext. reddish brown, int. blackish.
Fabric: medium; blackish.
Quality class: semi-coarse.
Vessel class: mugs/ollas.

134 (Inv. PRM000201)
Location and stratigraphy: Chamber 3, Zone 1.
Excavation: Candioli, 1969.
Description: straight rim sherd with two parallel cordons ending with two small knobs.
Surfaces: regular and smoothed; greyish brown.
Fabric: medium; grey.
Quality class: semi-coarse.
Vessel class: jars/dolia.

135 (Inv. PRM020784)
Location and stratigraphy: Chamber 3, Zone 1, US 13.
Excavation: MCR, 1998.

Description: wall sherd with two parallel cordons.
Surfaces: irregular and smoothed; reddish brown.
Fabric: medium; blackish.
Quality class: semi-coarse.
Vessel class: jars.

136 (Inv. PRM002314)
Location and stratigraphy: Chamber 2.
Excavation: GGR, 1972.
Description: distinct rim sherd on a convex wall of a close form vessel with two parallel horizontal cordons.
Surfaces: regular and smoothed; brown.
Fabric: medium; reddish.
Quality class: semi-coarse.
Vessel class: jars/dolia.

137 (Inv. PRM002284)
Location and stratigraphy: Chamber 2.
Excavation: CSL, 1970.
Description: rim sherd on a slightly inward-sloping wall with two parallel horizontal cordons.
Surfaces: irregular and smoothed; ext. greyish, int. reddish.
Fabric: medium; grey.
Quality class: semi-coarse.
Vessel class: jars/dolia.

138 (Inv. PRM002243)
Location and stratigraphy: outside the caves, on top of the landslide.
Excavation: Pasquali, 1975.
Description: thickened rim sherd on a slightly outward-sloping wall with two parallel horizontal cordons.
Surfaces: irregular and smoothed; dark grey.
Fabric: medium; brown.
Quality class: semi-coarse.
Vessel class: jars/dolia.

139 (Inv. PRM015766)
Location and stratigraphy: Chamber 1, US 0.
Excavation: MCR, 1999
Description: rim sherd on a slightly conchamber wall with cord decoration.
Surfaces: regular and burnished; dark grey.
Fabric: medium; reddish.
Quality class: semi-fine.
Vessel class: jars/dolia.

140 (Inv. PRM015741)
Location and stratigraphy: Chamber 3, Zone 1, Tomb 1, US 10.
Excavation: MCR, 1998
Description: straight thickened rim sherd with a horizontal cordon.
Surfaces: irregular and smoothed; brown.
Fabric: coarse; blackish.
Quality class: coarse.
Vessel class: jars/dolia.

141 (Inv. PRM015797)
Location and stratigraphy: Chamber 3, Zone 2.
Excavation: MCR, 1998
Description: straight rim sherd with a horizontal cordon.
Surfaces: irregular and smoothed; yellowish brown.
Fabric: medium; greyish.
Quality class: semi-coarse.
Vessel class: jars/dolia.

142 (Inv. PRM015744)
Location and stratigraphy: Chamber 3, Zone 1, US 13.
Excavation: MCR, 1998
Description: straight rim sherd with cord decoration.
Surfaces: irregular and smoothed; reddish brown.
Fabric: medium; blackish.
Quality class: semi-coarse.
Vessel class: jars.

143 (Inv. PRM015763)
Location and stratigraphy: Chamber 1, US 0.
Excavation: MCR, 1999.
Description: two joining straight rim sherds with cord decoration.
Surfaces: irregular and smoothed; ext. reddish, int. reddish brown.
Fabric: medium; dark grey.
Quality class: semi-coarse.
Vessel class: jars.

144 (Inv. PRM015751)
Location and stratigraphy: Chamber 3, Zone 1, Tomb 1, US 10.
Excavation: MCR, 1998.
Description: straight rim sherd with a horizontal cordon.
Surfaces: regular and smoothed; ext. brown, int. black.
Fabric: medium; greyish.
Quality class: semi-coarse.
Vessel class: jars.

145 (Inv. PRM015753)
Location and stratigraphy: Chamber 3, Zone 1, US 13.
Excavation: MCR, 1998.
Description: everted rim sherd with a horizontal cordon.
Surfaces: irregular and smoothed; reddish brown.
Fabric: medium; black.
Quality class: semi-coarse.
Vessel class: jars/dolia.

146 (Inv. PRM015756)
Location and stratigraphy: Chamber 3, Zone 1, US 13.
Excavation: MCR, 1998.
Description: straight rim sherd with a horizontal cordon.
Surfaces: ext. regular and burnished, int. regular and smoothed; greyish brown.
Fabric: medium; greyish, reddish near the outer surface.
Quality class: semi-fine.
Vessel class: beakers/jars

147 (Inv. PRM015733)
Location and stratigraphy: Chamber 3, Zone 1, US 13.
Excavation: MCR, 1998.
Description: rim sherd on slightly inward-sloping wall with a horizontal cordon.
Surfaces: irregular and smoothed; greyish brown.
Fabric: medium; black.
Quality class: semi-coarse.
Vessel class: beakers/jars

148 (Inv. PRM015693)
Location and stratigraphy: Chamber 1, US 0.
Excavation: MCR, 1999.
Description: straight rim sherd with a horizontal cordon.
Surfaces: regular and burnished; ext. reddish, int. brown.
Fabric: medium; reddish brown.
Quality class: semi-coarse.
Vessel class: dolia.

149 (Inv. PRM015694)
Location and stratigraphy: Chamber 1, US 0.
Excavation: MCR, 1999.
Description: straight rim sherd with a horizontal cordon.
Surfaces: irregular and smoothed; ext. reddish, int. brown.
Fabric: medium; blackish grey.
Quality class: semi-coarse.
Vessel class: jars/dolia.

150 (Inv. PRM015742)
Location and stratigraphy: Chamber 3, Zone 1, US 13.
Excavation: MCR, 1998.
Description: straight rim sherd with a horizontal cordon.
Surfaces: regular and smoothed; blackish brown.
Fabric: medium; greyish.
Quality class: semi-coarse.
Vessel class: jars.

151 (Inv. PRM015754)
Location and stratigraphy: Chamber 3, Zone 1, US 13.
Excavation: MCR, 1998.
Description: straight rim sherd on an inward-sloping wall with a horizontal cordon.
Surfaces: irregular and smoothed; ext. reddish brown, int. blackish brown.
Fabric: coarse; black.
Quality class: coarse.
Vessel class: jars.

152 (Inv. PRM021542)
Location and stratigraphy: Chamber 1, US 2, Square B2.
Excavation: MCR, 1999.
Description: rim sherd on an outward-sloping wall with a horizontal cordon.
Surfaces: irregular and smoothed; reddish brown.
Fabric: medium; brown.
Quality class: semi-coarse.
Vessel class: jars.

153 (Inv. PRM015758)
Location and stratigraphy: Chamber 3, Zone 2.
Excavation: MCR, 1998.
Description: rim sherd with a horizontal cordon.
Surfaces: irregular and smoothed; greyish.
Fabric: medium; greyish.
Quality class: semi-coarse.
Vessel class: jars/dolia.

154 (Inv. PRM002241)
Location and stratigraphy: outside the caves, on top of the landslide.
Excavation: Pasquali, 1975.
Description: rim sherd on a slightly outward-sloping wall with a horizontal cordon.
Surfaces: ext. irregular and burnished; reddish.
Fabric: medium; reddish.
Quality class: semi-coarse.
Vessel class: jars/dolia.

155 (Inv. PRM021703)
Location and stratigraphy: Chamber 1, US 2.
Excavation: MCR, 1999.
Description: rim sherd on a convex wall with a horizontal cordon.
Surfaces: irregular and smoothed; blackish brown.
Fabric: medium; blackish brown.
Quality class: semi-coarse.
Vessel class: jars/dolia.

156 (Inv. PRM021647)
Location and stratigraphy: Chamber 1, US 2, Square A2-B2.
Excavation: MCR, 1999.
Description: straight rim sherd with a horizontal cordon.
Surfaces: irregular and smoothed; brown.
Fabric: medium; brown.

Quality class: semi-coarse.
Vessel class: jars/dolia.

157 (Inv. PRM021422)
Location and stratigraphy: Chamber 3, Zone 2
Excavation: MCR, 1998.
Description: straight rim sherd with a horizontal cordon.
Surfaces: irregular and smoothed; reddish.
Fabric: medium; brown.
Quality class: semi-coarse.
Vessel class: beakers/jars.

158 (Inv. PRM015736)
Location and stratigraphy: Chamber 3, Zone 1, US 13.
Excavation: MCR, 1998.
Description: slightly everted rim sherd with a horizontal cordon.
Surfaces: regular and smoothed; reddish.
Fabric: medium; reddish.
Quality class: semi-coarse.
Vessel class: beakers.

159 (Inv. PRM015804)
Location and stratigraphy: Chamber 1, US 2, Square A2-B2.
Excavation: MCR, 1999.
Description: straight rim sherd with a horizontal cordon.
Surfaces: irregular and smoothed; ext. dark grey and reddish, int. brown.
Fabric: medium; light grey.
Quality class: semi-coarse.
Vessel class: jars/dolia.

160 (Inv. PRM002251)
Location and stratigraphy: outside the caves, on top of the landslide.
Excavation: Pasquali, 1975
Description: inward-sloping wall sherd with a slightly horned handle set on two parallel horizontal cordons.
Surfaces: irregular and coarse; reddish.
Fabric: medium; greyish.
Quality class: coarse.
Vessel class: ollas/dolia.

161 (Inv. PRM002344)
Location and stratigraphy: terraces next to the castle in a southerly direction.
Excavation: Pasquali-Rauss, 1986.
Description: straight rim sherd on a very thin wall with a loop handle.
Surfaces: regular and coarse; reddish brown.
Fabric: coarse; black.
Quality class: coarse.
Vessel class: beakers.

162 (Inv. PRM021589)
Location and stratigraphy: Chamber 1, US 5.
Excavation: MCR, 1999.
Description: elbow handle sherd (upper part) of a very small vessel.
Surfaces: irregular and smoothed; reddish.
Fabric: fine; reddish.
Quality class: semi-fine.
Vessel class: unknown.

163 (Inv. PRM002340)
Location and stratigraphy: outside the caves, northward, next to the path to the castle.
Excavation: Pasquali-Rauss, 1987.
Description: strap handle sherd (middle part) with raised margins.
Surfaces: irregular and smoothed; reddish brown.
Fabric: medium; brown.
Quality class: semi-coarse.
Vessel class: unknown.

164 (Inv. PRM002280)
Location and stratigraphy: Chamber 2.
Excavation: CSL, 1970.
Description: strap handle sherd (lower part) with clay pivot.
Surfaces: regular and smoothed; brown.
Fabric: medium; brown, reddish near the surfaces.
Quality class: semi-coarse.
Vessel class: unknown.

165 (Inv. PRM015767)
Location and stratigraphy: Chamber 1, US 2, Square B2.
Excavation: MCR, 1999.
Description: straight rim sherd with handle attachment (upper part).
Surfaces: irregular and smoothed; greyish.
Fabric: medium; greyish.
Quality class: semi-coarse.
Vessel class: unknown.

166 (Inv. PRM015787)
Location and stratigraphy: Chamber 1, US 2, Square B2.
Excavation: MCR, 1999.
Description: elbow handle sherd with a short axe-shaped appendage.
Surfaces: regular and smoothed; reddish.
Fabric: fine; reddish.
Quality class: semi-fine.
Vessel class: unknown.

167 (Inv. PRM015695)
Location and stratigraphy: Chamber 1, US 2, Square A2.
Excavation: MCR, 1999.
Description: elbow handle sherd with a short double-button appendage.
Surfaces: regular and burnished; black.

191 (Inv. PRM015728)
Location and stratigraphy: Chamber 3, Zone 1, Tomb 1, US 10.
Excavation: MCR, 1998.
Description: rim sherd on an inward-sloping wall.
Surfaces: irregular and burnished; brown.
Fabric: medium; greyish, reddish near the surfaces.
Quality class: semi-coarse.
Vessel class: beakers.

192 (Inv. PRM015726)
Location and stratigraphy: Chamber 3, Zone 1, Tomb 1, US 10.
Excavation: MCR, 1998.
Description: slightly everted rim sherd.
Surfaces: regular and burnished; greyish.
Fabric: medium; blackish.
Quality class: semi-coarse.
Vessel class: beakers.

193 (Inv. PRM015727)
Location and stratigraphy: Chamber 3, Zone 1, US 13.
Excavation: MCR, 1998.
Description: straight rim sherd.
Surfaces: irregular and smoothed; dark grey.
Fabric: medium; greyish.
Quality class: semi-coarse.
Vessel class: beakers/jars.

194 (Inv. PRM015781)
Location and stratigraphy: Chamber 1, US 2, Square A2-B2.
Excavation: MCR, 1999.
Description: rim sherd on a slightly outward-sloping wall.
Surfaces: ext. regular and burnished, int. regular and smoothed; ext. brown, int. grey.
Fabric: medium; greyish, reddish near the surfaces.
Quality class: semi-coarse.
Vessel class: beakers.

195 (Inv. PRM015746)
Location and stratigraphy: Chamber 3, Zone 1, Tomb 1, US 10.
Excavation: MCR, 1998.
Description: rim sherd on a slightly convex wall.
Surfaces: irregular and smoothed; reddish grey.
Fabric: medium; black and reddish.
Quality class: semi-coarse.
Vessel class: bowls.

196 (Inv. PRM015747)
Location and stratigraphy: Chamber 3, Zone 1, Tomb 1, US 10.
Excavation: MCR, 1998.
Description: rim sherd on an inward-sloping wall decorated with stick impressions.
Surfaces: irregular and smoothed; ext. brown, int. reddish.
Fabric: medium; black, reddish near the outer surface.
Quality class: semi-coarse.
Vessel class: beakers/jars.

197 (Inv. PRM015690)
Location and stratigraphy: Chamber 1, US 0.
Excavation: MCR, 1999.
Description: thickened rim sherd on an outward-sloping wall.
Surfaces: irregular and smoothed; brown.
Fabric: medium; greyish, reddish near the outer surface.
Quality class: semi-coarse.
Vessel class: ollas.

198 (Inv. PRM015760)
Location and stratigraphy: access corridor to Chamber 1 (surface cleaning).
Excavation: MCR, 1998.
Description: straight rim sherd on a slightly convex wall.
Surfaces: irregular and smoothed; reddish brown.
Fabric: medium; greyish.
Quality class: semi-coarse.
Vessel class: ollas.

199 (Inv. PRM020929)
Location and stratigraphy: inside the caves, surface cleaning.
Excavation: MCR, 1998.
Description: straight rim sherd with an impressed fingertips decoration.
Surfaces: irregular and smoothed; ext. brown, int. reddish.
Fabric: medium; brown.
Quality class: semi-coarse.
Vessel class: unknown.

200 (Inv. PRM015703)
Location and stratigraphy: Chamber 3, Zone 1, Tomb 1, US 10.
Excavation: MCR, 1998.
Description: straight rim sherd on a slightly inward-sloping wall.
Surfaces: irregular and smoothed; reddish.
Fabric: medium; reddish.
Quality class: semi-coarse.
Vessel class: beakers.

201 (Inv. PRM015780)
Location and stratigraphy: Chamber 1, US 2, Square B2.
Excavation: MCR, 1999.
Description: rim sherd on a slightly convex wall.

Surfaces: ext. regular and smoothed, int. regular and coarse; ext. reddish brown, int. blackish.
Fabric: fine; blackish.
Quality class: semi-fine.
Vessel class: beakers/jars.

202 (Inv. PRM015739)
Location and stratigraphy: Chamber 3, Zone 1, US 9.
Excavation: MCR, 1998.
Description: straight rim sherd.
Surfaces: irregular and smoothed; reddish.
Fabric: coarse; reddish.
Quality class: coarse.
Vessel class: jars/dolia.

203 (Inv. PRM028761)
Location and stratigraphy: Chamber 2.
Excavation: GGR, 1972.
Description: straight rim sherd on a slightly convex wall.
Surfaces: regular and burnished; ext. greyish brown, int. greyish.
Fabric: coarse; grey.
Quality class: semi-coarse.
Vessel class: beakers.

204 (Inv. PRM030990)
Location and stratigraphy: Chamber 1.
Excavation: MCR, 2018 (collected on the edge of an illegal excavation during an inspection).
Description: five joining potsherds of a truncated cone shape vessel with a fragmentary lug handle.
Surfaces: regular and smoothed; ext. brown and grey, int. reddish and black.
Fabric: coarse; greyish brown.
Quality class: semi-coarse.
Vessel class: beakers.

205 (Inv. PRM028775)
Location and stratigraphy: Chamber 2 or 3.
Excavation: GGR, 1972.
Description: thickened rim sherd on a slightly convex wall with a horizontal cordon.
Surfaces: irregular and burnished; reddish brown.
Fabric: medium; grey and reddish.
Quality class: semi-coarse.
Vessel class: beakers/jars.

206 (Inv. PRM030991)
Location and stratigraphy: Chamber 1.
Excavation: MCR, 2018 (collected on the edge of an illegal excavation during an inspection).
Description: open form vessel sherd with slightly everted rim and an elbow handle. Inside there are traces of carbonized organic material.
Surfaces: irregular and smoothed; ext. reddish and grey, int. blackish.
Fabric: medium; blackish.
Quality class: semi-coarse.
Vessel class: beakers/jars.

207 (Inv. PRM028722)
Location and stratigraphy: Chamber 1.
Excavation: MCR, 2016 (collected on the edge of an illegal excavation during an inspection).
Description: straight rim sherd with a horizontal cordon.
Surfaces: regular and smoothed; ext. reddish, int. greyish.
Fabric: medium; reddish.
Quality class: semi-coarse.
Vessel class: jars (?).

208 (Inv. PRM028719)
Location and stratigraphy: Chamber 1.
Excavation: MCR, 2016 (collected on the edge of an illegal excavation during an inspection).
Description: rim sherd on a convex wall with a horizontal cordon.
Surfaces: regular and burnished; ext. reddish, int. reddish grey.
Fabric: medium; reddish grey.
Quality class: semi-coarse.
Vessel class: jars.

209 (Inv. PRM028724)
Location and stratigraphy: Chamber 1.
Excavation: MCR, 2016 (collected on the edge of an illegal excavation during an inspection).
Description: rim sherd on a convex wall with a cord decoration.
Surfaces: regular and smoothed; ext. reddish grey, int. grey.
Fabric: fine; grey.
Quality class: semi-coarse.
Vessel class: jars.

210 (Inv. PRM028767)
Location and stratigraphy: Chamber 2 or 3.
Excavation: GGR, 1972.
Description: inverted rim sherd on a convex wall with a horizontal cordon.
Surfaces: irregular and smoothed; grey.
Fabric: medium; grey.
Quality class: semi-coarse.
Vessel class: jars.

211 (Inv. PRM028707)
Location and stratigraphy: Chamber 1.
Excavation: MCR, 2016 (collected on the edge of an illegal excavation during an inspection).
Description: thinned rim sherd on an outward-sloping wall with a horizontal cordon

Surfaces: regular and smoothed; ext. greyish brown, int. greyish.
Fabric: medium; grey.
Quality class: semi-coarse.
Vessel class: jars.

212 (Inv. PRM028742)
Location and stratigraphy: Chamber 3.
Excavation: MCR, 2004 (collected on the surface).
Description: rim sherd on a convex wall with traces of a circular knob attachment.
Surfaces: irregular and burnished; ext. reddish brown, int. greyish.
Fabric: medium; grey.
Quality class: semi-coarse.
Vessel class: jars.

213 (Inv. PRM028718)
Location and stratigraphy: Chamber 1.
Excavation: MCR, 2016 (collected on the edge of an illegal excavation during an inspection).
Description: straight rim sherd.
Surfaces: irregular and smoothed; ext. greyish, int. reddish.
Fabric: coarse; dark grey.
Quality class: semi-coarse.
Vessel class: jars/dolia.

214 (Inv. PRM030992)
Location and stratigraphy: Chamber 1.
Excavation: MCR, 2018 (collected on the edge of an illegal excavation during an inspection).
Description: rim sherd on an outward-sloping wall with a horizontal cordon.
Surfaces: regular and smoothed; ext. reddish, int. brown.
Fabric: medium; grey.
Quality class: semi-coarse.
Vessel class: jars.

215 (Inv. PRM028766)
Location and stratigraphy: Chamber 2 or 3.
Excavation: GGR, 1972.
Description: rim sherd on a slightly outward-sloping wall with a horizontal cordon.
Surfaces: irregular and smoothed; ext. greyish, int. grey.
Fabric: medium; grey.
Quality class: semi-coarse.
Vessel class: jars/dolia.

216 (Inv. PRM028723)
Location and stratigraphy: Chamber 1.
Excavation: MCR, 2016 (collected on the edge of an illegal excavation during an inspection).
Description: slightly thickened rim sherd on an inward-sloping wall with cord decoration.
Surfaces: regular and burnished; ext. reddish, int. reddish grey.
Fabric: medium; grey.
Quality class: semi-coarse.
Vessel class: jars/dolia.

217 (Inv. PRM028702)
Location and stratigraphy: Chamber 1.
Excavation: MCR, 2016 (collected on the edge of an illegal excavation during an inspection).
Description: rim sherd on an outward-sloping wall with a small knob and a horizontal cordon.
Surfaces: regular and smoothed; greyish.
Fabric: medium; grey.
Quality class: semi-coarse.
Vessel class: jars/dolia.

218 (Inv. PRM028720)
Location and stratigraphy: Chamber 1.
Excavation: MCR, 2016 (collected on the edge of an illegal excavation during an inspection).
Description: rim sherd on an outward-sloping wall with a horizontal cordon.
Surfaces: irregular and smoothed; ext. reddish brown, int. greyish brown.
Fabric: coarse; greyish.
Quality class: semi-coarse.
Vessel class: dolia.

219 (Inv. PRM028721)
Location and stratigraphy: Chamber 1.
Excavation: MCR, 2016 (collected on the edge of an illegal excavation during an inspection).
Description: slightly everted rim sherd on a slightly convex wall with a horizontal cordon.
Surfaces: irregular and smoothed; ext. reddish brown, int. reddish.
Fabric: coarse; dark grey.
Quality class: semi-coarse.
Vessel class: dolia.

220 (Inv. PRM028701)
Location and stratigraphy: Chamber 1.
Excavation: MCR, 2016 (collected on the edge of an illegal excavation during an inspection).
Description: rim sherd on an outward-sloping wall with two parallel horizontal cordon.
Surfaces: irregular and smoothed; ext. dark grey, int. reddish grey.
Fabric: coarse; dark grey.
Quality class: semi-coarse.
Vessel class: dolia.

221 (Inv. PRM028715)
Location and stratigraphy: Chamber 1.
Excavation: MCR, 2016 (collected on the edge of an illegal excavation during an inspection).

Description: slightly everted rim sherd on an inward-sloping wall.
Surfaces: regular and burnished; grey.
Fabric: medium; dark grey.
Quality class: semi-fine
Vessel class: dolia.

222 (Inv. PRM028763)
Location and stratigraphy: Chamber 2 or 3.
Excavation: GGR, 1972.
Description: straight rim sherd on a convex wall.
Surfaces: regular and burnished; reddish.
Fabric: medium; grey.
Quality class: semi-coarse.
Vessel class: bowls.

223 (Inv. PRM031029)
Location and stratigraphy: Chamber 3, Zone 1, US 3.
Excavation: MCR, 1998.
Description: hemispherical bowl sherd with a vertical lug handle and a cord decoration.
Surfaces: regular and burnished; light brown.
Fabric: fine; light brown.
Quality class: semi-fine.
Vessel class: bowls.

224 (Inv. PRM028762)
Location and stratigraphy: Chamber 2 or 3.
Excavation: GGR, 1972.
Description: slightly everted rim on a convex wall.
Surfaces: regular and burnished; grey.
Fabric: fine; grey.
Quality class: fine.
Vessel class: bowls.

225 (Inv. PRM028714)
Location and stratigraphy: Chamber 1.
Excavation: MCR, 2016 (collected on the edge of an illegal excavation during an inspection).
Description: slightly everted rim on an inward-sloping wall.
Surfaces: regular and burnished; ext. grey, int. grey and reddish.
Fabric: fine; reddish grey.
Quality class: fine.
Vessel class: mugs.

226 (Inv. PRM028700)
Location and stratigraphy: Chamber 1.
Excavation: MCR, 2016 (collected on the edge of an illegal excavation during an inspection).
Description: very small fragmentary globular mug with an everted rim and traces of a handle attachments.
Surfaces: regular and burnished; reddish.
Fabric: fine; reddish.
Quality class: semi-fine.
Vessel class: miniaturistic mugs.

227 (Inv. PRM000205)
Location and stratigraphy: Chamber 3, Zone 1.
Excavation: Candioli, 1969.
Description: three joining distinct base sherds with a slightly convex wall.
Surfaces: irregular and smoothed; blackish brown (int. base surface: reddish).
Fabric: medium; black.
Quality class: semi-coarse.
Vessel class: beakers.

228 (Inv. PRM000215)
Location and stratigraphy: Chamber 3, Zone 1.
Excavation: Candioli, 1969.
Description: convex base sherd with rounded angle and convex wall.
Surfaces: regular and smoothed; ext. black, int. blackish.
Fabric: medium; blackish brown.
Quality class: semi-coarse.
Vessel class: mugs.

229 (Inv. PRM000223)
Location and stratigraphy: Chamber 3, Zone 1.
Excavation: Candioli, 1969.
Description: flattish base sherd with an outward-sloping wall.
Surfaces: irregular and smoothed; reddish brown.
Fabric: medium; black.
Quality class: semi-coarse.
Vessel class: beakers.

230 (Inv. PRM000232)
Location and stratigraphy: Chamber 3, Zone 1.
Excavation: Candioli, 1969.
Description: distinct flattish base sherd with an outward-sloping wall.
Surfaces: irregular and smoothed; brown.
Fabric: medium; blackish brown.
Quality class: semi-coarse.
Vessel class: jars.

231 (Inv. PRM002211)
Location and stratigraphy: outside the caves, on top of the landslide.
Excavation: Pasquali, 1975.
Description: flattish base sherd with an outward-sloping wall.
Surfaces: regular and burnished; blackish brown.
Fabric: medium; black.
Quality class: semi-coarse.
Vessel class: beakers.

232 (Inv. PRM002239)
Location and stratigraphy: outside the caves, on top of the landslide.
Excavation: Pasquali, 1975.
Description: flattish base sherd with an outward-sloping wall.
Surfaces: irregular and smoothed; reddish brown.
Fabric: medium; black.
Quality class: semi-coarse.
Vessel class: jars.

233 (Inv. PRM000231)
Location and stratigraphy: Chamber 3, Zone 1.
Excavation: Candioli, 1969.
Description: flattish base sherd with an outward-sloping wall.
Surfaces: regular and smoothed; reddish.
Fabric: medium; blackish.
Quality class: semi-coarse.
Vessel class: dolia.

234 (Inv. PRM002286)
Location and stratigraphy: Chamber 2.
Excavation: CSL, 1970.
Description: two joining flattish base sherd with a slightly outward-sloping wall.
Surfaces: irregular and smoothed; ext. reddish brown, int. brown.
Fabric: medium; brown.
Quality class: semi-coarse.
Vessel class: jars.

235 (Inv. PRM002320)
Location and stratigraphy: unknown.
Excavation: GGR, 1972.
Description: umbilicate base sherd of a small vessel.
Surfaces: ext. regular and smoothed, int. irregular and coarse; grey.
Fabric: coarse; grey.
Quality class: semi-coarse.
Vessel class: mugs.

236 (Inv. PRM015769)
Location and stratigraphy: Chamber 1, US 1.
Excavation: MCR, 1999.
Description: convex base sherd.
Surfaces: regular and burnished; ext. blackish brown, int. black.
Fabric: medium; brown.
Quality class: semi-fine.
Vessel class: mugs.

237 (Inv. PRM015791)
Location and stratigraphy: Chamber 1, US 2, Square B2.
Excavation: MCR, 1999.
Description: umbilicate base sherd.
Surfaces: regular and smoothed; ext. blackish brown, int. black.
Fabric: medium; black.
Quality class: semi-coarse.
Vessel class: mugs.

238 (Inv. PRM002359)
Location and stratigraphy: Chamber 1, Sondage 2, spit 0÷30 cm.
Excavation: CSL, 1974.
Description: flattish base sherd with a slightly outward-sloping wall.
Surfaces: irregular and coarse; greyish.
Fabric: medium; brown.
Quality class: coarse.
Vessel class: dolia.

239 (Inv. PRM015711)
Location and stratigraphy: Chamber 3, Zone 2.
Excavation: MCR, 1998.
Description: flattish base sherd with an almost vertical wall.
Surfaces: irregular and smoothed; reddish.
Fabric: medium; reddish.
Quality class: semi-coarse.
Vessel class: beakers.

240 (Inv. PRM015691)
Location and stratigraphy: Chamber 1, US 2, Square B3.
Excavation: MCR, 1999.
Description: flattish base sherd with an outward-sloping wall.
Surfaces: ext. irregular and burnished, int. Irregular and coarse; ext. greyish brown, int. reddish.
Fabric: medium; greyish.
Quality class: semi-coarse.
Vessel class: jars.

241 (Inv. PRM015713)
Location and stratigraphy: Chamber 3, Zone 1, US 13.
Excavation: MCR, 1998.
Description: flattish base sherd with a conchamber wall.
Surfaces: irregular and smoothed; black.
Fabric: medium; black.
Quality class: semi-coarse.
Vessel class: jars.

242 (Inv. PRM015710)
Location and stratigraphy: Chamber 3, Zone 1, Tomb 1, US 9.
Excavation: MCR, 1998.
Description: flattish base sherd with a slightly outward-sloping wall.
Surfaces: irregular and smoothed; reddish.
Fabric: medium; reddish.

Quality class: semi-coarse.
Vessel class: beakers.

243 (Inv. PRM015689)
Location and stratigraphy: Chamber 1, US 3, Square B2-A2.
Excavation: MCR, 1999.
Description: flattish base sherd with a slightly convex wall.
Surfaces: irregular and coarse; ext. blackish brown, int. reddish black.
Fabric: coarse; black.
Quality class: coarse.
Vessel class: jars.

244 (Inv. PRM015774)
Location and stratigraphy: Chamber 1, US 2, Square B3.
Excavation: MCR, 1999.
Description: flattish base sherd with an outward-sloping wall.
Surfaces: irregular and smoothed; reddish.
Fabric: medium; dark grey.
Quality class: semi-coarse.
Vessel class: dolia.

245 (Inv. PRM015775)
Location and stratigraphy: Chamber 1, US 2, Square A2-B2.
Excavation: MCR, 1999.
Description: flattish base sherd with an outward-sloping wall.
Surfaces: irregular and smoothed; reddish.
Fabric: medium; dark grey.
Quality class: semi-coarse.
Vessel class: dolia.

246 (Inv. PRM015799)
Location and stratigraphy: Chamber 1, US 2, Square A2.
Excavation: MCR, 1999.
Description: base sherd with an applied cord decoration (a cross in a circle) on the lower surface, which acts as a foot.
Surfaces: ext. regular and burnished, int. regular and smoothed; dark grey.
Fabric: medium; dark grey.
Quality class: semi-coarse.
Vessel class: bowls/large bowls.

247 (Inv. PRM015778)
Location and stratigraphy: Chamber 1, US 2, Square B3.
Excavation: MCR, 1999.
Description: flattish base sherd.
Surfaces: irregular and smoothed; brown.
Fabric: medium; dark grey.
Quality class: semi-coarse.
Vessel class: dolia.

248 (Inv. PRM015712)
Location and stratigraphy: Chamber 3, Zone 1, Tomb 1, US 10.
Excavation: MCR, 1998.
Description: base sherd with a conchamber wall of a very small vessel.
Surfaces: irregular and smoothed; reddish.
Fabric: medium; reddish.
Quality class: semi-coarse.
Vessel class: mugs or beakers.

249 (Inv. PRM015776)
Location and stratigraphy: Chamber 1, US 2, Square B2.
Excavation: MCR, 1999.
Description: base sherd with an outward-sloping wall.
Surfaces: irregular and smoothed; ext. reddish brown, int. grey.
Fabric: medium; grey.
Quality class: semi-coarse.
Vessel class: beakers.

250 (Inv. PRM015793)
Location and stratigraphy: Chamber 1, US 2, Square B2.
Excavation: MCR, 1999.
Description: base sherd with an almost vertical wall.
Surfaces: regular and smoothed; ext. reddish brown, int. reddish.
Fabric: medium; grey.
Quality class: semi-coarse.
Vessel class: dolia.

251 (Inv. PRM020753)
Location and stratigraphy: access corridor to Chamber 1 (surface cleaning).
Excavation: MCR, 1998.
Description: distinct base sherd with an outward-sloping wall.
Surfaces: irregular and smoothed; reddish.
Fabric: medium; brown.
Quality class: semi-coarse.
Vessel class: jars.

252 (Inv. PRM015798)
Location and stratigraphy: Chamber 1, US 2, Square B2.
Excavation: MCR, 1999.
Description: distinct flattish base sherd with an outward-sloping wall.
Surfaces: regular and smoothed; ext. brown, int. reddish.
Fabric: coarse; black.
Quality class: coarse.
Vessel class: jars.

253 (Inv. PRM020946)
Location and stratigraphy: Chamber 1, US 0.
Excavation: MCR, 1999.

Description: flattish base sherd with an almost vertical wall.
Surfaces: irregular and smoothed; ext. brown, int. reddish.
Fabric: medium; brown.
Quality class: semi-coarse.
Vessel class: jars.

254 (Inv. PRM021541)
Location and stratigraphy: Chamber 1, US 2, Square B2.
Excavation: MCR, 1999.
Description: flattish base sherd with slightly conchamber wall.
Surfaces: irregular and coarse; reddish.
Fabric: medium; brown.
Quality class: coarse.
Vessel class: jars.

255 (Inv. PRM021666)
Location and stratigraphy: Chamber 1, US 2, Square A2-B2.
Excavation: MCR, 1999.
Description: base sherd.
Surfaces: irregular and burnished; ext. reddish, int. black.
Fabric: medium; brown.
Quality class: semi-coarse.
Vessel class: jars.

256 (Inv. PRM021685)
Location and stratigraphy: Chamber 1, US 3, Square B2.
Excavation: MCR, 1999.
Description: slightly convex base sherd.
Surfaces: irregular and smoothed; blackish.
Fabric: medium; brown.
Quality class: semi-coarse.
Vessel class: jars.

257 (Inv. PRM021432)
Location and stratigraphy: Chamber 1, US 3, Square B2.
Excavation: MCR, 1999.
Description: distinct base sherd.
Surfaces: irregular and smoothed; ext. blackish, int. reddish brown.
Fabric: medium; blackish.
Quality class: semi-coarse.
Vessel class: dolia.

258 (Inv. PRM021625)
Location and stratigraphy: Chamber 1, US 0.
Excavation: MCR, 1999.
Description: base sherd with an outward-sloping wall.
Surfaces: irregular and coarse; reddish.
Fabric: medium; blackish.
Quality class: coarse.
Vessel class: dolia.

259 (Inv. PRM002309)
Location and stratigraphy: unknown.
Excavation: Avanzini, 1986.
Description: discoid spindle whorl sherd.
Surfaces: irregular and smoothed; reddish brown.
Fabric: medium; brown.

260 (Inv. PRM012746)
Location and stratigraphy: Chamber 3, Zone 1, Tomb 2 (US 18).
Excavation: MCR, 1998.
Description: discoid spindle whorl sherd.
Surfaces: irregular and smoothed; reddish.
Fabric: medium; reddish.

261 (Inv. PRM015706)
Location and stratigraphy: Chamber 3, Zone 1, Tomb 1, US 10.
Excavation: MCR, 1998.
Description: discoid convex-conchamber spindle whorl sherd.
Surfaces: irregular and coarse; reddish brown.
Fabric: medium; reddish.

262 (Inv. PRM015707)
Location and stratigraphy: Chamber 3, Zone 1, US 13.
Excavation: MCR, 1998.
Description: discoid spindle whorl sherd.
Surfaces: irregular and smoothed; reddish.
Fabric: medium; reddish.

263 (Inv. PRM015708)
Location and stratigraphy: Chamber 3, Zone 1, US 13.
Excavation: MCR, 1998.
Description: discoid convex-conchamber spindle whorl sherd with a impressed decoration which drawing a circular line of points near the edge of the conchamber surface.
Surfaces: irregular and coarse; reddish.
Fabric: medium; reddish.

264 (Inv. PRM015708)
Location and stratigraphy: Chamber 3, Zone 1.
Excavation: Candioli, 1969.
Description: sub-cylindrical loom weight sherd.
Surfaces: regular and coarse; reddish brown.
Fabric: coarse; black.

265 (Inv. PRM000202)
Location and stratigraphy: Chamber 3, Zone 1.
Excavation: Candioli, 1969.
Description: fragmentary conical tuyère.
Surfaces: irregular and burnished; greyish brown.
Fabric: medium; brown.

266 (Inv. PRM028827)
Location and stratigraphy: outside the caves, on top of the landslide.
Excavation: Pasquali, 1975
Description: stone burnisher with evident use-wear traces.

267 (Inv. PRM002254)
Location and stratigraphy: outside the caves, on top of the landslide.
Excavation: Pasquali, 1975
Description: sickle blade with invasive retouch, bilateral on dorsal face and unilateral on ventral face. Presence of bulb-of-percussion and polished use-wear traces on the side with bifacial flaking.
Colour: 2.5Y - 6/2 (light brownish gray).

268 (Inv. PRM002255)
Location and stratigraphy: outside the caves, on top of the landslide.
Excavation: Pasquali, 1975
Description: sickle blade with unilateral and bifacial invasive retouch.
Colour: fades from white to dark gray-blackish.

269 (Inv. PRM002256)
Location and stratigraphy: outside the caves, on top of the landslide.
Excavation: Pasquali, 1975
Description: sickle blade with bilateral and bifacial invasive retouch. Presence of bulb-of-percussion.
Colour: Gley 1 - 4/ (dark gray).

270 (Inv. PRM002257)
Location and stratigraphy: outside the caves, on top of the landslide.
Excavation: Pasquali, 1975
Description: sickle blade with unilateral and bifacial invasive retouch; marginal and unilateral on dorsal face. Presence of bulb-of-percussion and cortex which cover almost all the dorsal face. Polished use-wear traces on the side with bifacial flaking.
Colour: Gley 1 (fades from greyish green to grey).

271 (Inv. PRM002258)
Location and stratigraphy: outside the caves, on top of the landslide.
Excavation: Pasquali, 1975
Description: sickle blade with unilateral and bifacial invasive retouch; a very light invasive retouch is present on the other side. Polished use-wear traces on the more retouched side.
Colour: 5Y – 4/1 (dark gray).

272 (Inv. PRM002259)
Location and stratigraphy: outside the caves, on top of the landslide.
Excavation: Pasquali, 1975
Description: sickle blade with unilateral and bifacial invasive retouch.
Colour: 2.5 YR – 4/2 (dark grayish brown).

273 (Inv. PRM002260)
Location and stratigraphy: outside the caves, on top of the landslide.
Excavation: Pasquali, 1975
Description: fragmentary sickle blade with unilateral and bifacial invasive retouch. Polished use-wear traces on the retouched side.
Colour: 5Y – 5/1 (gray).

274 (Inv. PRM002266)
Location and stratigraphy: outside the caves, on top of the landslide.
Excavation: Pasquali, 1975
Description: sickle blade with unilateral and bifacial invasive retouch; presence of cortex on the other side. Slight polished use-wear traces on the retouched side.
Colour: 5Y- 7/1 (light gray).

275 (Inv. PRM002267)
Location and stratigraphy: outside the caves, on top of the landslide.
Excavation: Pasquali, 1975
Description: sickle blade with bilateral and bifacial invasive retouch. Presence of whitish patination covering the entire surface.
Colour: white

276 (Inv. PRM002268)
Location and stratigraphy: outside the caves, on top of the landslide.
Excavation: Pasquali, 1975
Description: sickle blade with unilateral and bifacial invasive retouch. Polished use-wear traces on the retouched side. Presence of cortex.
Colour: Gley 2 – 5/1 (greenish gray).

277 (Inv. PRM002279)
Location and stratigraphy: Chamber 2.
Excavation: CSL, 1970.
Description: sickle blade with unilateral and bifacial invasive retouch. Polished use-wear traces on the retouched side.
Colour: 2.5 Y – 6/2 (light brownish gray).

278 (Inv. PRM002329)
Location and stratigraphy: terraces next to the castle in a southerly direction.
Excavation: Pasquali-Rauss, 1986.
Description: sickle blade with bilateral invasive retouch on the dorsal face.
Colour: Gley 1 – 4/ (dark gray).

279 (Inv. PRM002330)
Location and stratigraphy: terraces next to the castle in a southerly direction.
Excavation: Pasquali-Rauss, 1986.
Description: sickle blade with bilateral covering retouch on the dorsal face. Presence of whitish patination.
Colour: Gley 1 – 5/ (gray).

280 (Inv. PRM002342)
Location and stratigraphy: outside the caves, northward, next to the path to the castle.
Excavation: Pasquali-Rauss, 1986.
Description: sickle blade with unilateral and bifacial invasive retouch. Polished use-wear traces on the retouched side. Presence of bulb-of-percussion.
Colour: 2.5 YR – 4/1 (dark gray).

281 (Inv. PRM021886)
Location and stratigraphy: Chamber 1, US 2, Square B3.
Excavation: MCR, 1999.
Description: fragmentary sickle blade (altered and broken by heat) with bilateral invasive retouch on ventral face and unilateral invasive retouch on dorsal face. Slight polished use-wear traces.
Colour: Gley 1 – 5/ (gray).

282 (Inv. PRM015805)
Location and stratigraphy: Chamber 1, US 5, Square B2.
Excavation: MCR, 1999.
Description: sickle blade with unilateral and bifiacial invasive retouch. Presence of cortex.
Colour: 2.5Y – 5/2 (grayish brown).

283 (Inv. PRM021869)
Location and stratigraphy: Chamber 1, US 0.
Excavation: MCR, 1999.
Description: sickle blade with unilateral and bifacial invasive retouch. Presence of cortex and of a greyish patination. Polished use-wear traces on the retouched side.
Colour: Gley 1 – 6/1 (greenish gray).

284 (Inv. PRM021879)
Location and stratigraphy: Chamber 1, US 0.
Excavation: MCR, 1999.
Description: sickle blade with unilateral and bifacial invasive retouch. Presence of cortex. Polished use-wear traces on the retouched side.
Colour: 5Y – 4/1 (dark gray).

285 (Inv. PRM002260)
Location and stratigraphy: outside the caves, on top of the landslide.
Excavation: Pasquali, 1975.
Description: flake with unilateral slight retouch on ventral face.
Colour: 2.5 YR – 5/2 (grayish brown).

286 (Inv. PRM021832)
Location and stratigraphy: Chamber 1, US 0.
Excavation: MCR, 1999.
Description: side scraper with bifacial invasive retouch.
Colour: 5Y – 5/1 (gray).

287 (Inv. PRM028837)
Location and stratigraphy: outside the caves, northward, next to the path to the castle.
Excavation: Pasquali-Rauss, 1987
Description: fragmentary side scraper with bilateral and bifacial invasive retouch.
Colour: 2.5Y – between 7/1 and 6/1

288 (Inv. PRM021863)
Location and stratigraphy: Chamber 1, US 2, Square A2.
Excavation: MCR, 1999.
Description: side scraper with unilateral fine marginal retouch on the ventral face.
Colour: 2.5Y – 6/3 (light yellowish brown).

289 (Inv. PRM002261)
Location and stratigraphy: outside the caves, on top of the landslide.
Excavation: Pasquali, 1975.
Description: flake with unilateral slight invasive retouch on the ventral face.
Colour: 10YR - 5/3 (brown).

290 (Inv. PRM021758)
Location and stratigraphy: inside the caves (surface cleaning).
Excavation: MCR, 1998.
Description: flake with unilateral fine marginal retouch on the dorsal face.
Colour: 5Y – 5/3 (olive).

291 (Inv. PRM015800)
Location and stratigraphy: Chamber 1, US 5, Square B2.
Excavation: MCR, 1999.
Description: large flake with a slight fine marginal retouch on the ventral face.
Colour: 5YR – 5/4 (reddish brown).

292 (Inv. PRM021796)
Location and stratigraphy: Chamber 3, Zone 1, Tomb 1, US 9.
Excavation: MCR, 1998.
Description: flake with ventral lateral and distal fine marginal retouch.
Colour: 2.5YR – 5/3 (reddish brown).

293 (Inv. PRM021873)
Location and stratigraphy: Chamber 1, US 2, Square B2.
Excavation: MCR, 1999.
Description: flake with dorsal fine marginal retouch. Presence of bulb-of-percussion.
Colour: 5YR – 4/4 (reddish brown).

294 (Inv. PRM002262)
Location and stratigraphy: outside the caves, on top of the landslide.
Excavation: Pasquali, 1975.
Description: end scraper with dorsal unilateral fine marginal retouch. Presence of cortex.
Colour: Gley 1 – 4/ (dark gray).

295 (Inv. PRM002264)
Location and stratigraphy: outside the caves, on top of the landslide.
Excavation: Pasquali, 1975.
Description: sub-circular end scraper with dorsal invasive retouch. Presence of whitish patination.
Colour: 2.5YR - 5/2 (grayish brown).

296 (Inv. PRM015797)
Location and stratigraphy: Chamber 2.
Excavation: MCR, 1998.
Description: core with cortex.
Colour: 7.5YR – 5/4 (brown).

297 (Inv. PRM021803)
Location and stratigraphy: Chamber 1, US 0.
Excavation: MCR, 1999.
Description: end scraper with distal dorsal invasive retouch. Presence of cortex.
Colour: 5YR – 4/4 (reddish brown).

298 (Inv. PRM015795)
Location and stratigraphy: Chamber 3, Zone 1, US 13.
Excavation: MCR, 1998.
Description: blade with cortex.
Colour: 2.5YR – 5/2 (grayish brown).

299 (Inv. PRM012592)
Location and stratigraphy: Chamber 3, Zone 1, US 13.
Excavation: MCR, 1998.
Description: end scraper with unilateral fine marginal retouch on the ventral face.
Colour: 7.5YR – 6/4 (light brown).

300 (Inv. PRM002331)
Location and stratigraphy: terraces next to the castle in a southerly direction.
Excavation: Pasquali-Rauss, 1986.
Description: fragmentary barbed arrowhead with dorsal covering retouch and ventral invasive retouch.
Colour: 10 R – 6/1 (reddish gray).

301 (Inv. PRM028861)
Location and stratigraphy: outside the caves, on top of the landslide.
Excavation: Pasquali, 1975
Description: end scraper with bifacial covering retouch.
Colour: 10R 4/3 (weak red)

302 (Inv. PRM002328)
Location and stratigraphy: terraces next to the castle in a southerly direction.
Excavation: Pasquali-Rauss, 1986.
Description: long blade with a few retouches, probably only accidental or due to use-wear. Presence of cortex.
Colour: Gley 1 – 4/ (dark gray).

303 (Inv. PRM015794)
Location and stratigraphy: Chamber 3, Zone 1, US 13.
Excavation: MCR, 1998.
Description: fragmentary barbed arrowhead (the tip is missing) with unilateral fine marginal retouch on ventral surface and with a similar kind of retouch on the other face. Presence of cortex near the barbs.
Colour: 10YR – 7/2 (light gray).

304 (Inv. PRM028840)
Location and stratigraphy: outside the caves, northward, next to the path to the castle.
Excavation: Pasquali-Rauss, 1987
Description: small tanged arrowhead with bifacial covering retouch.
Colour: 2.5Y – 5/2 (grayish brown)

305 (Inv. PRM021887)
Location and stratigraphy: Chamber 1, US 2, Square B3.
Excavation: MCR, 1999.
Description: small triangular hollow-based arrowhead with bifacial covering retouch.
Colour: 10YR – 6/3 (pale brown).

306 (Inv. PRM015796)
Location and stratigraphy: Chamber 3, Zone 1, Tomb 1, US 10.
Excavation: MCR, 1998.
Description: fragmentary arrowhead with squared barbs and covering retouch. Altered and broken by heat (the tip and a piece of barb are missing)
Colour: greyish.

307 (Inv. PRM021837)
Location and stratigraphy: Chamber 3, Zone 2.
Excavation: MCR, 1998.
Description: hollow-based arrowhead with bifacial invasive retouch. Presence of whitish patination on both the faces.
Colour: 2.5YR – 5/4 (reddish brown).

308 (Inv. PRM021990)
Location and stratigraphy: Chamber 1, US 0.
Excavation: MCR, 1999.
Description: sandstone tool with central groove (arrowshaft smoother).

309 (Inv. PRM015698)
Location and stratigraphy: Chamber 1, US 3, Square A3.
Excavation: MCR, 1999.
Description: sub-rectangular stone brassard (wristguard) with enlarged endings and two rounded pierced holes.

310 (Inv. PRM002319)
Location and stratigraphy: Chamber 2.
Excavation: GGR, 1972.
Description: bone awl.

311 (Inv. PRM002307)
Location and stratigraphy: unknown.
Excavation: GGR, 1970.
Description: fragmentary tool in red deer antler cut, burnished and pierced.

312 (Inv. PRM002333)
Location and stratigraphy: unknown.
Excavation: unknown.
Description: fragmentary bone awl.

313 (Inv. PRM028817)
Location and stratigraphy: Chamber 1, US 3, Sqare A2-B2.
Excavation: MCR, 1999
Description: bone awl made from bear fibula.

314 (Inv. PRM028816)
Location and stratigraphy: inside the caves (on the surface).
Excavation: occasional find (Andrea Miorandi, 1992).
Description: bone spatula obtained from a diaphysis, partially altered by heat.

315 (Inv. PRM028818)
Location and stratigraphy: Chamber 3, US 10.
Excavation: MCR, 1998
Description: small fragmentary bone spatula.

316 (Inv. PRM021992)
Location and stratigraphy: Chamber 1, Zone 1 (at the end of the cavity).
Excavation: MCR, 1999.
Description: small triangular bone awl.

317 (Inv. PRM012593)
Location and stratigraphy: access corridor to Chamber 1 (surface cleaning).
Excavation: MCR, 1998.
Description: bone pin/needle with enlarged and pierced head obtained from a diaphyseal fragment (perhaps of a large herbivore).

318 (Inv. PRM002343)
Location and stratigraphy: terraces next to the castle in a southerly direction.
Excavation: Pasquali-Rauss, 1986.
Description: bone awl.

319 (Inv. PRM021991)
Location and stratigraphy: Chamber 1, US 0.
Excavation: MCR, 1999.
Description: bone awl with a pierced hole at the base.

320 (Inv. PRM012598)
Location and stratigraphy: Chamber 3, Zone 1, US 13.
Excavation: MCR, 1998.
Description: fragmentary pierced sub-rectangular shell bead.

321 (Inv. PRM012600)
Location and stratigraphy: Chamber 3, Zone 1, Tomb 1, US 10.
Excavation: MCR, 1998.
Description: fragmentary pierced sub-rectangular shell bead.

322 (Inv. PRM012594)
Location and stratigraphy: Chamber 3, Zone 1, US 13.
Excavation: MCR, 1998.
Description: pierced triangular shell bead.

323 (Inv. PRM012597)
Location and stratigraphy: Chamber 3, Zone 1, US 13.
Excavation: MCR, 1998.
Description: pierced sub-circular stone bead.

324 (Inv. PRM012595)
Location and stratigraphy: Chamber 3, Zone 1, US 13.
Excavation: MCR, 1998.
Description: pierced sub-circular stone bead.

325 (Inv. PRM012596)
Location and stratigraphy: Chamber 3, Zone 1, US 13.
Excavation: MCR, 1998.
Description: pierced sub-circular shell bead.

326 (Inv. PRM012599)
Location and stratigraphy: Chamber 3, Zone 1, Tomb 1, US 10.
Excavation: MCR, 1998.
Description: pierced sub-circular shell bead.

327 (Inv. PRM031074)
Location and stratigraphy: Chamber 3, Zone 1, Tomb 2 (US 18), over the human bones.
Excavation: MCR, 1998.
Description: pierced sub-circular stone(?) bead with a sub-quadrangular cross-section.

328 (Inv. PRM031075)
Location and stratigraphy: Chamber 3, Zone 1, US 8.
Excavation: MCR, 1998.
Description: fragmentary pierced sub-circular shell bead.

329 (Inv. PRM031076)
Location and stratigraphy: Chamber 3, Zone 1, US 8.
Excavation: MCR, 1998.
Description: fragmentary pierced sub-circular shell bead.

330 (Inv. PRM031078)
Location and stratigraphy: Chamber 3, Zone 1, Tomb 1, US 9.
Excavation: MCR, 1998.
Description: fragmentary pierced sub-circular stone bead with a sub-circular cross-section.

331 (Inv. PRM021970)
Location and stratigraphy: Chamber 3, Zone 1, Tomb 1, US 10.
Excavation: MCR, 1998.
Description: small piece of slag.

Plates

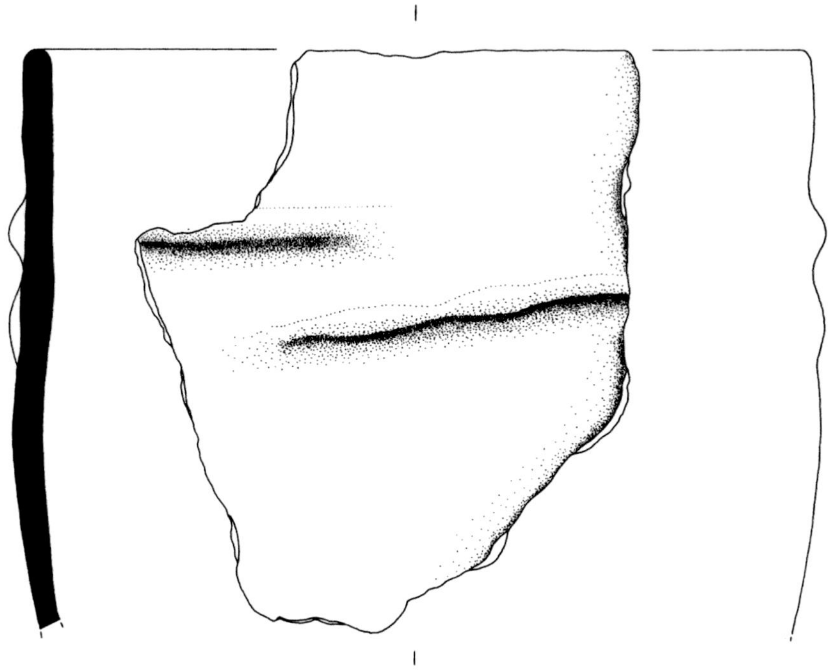

1

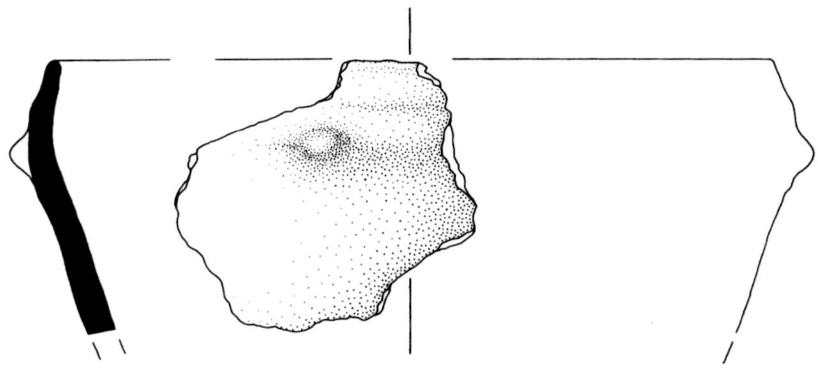

2

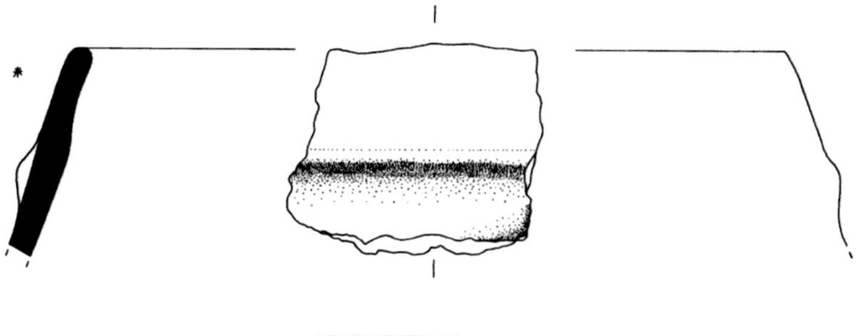

3

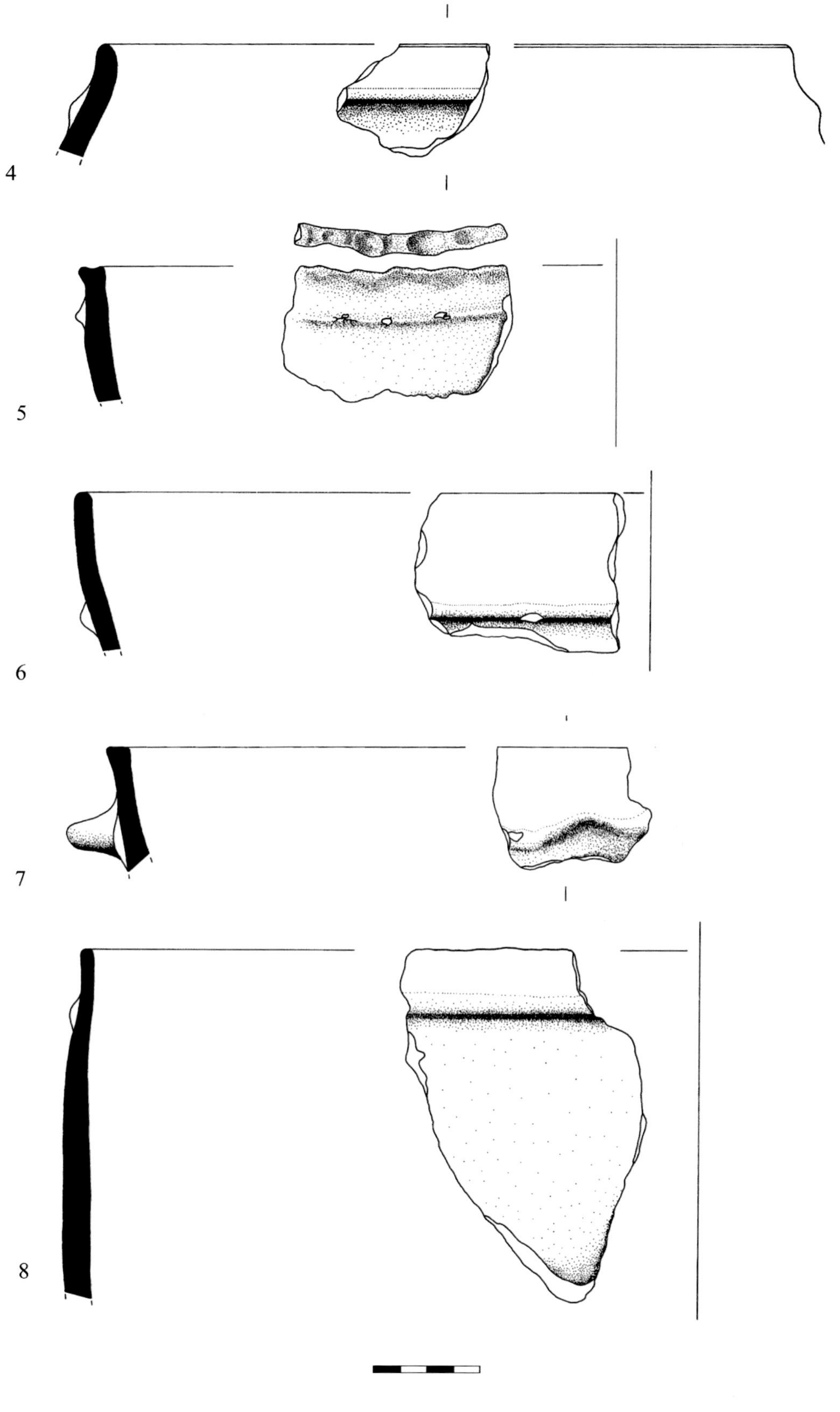

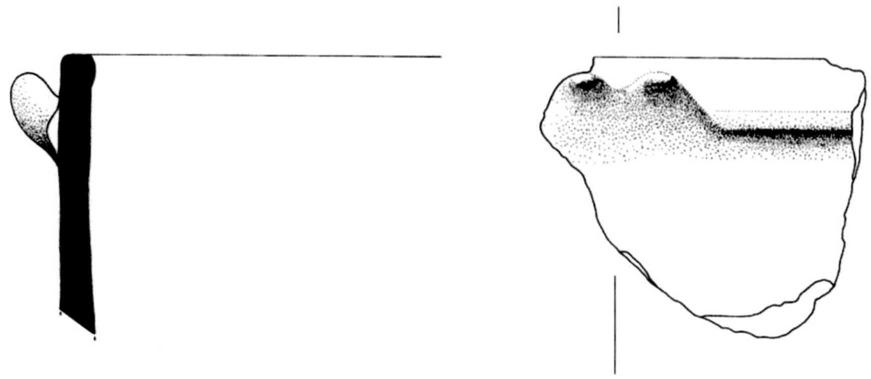

9

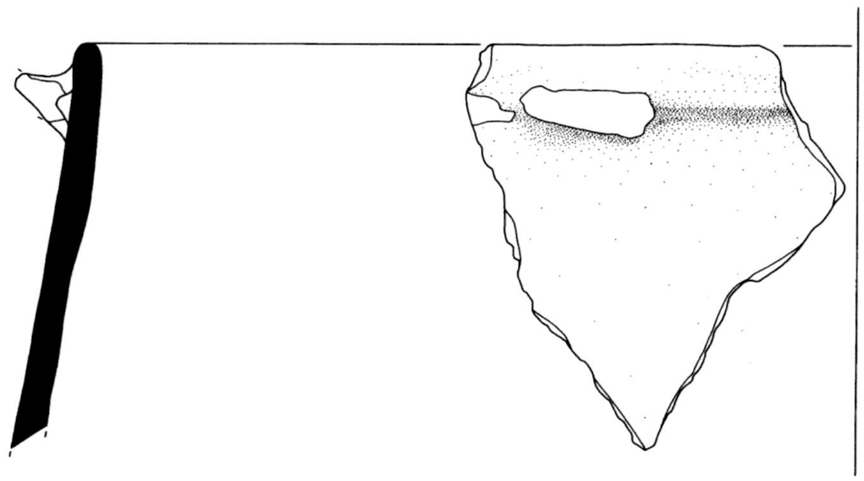

10

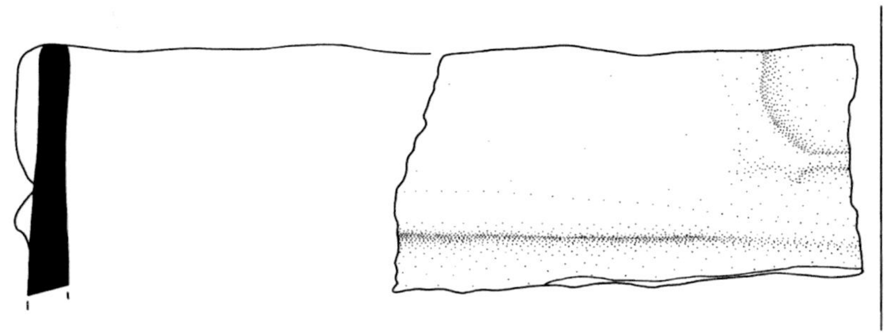

11

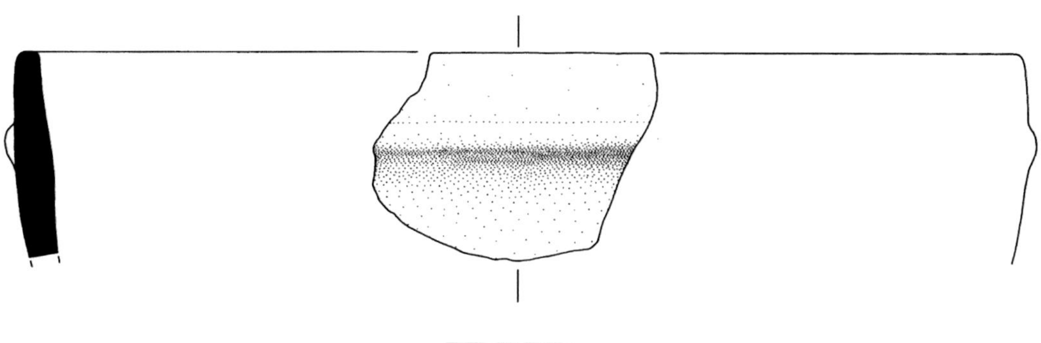

12

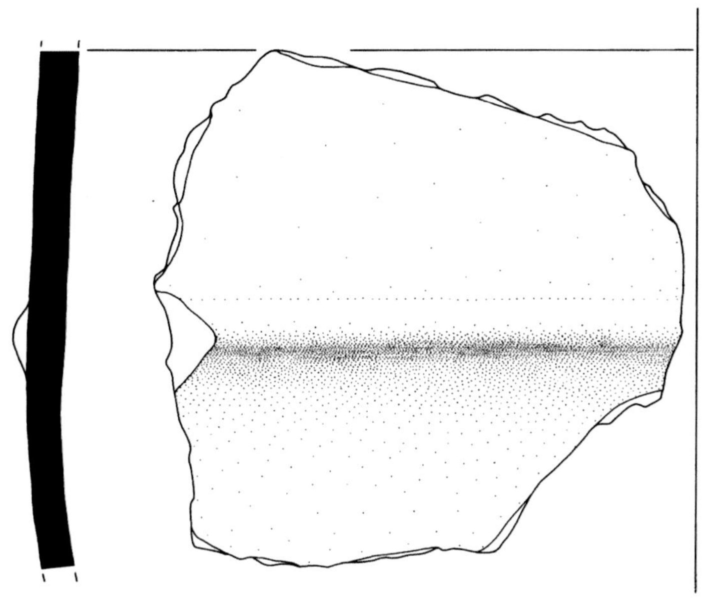

13

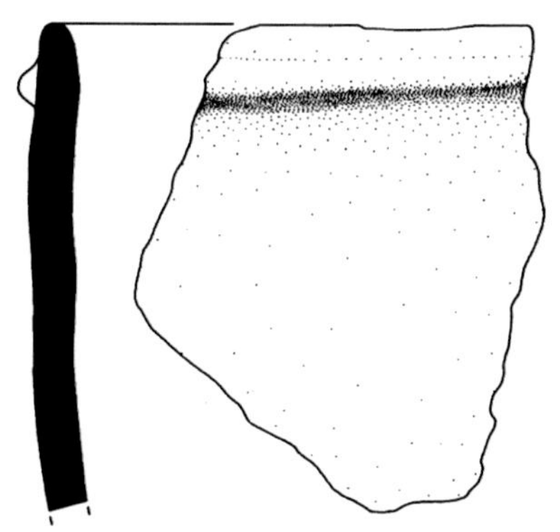

14

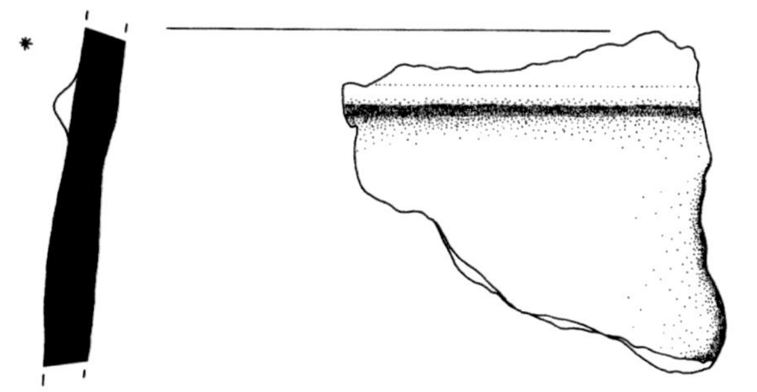

15

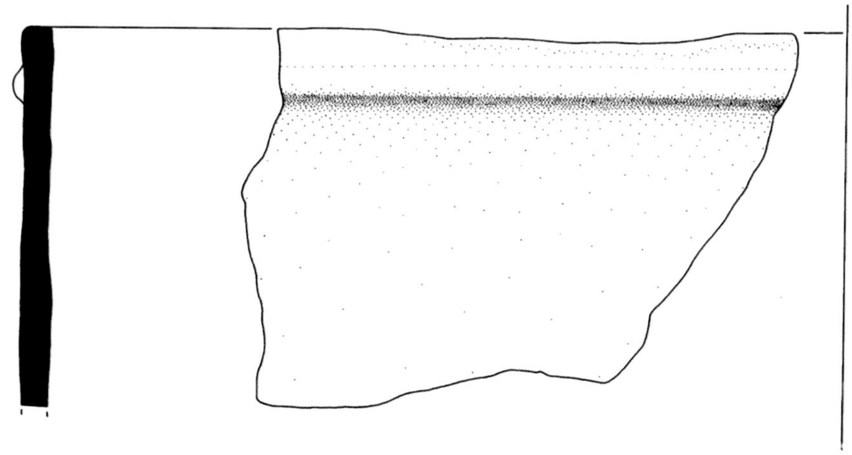

16

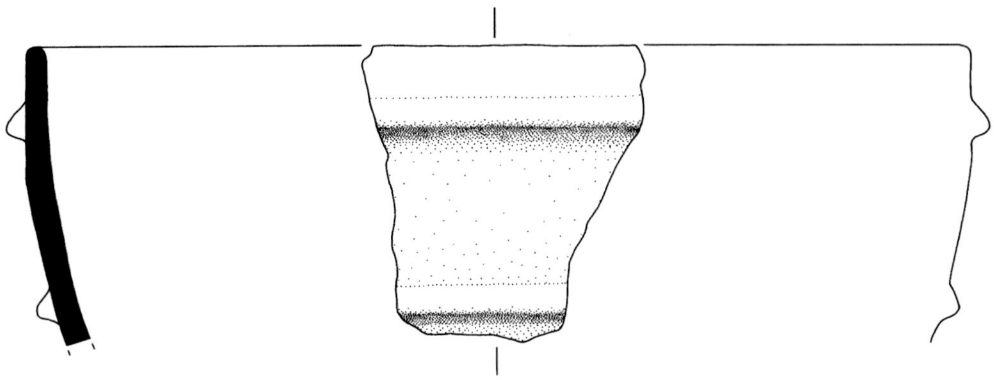

17

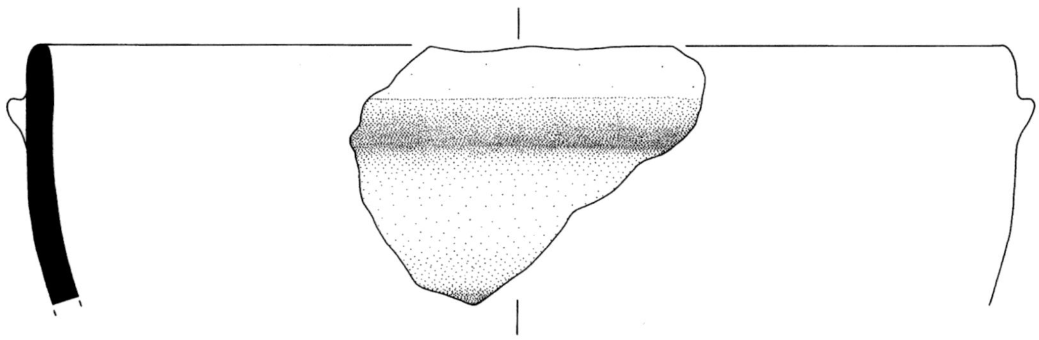

18

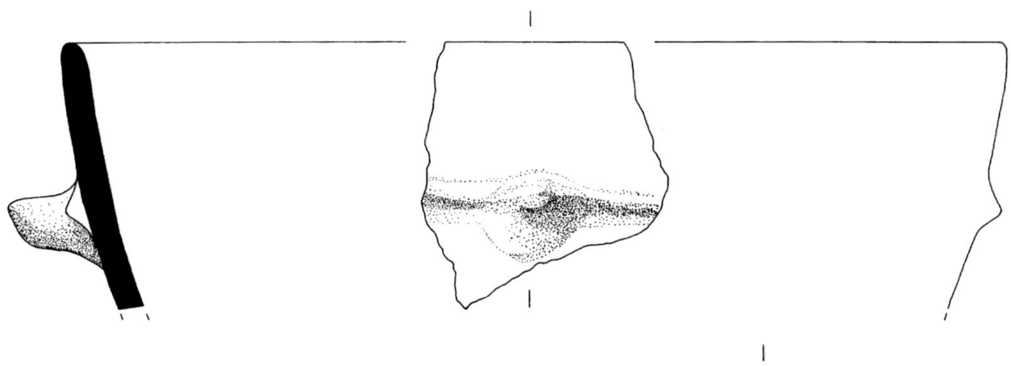

19

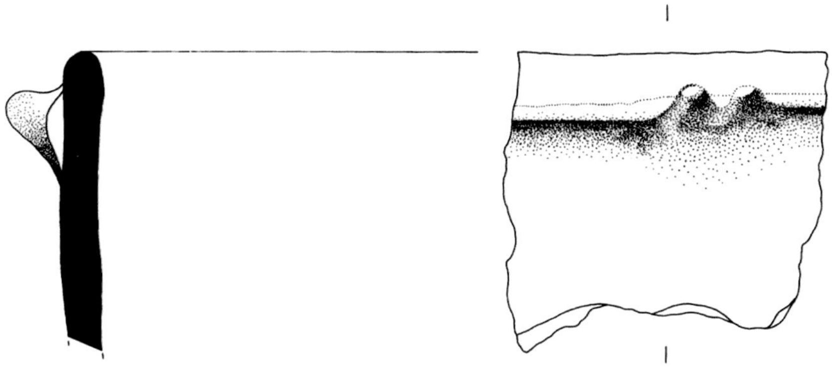

20

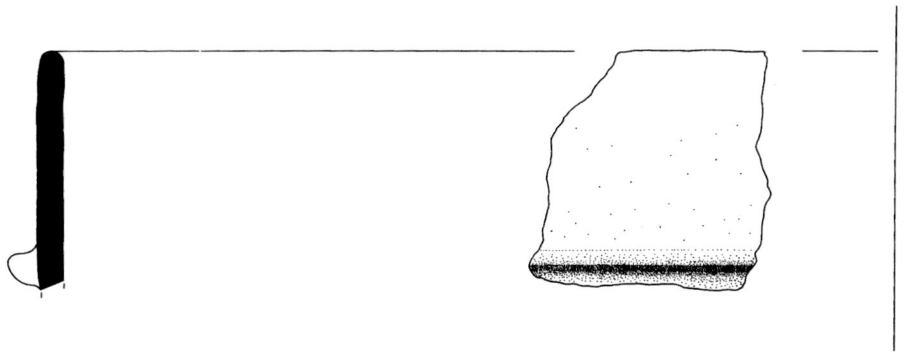

21

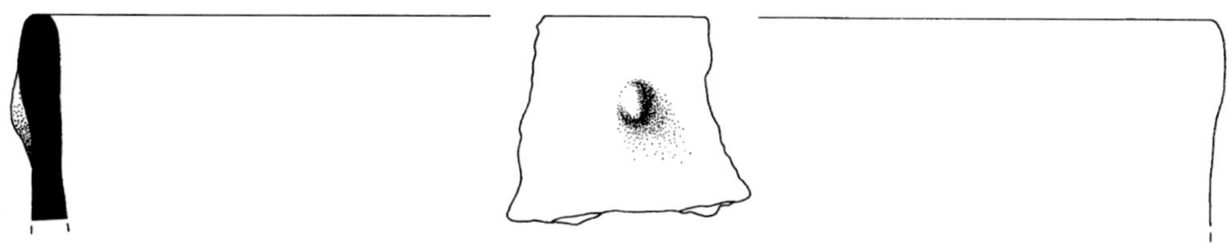

22

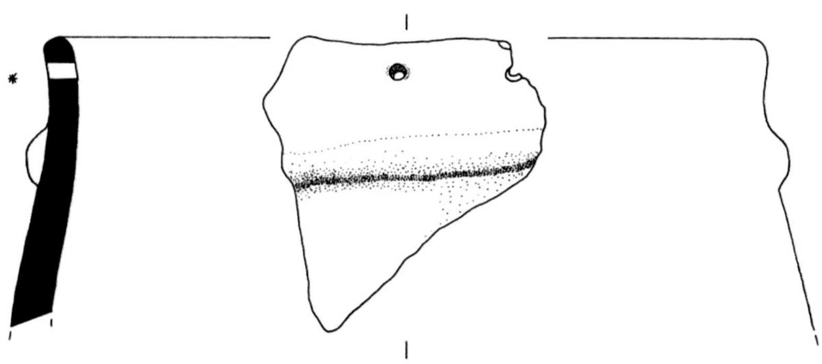

23

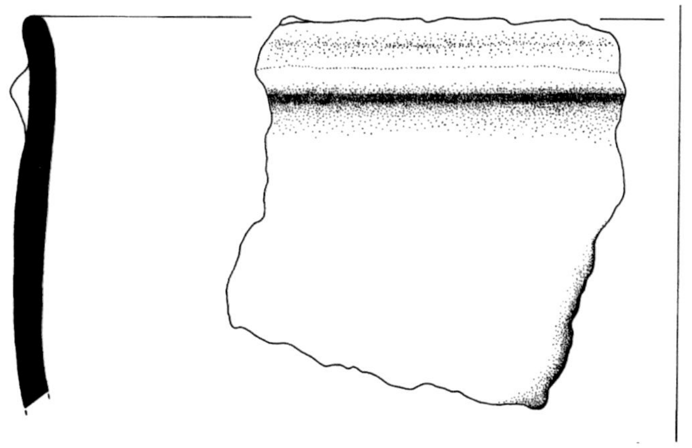

24

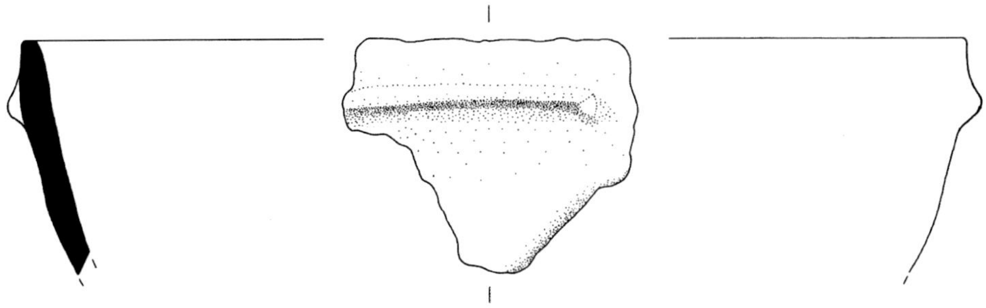

25

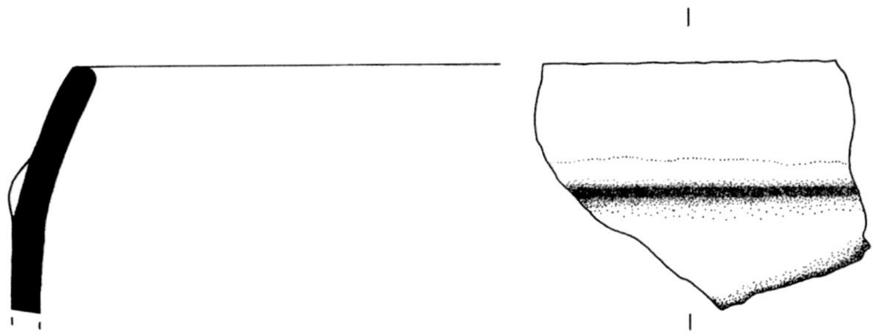

26

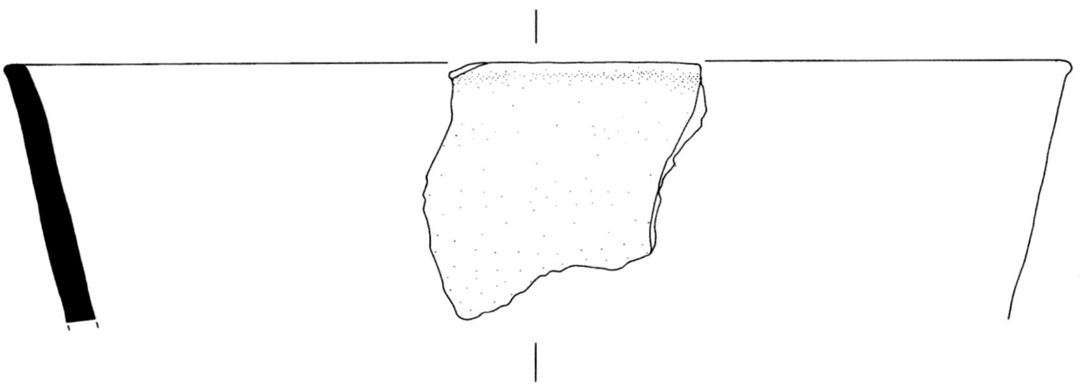

27

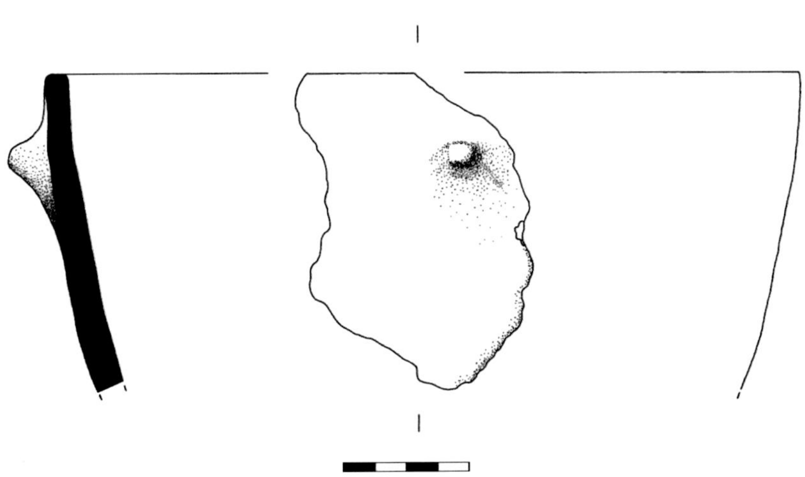

28

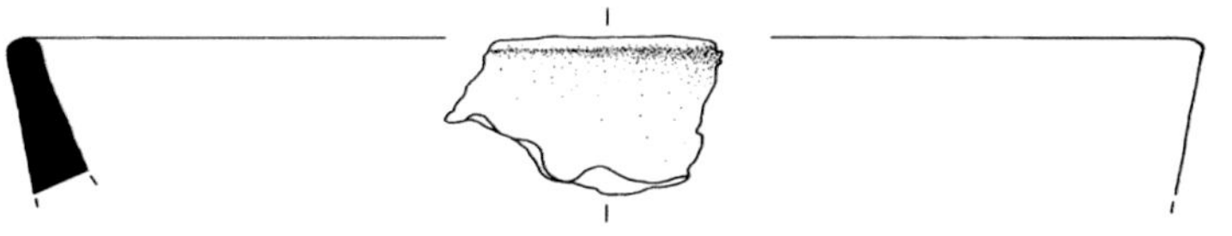
29

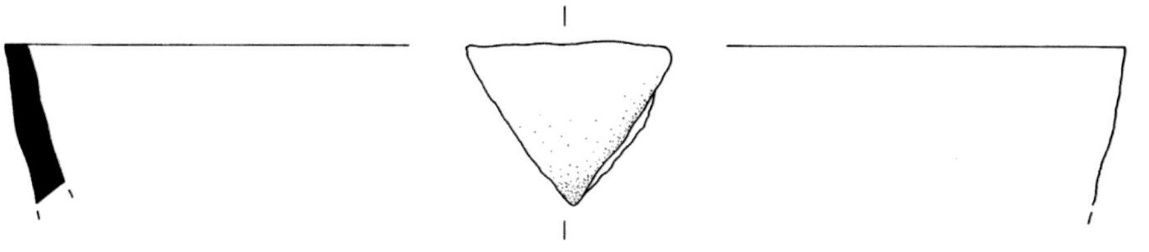
30

31

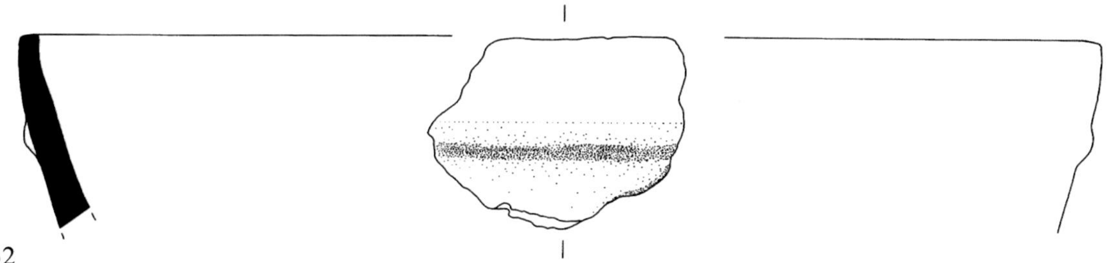
32

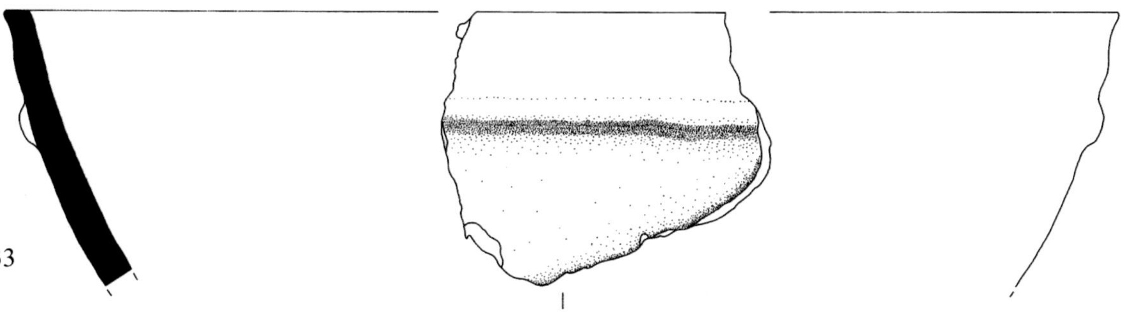
33

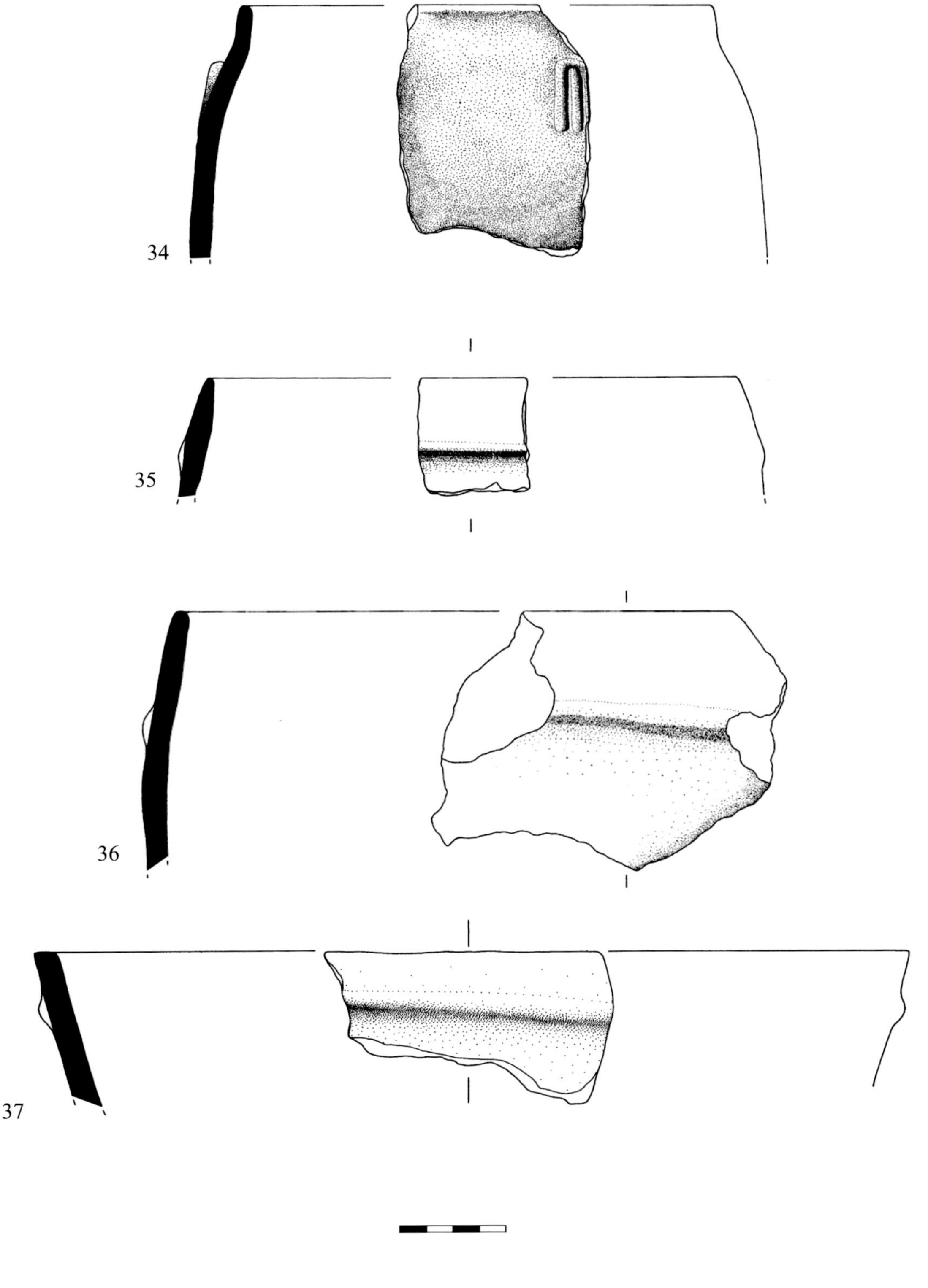
34
35
36
37

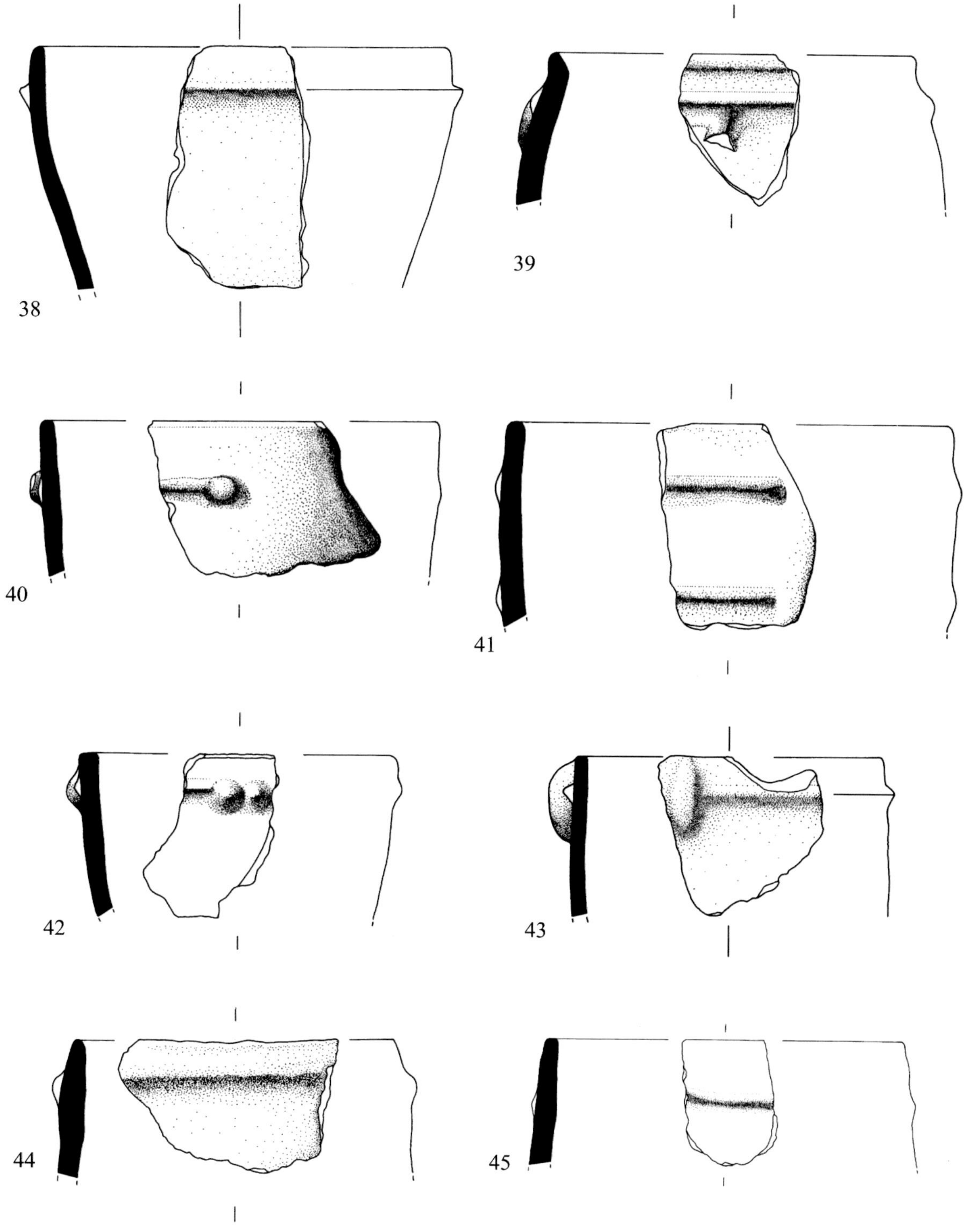
38
39
40
41
42
43
44
45

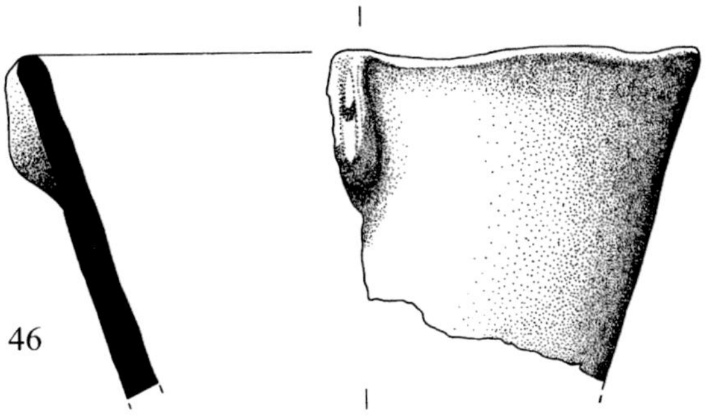

46

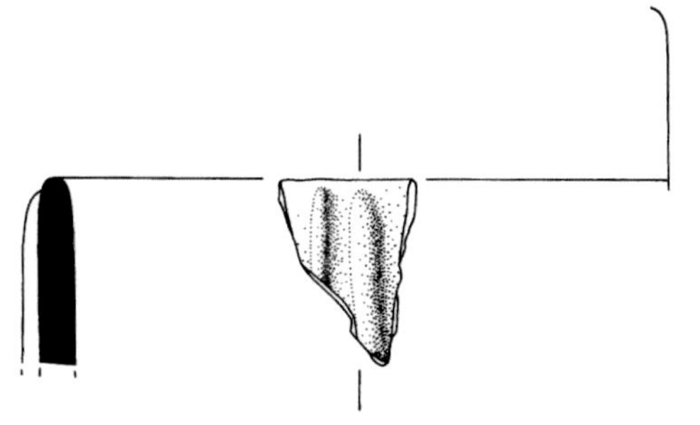

47

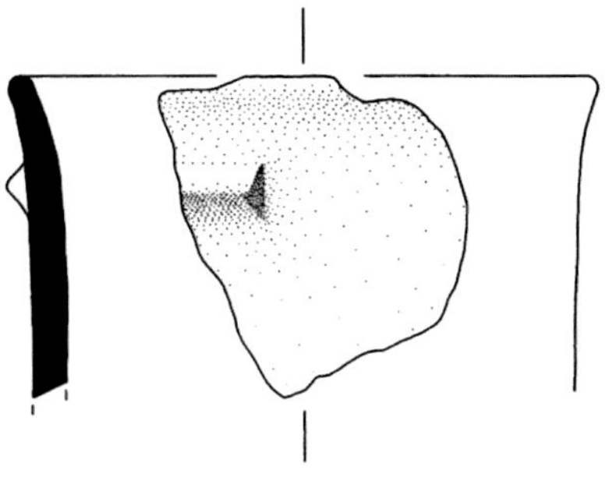

48

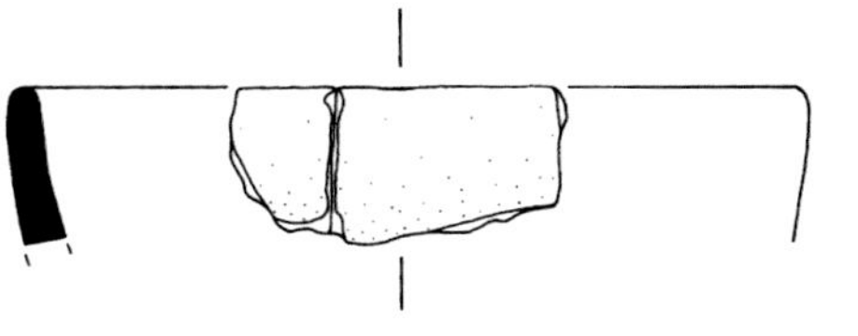

49

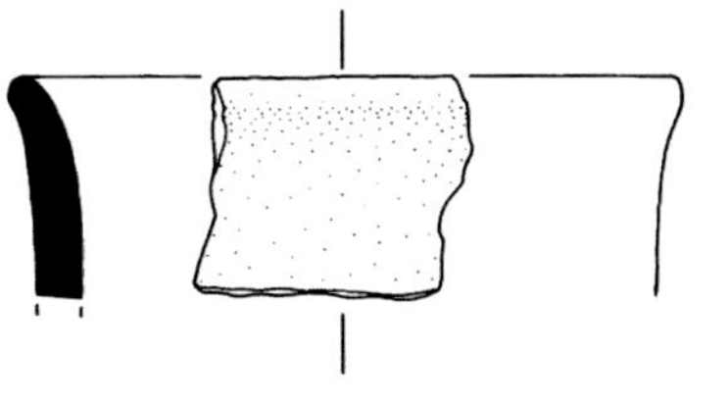

50

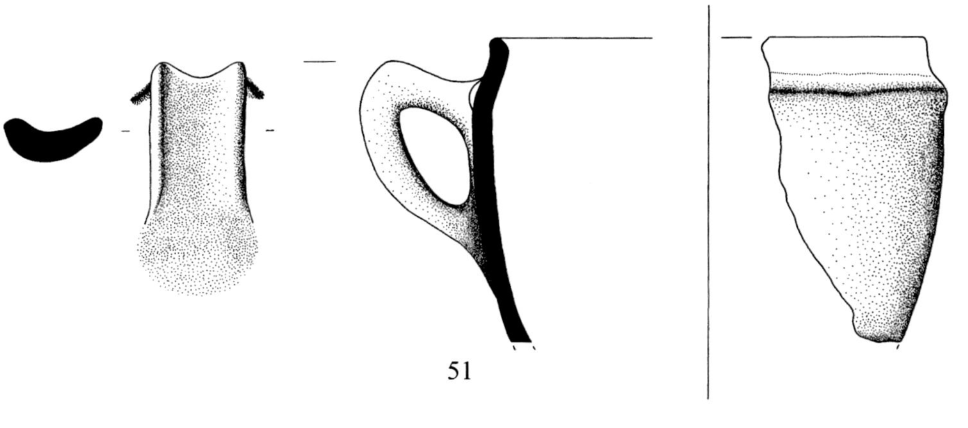

51

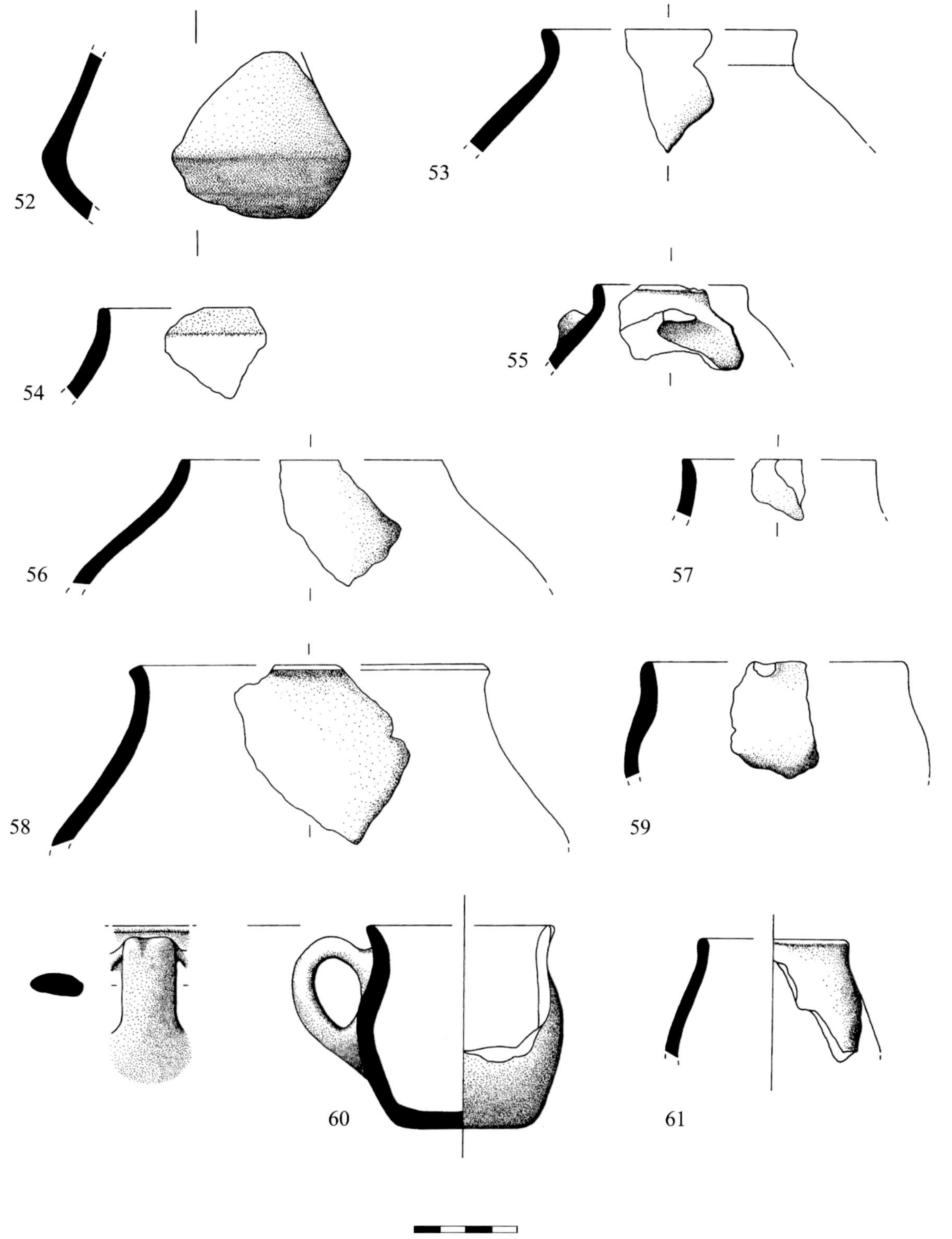
52
53
54
55
56
57
58
59
60
61

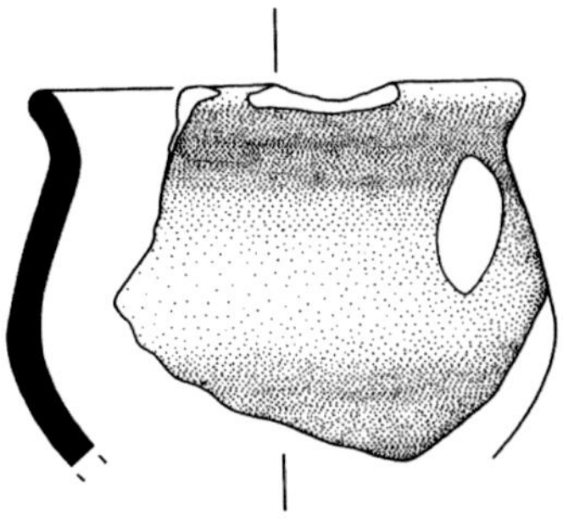

62

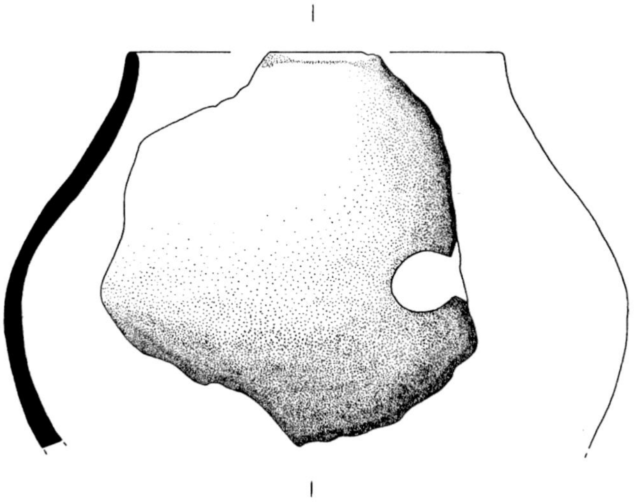

63

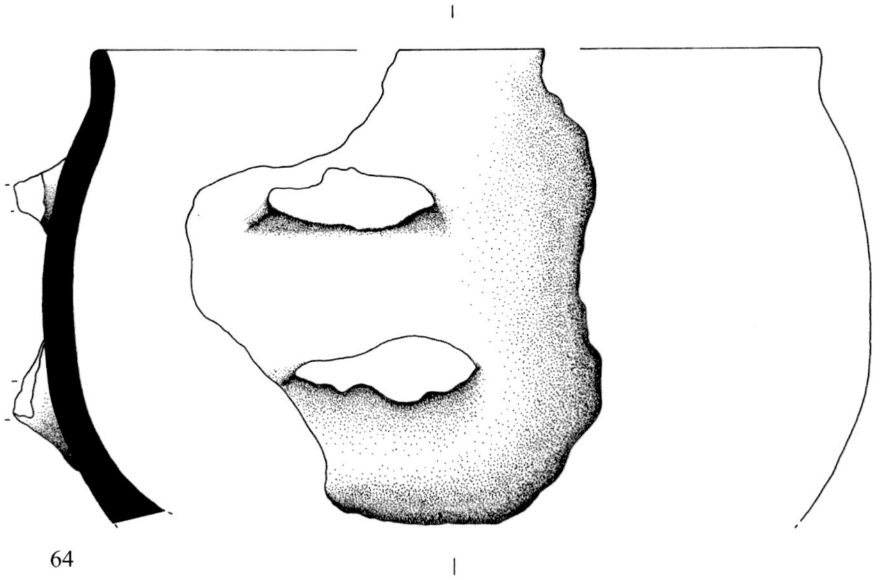

64

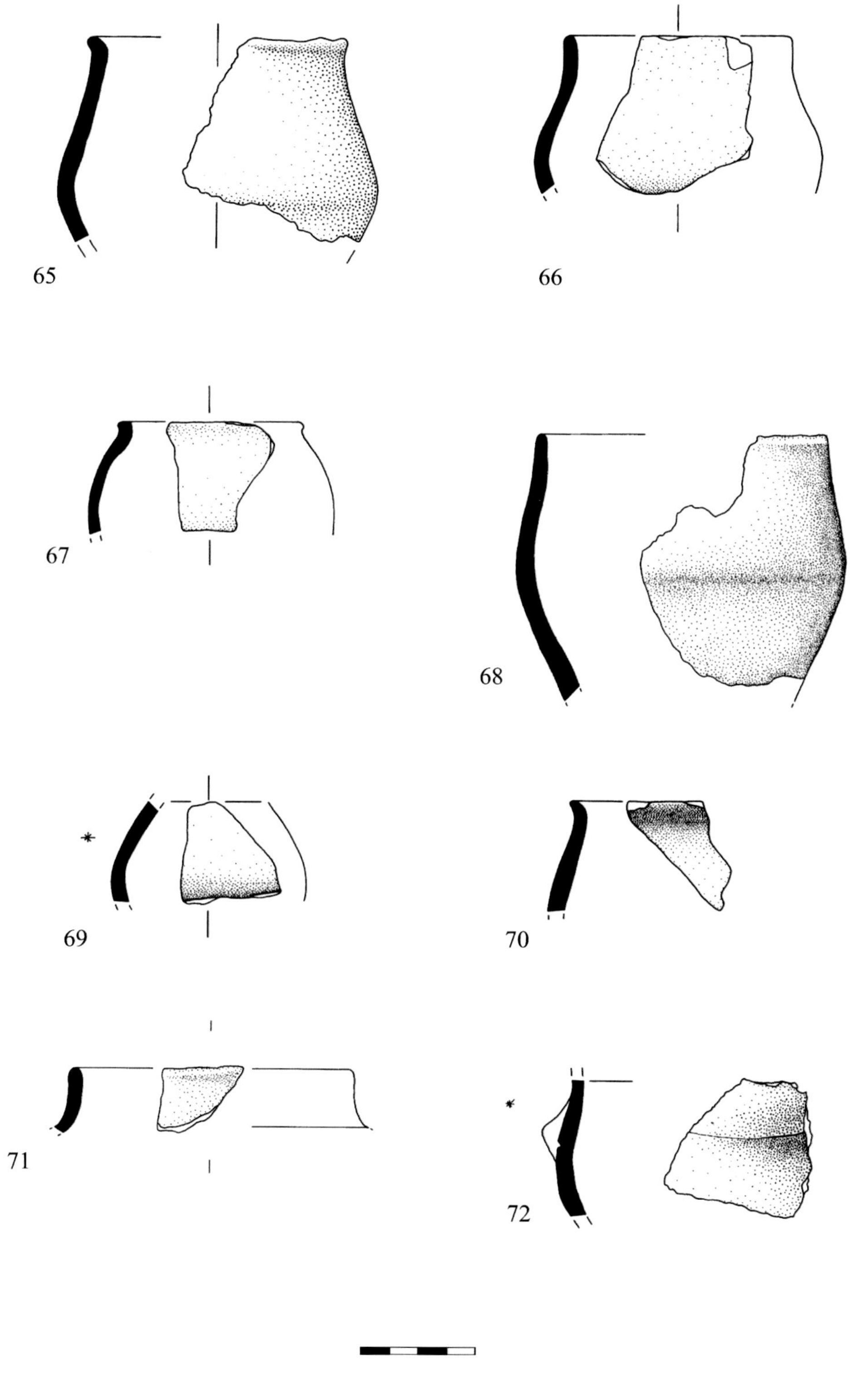
65
66
67
68
69
70
71
72

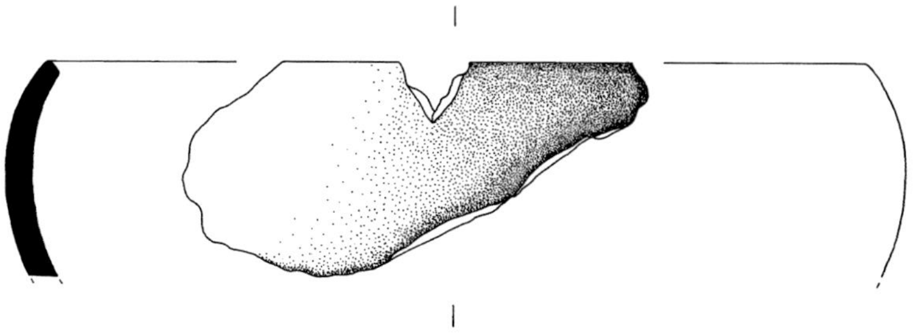

73

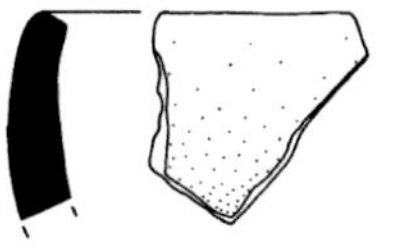

74

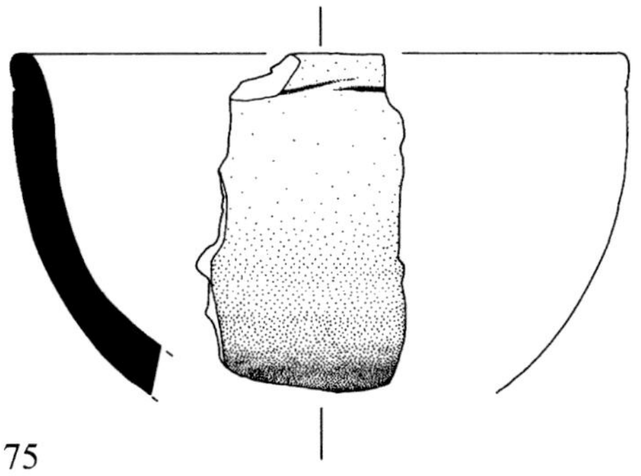

75

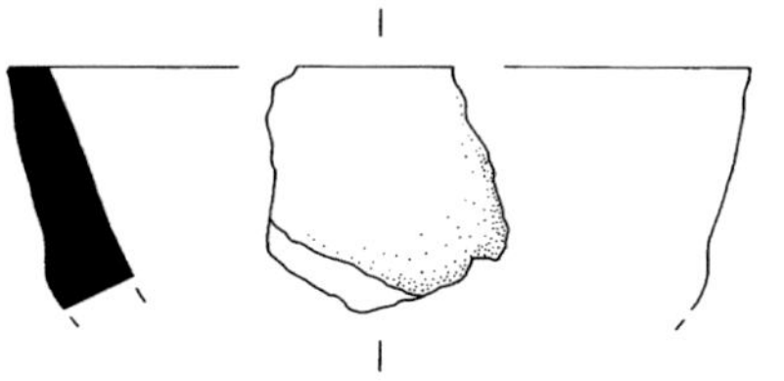

76

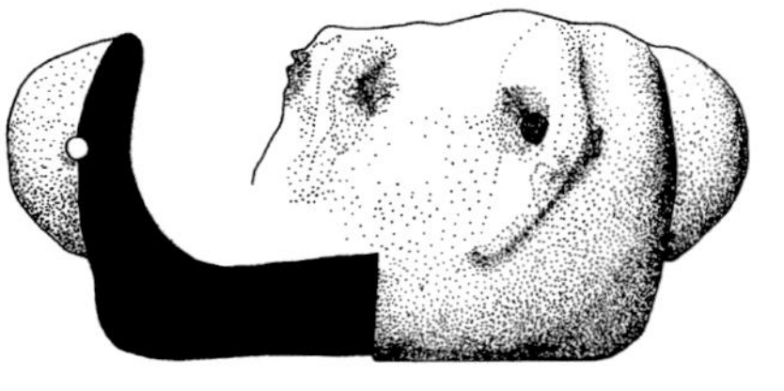

77

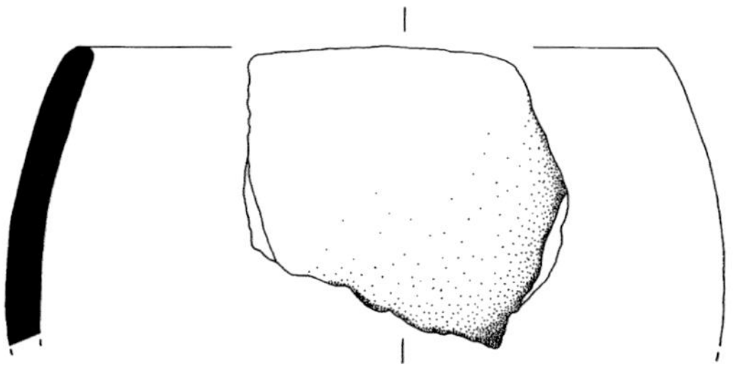

78

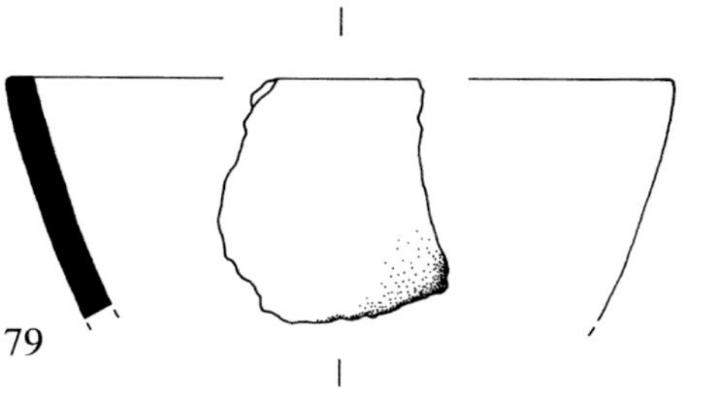

79

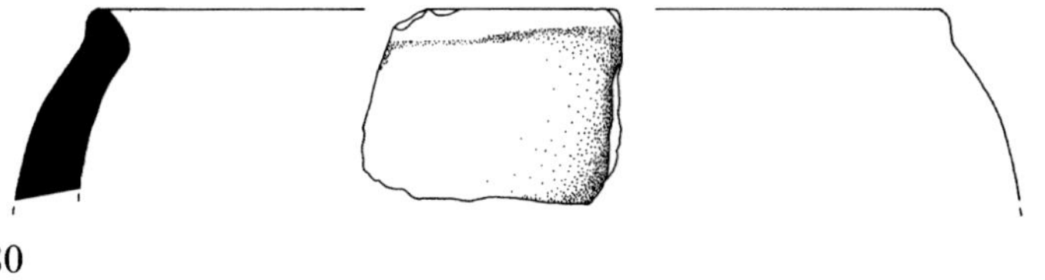

80

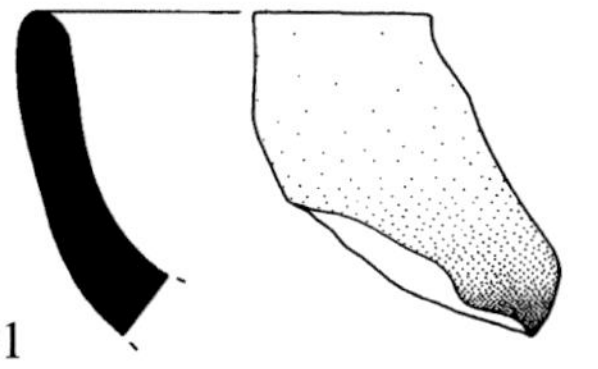

81

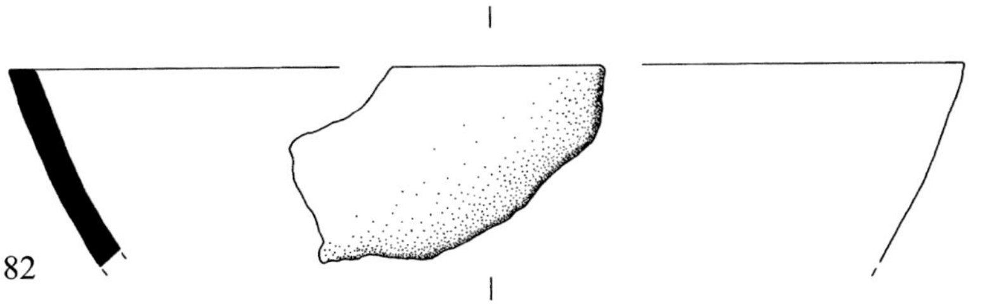

82

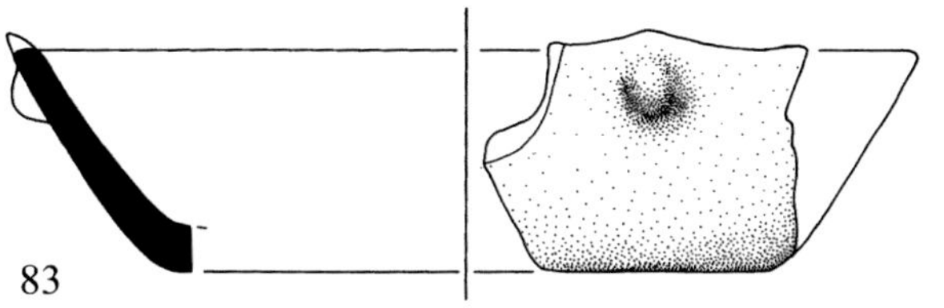

83

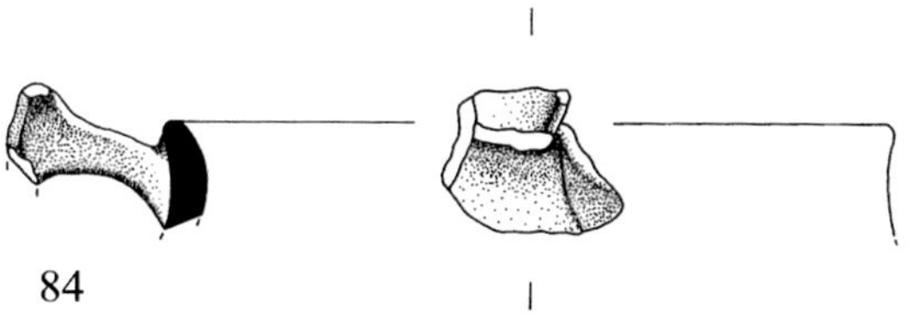

84

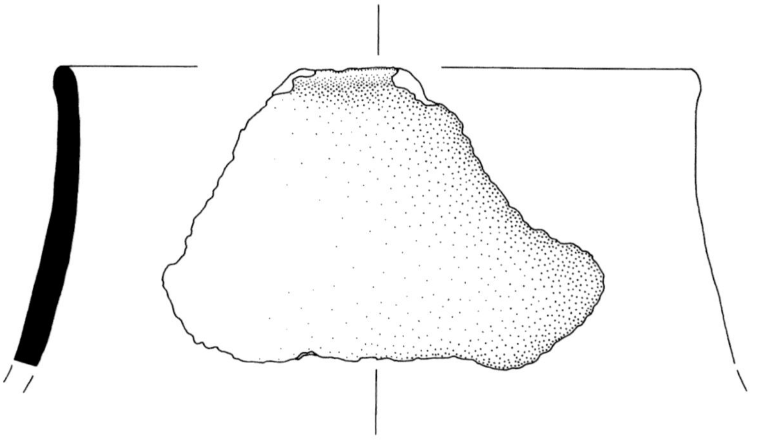

85

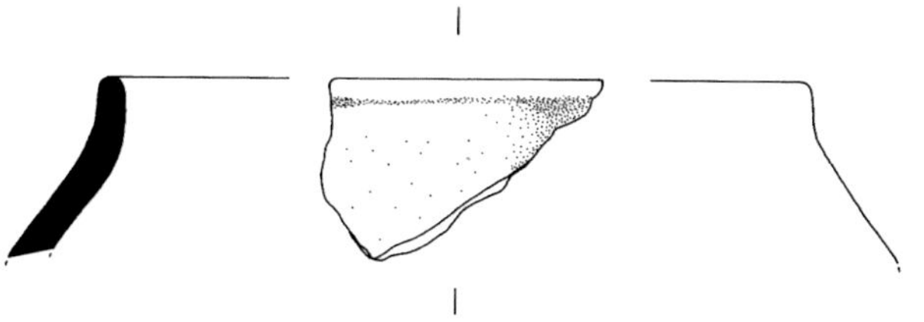

86

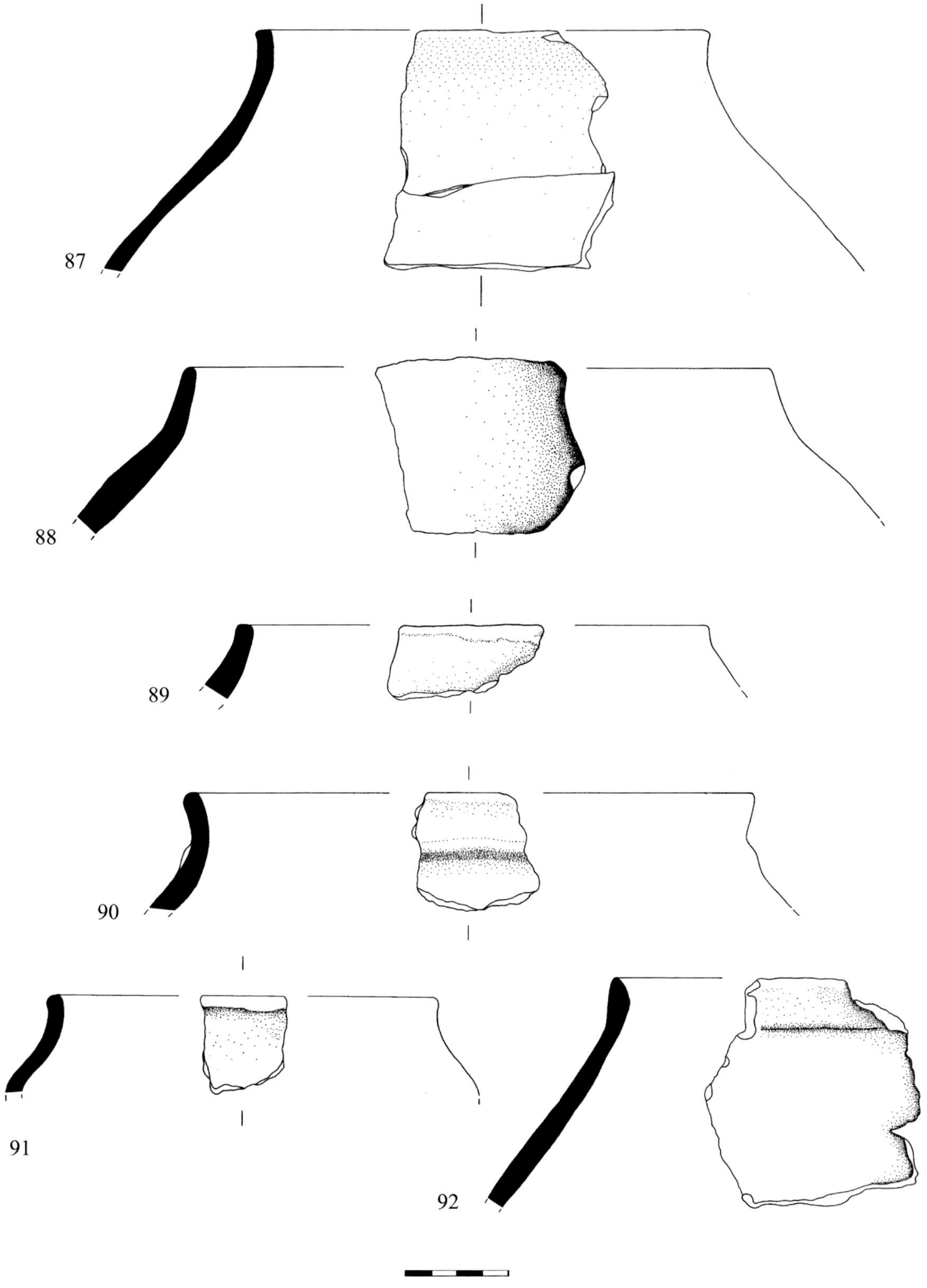
87
88
89
90
91
92

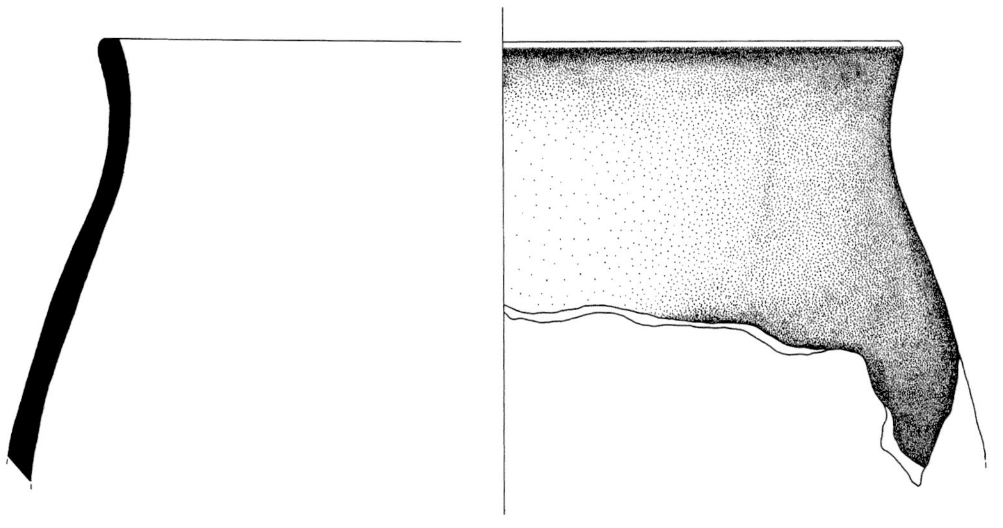

93

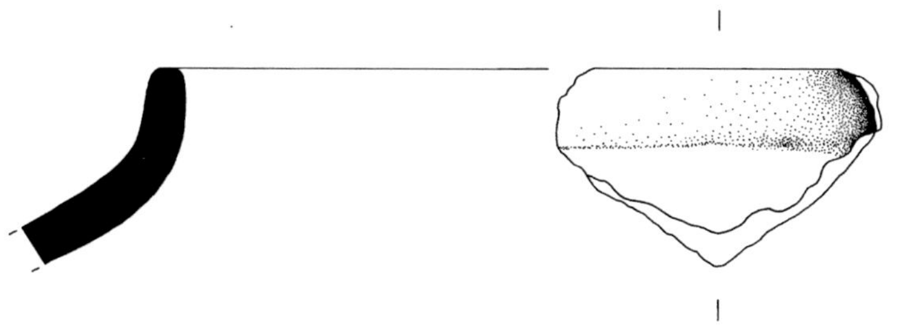

94

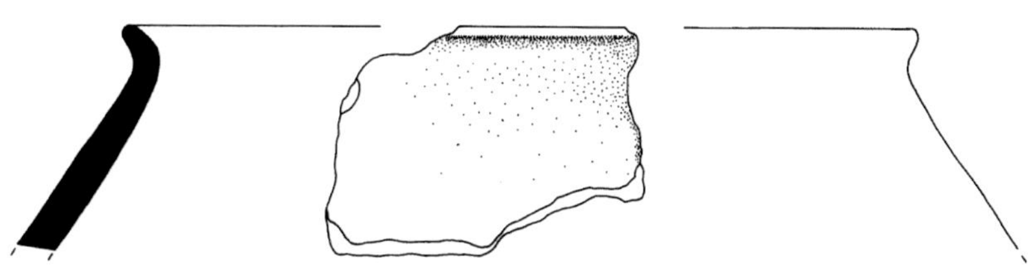

95

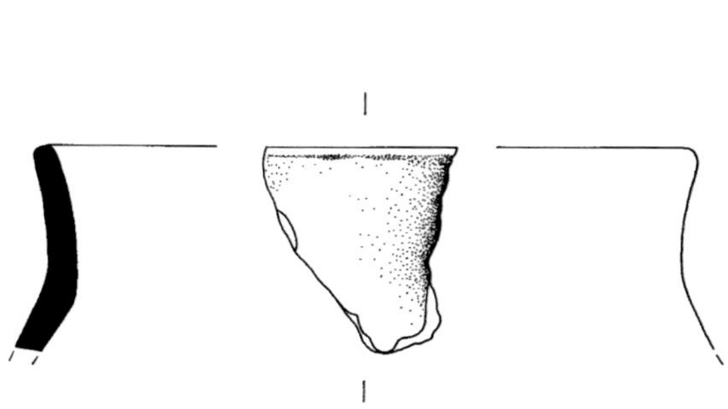

96

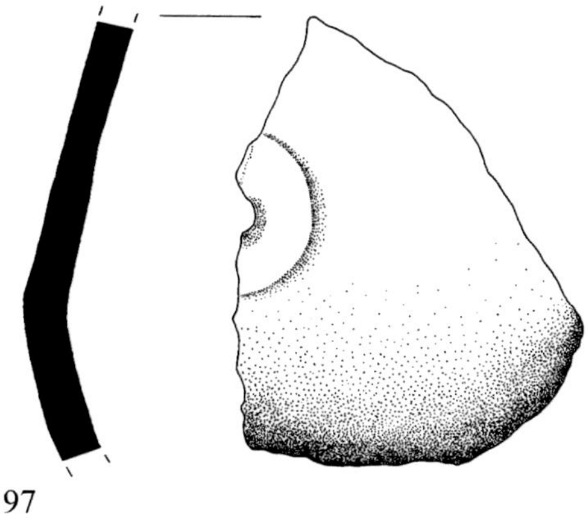

97

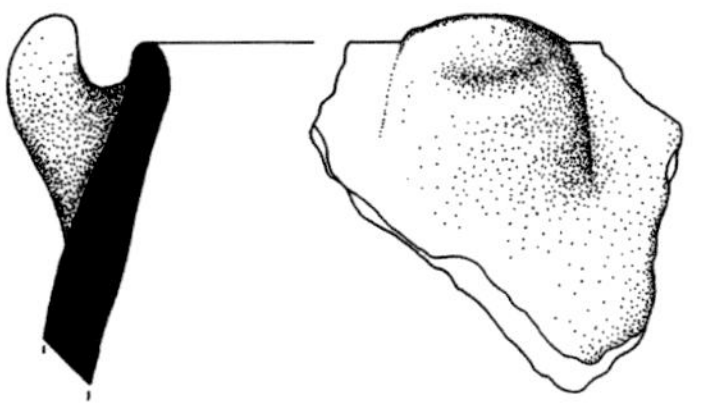
98

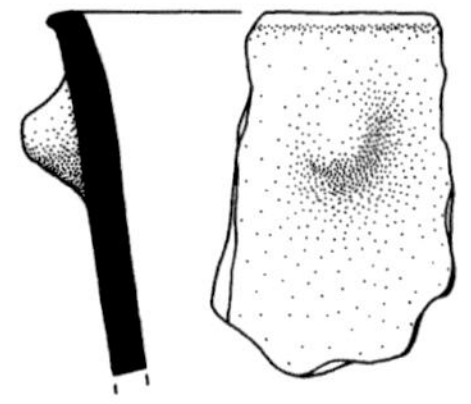
99

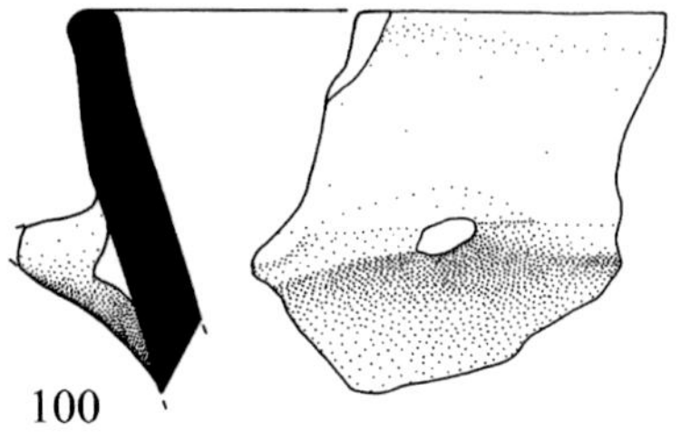
100

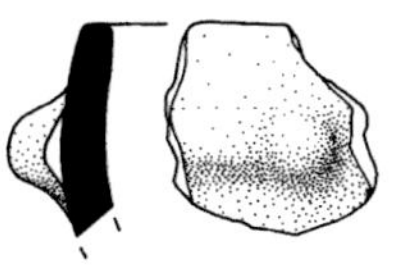
101

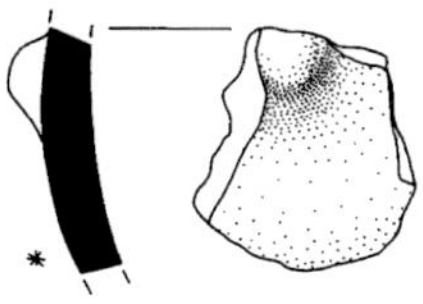
102

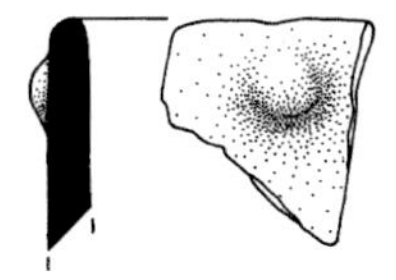
103

104

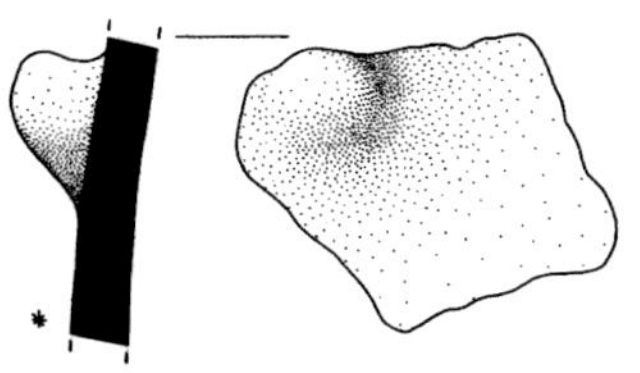
105

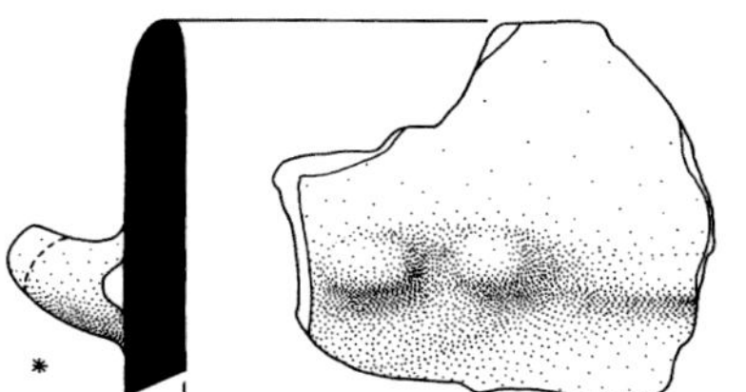
106

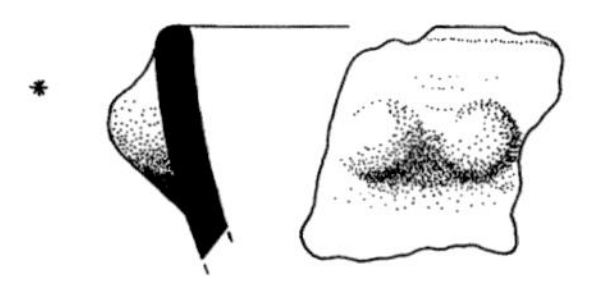
107

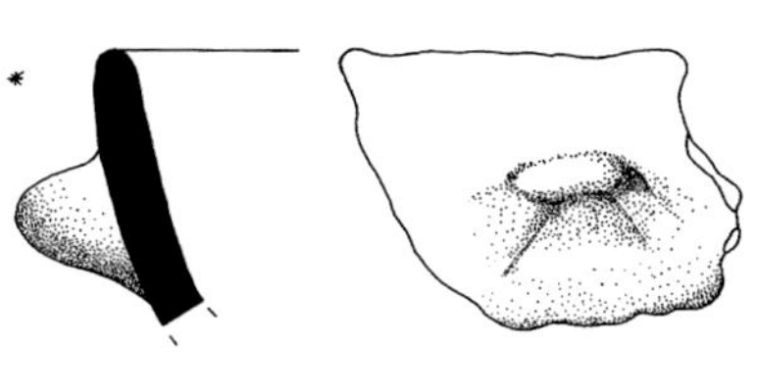
108

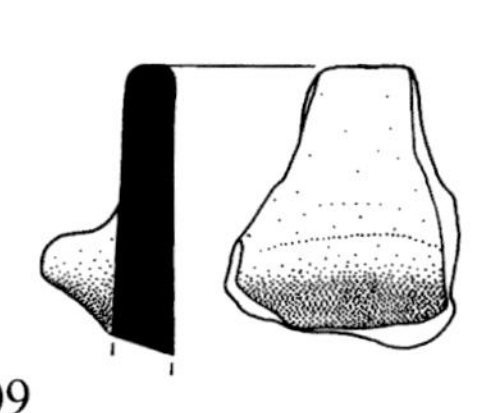
109

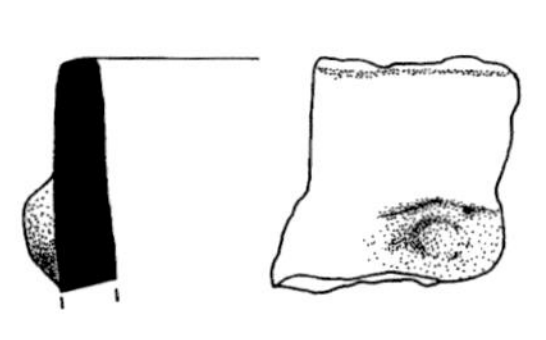
110

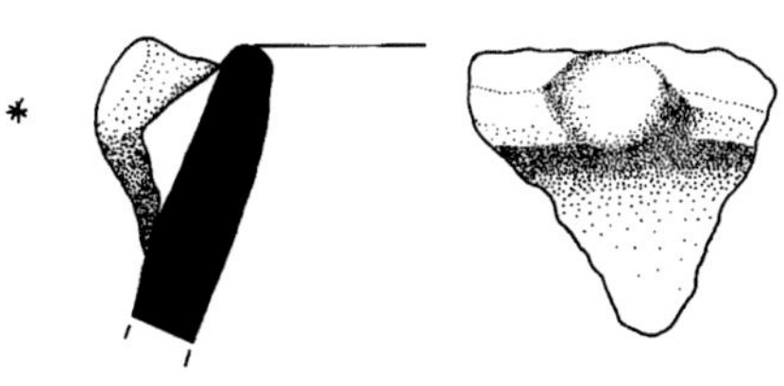
111

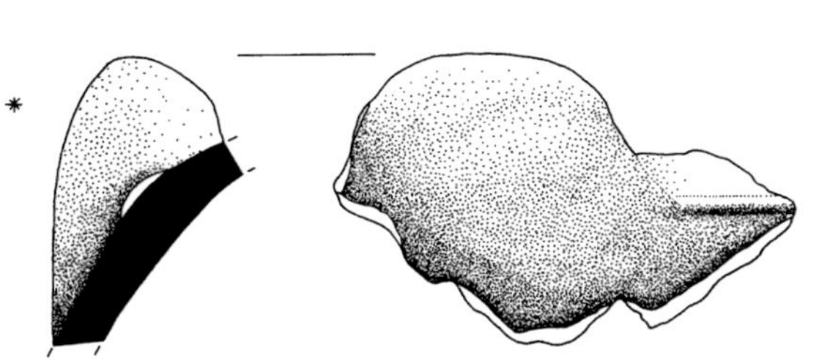
112

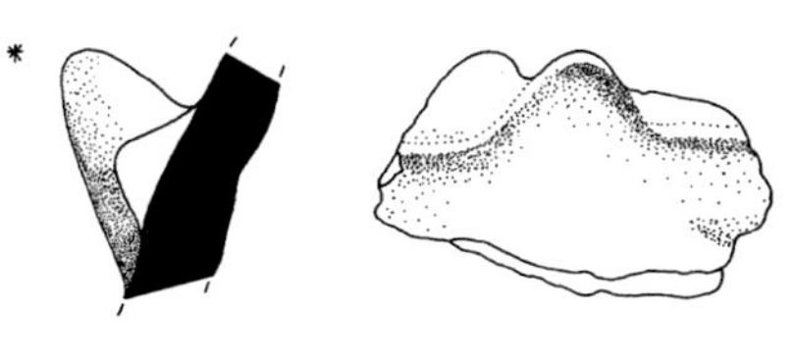
113

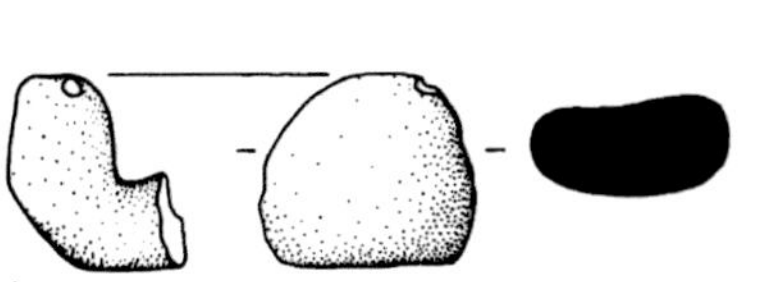
114

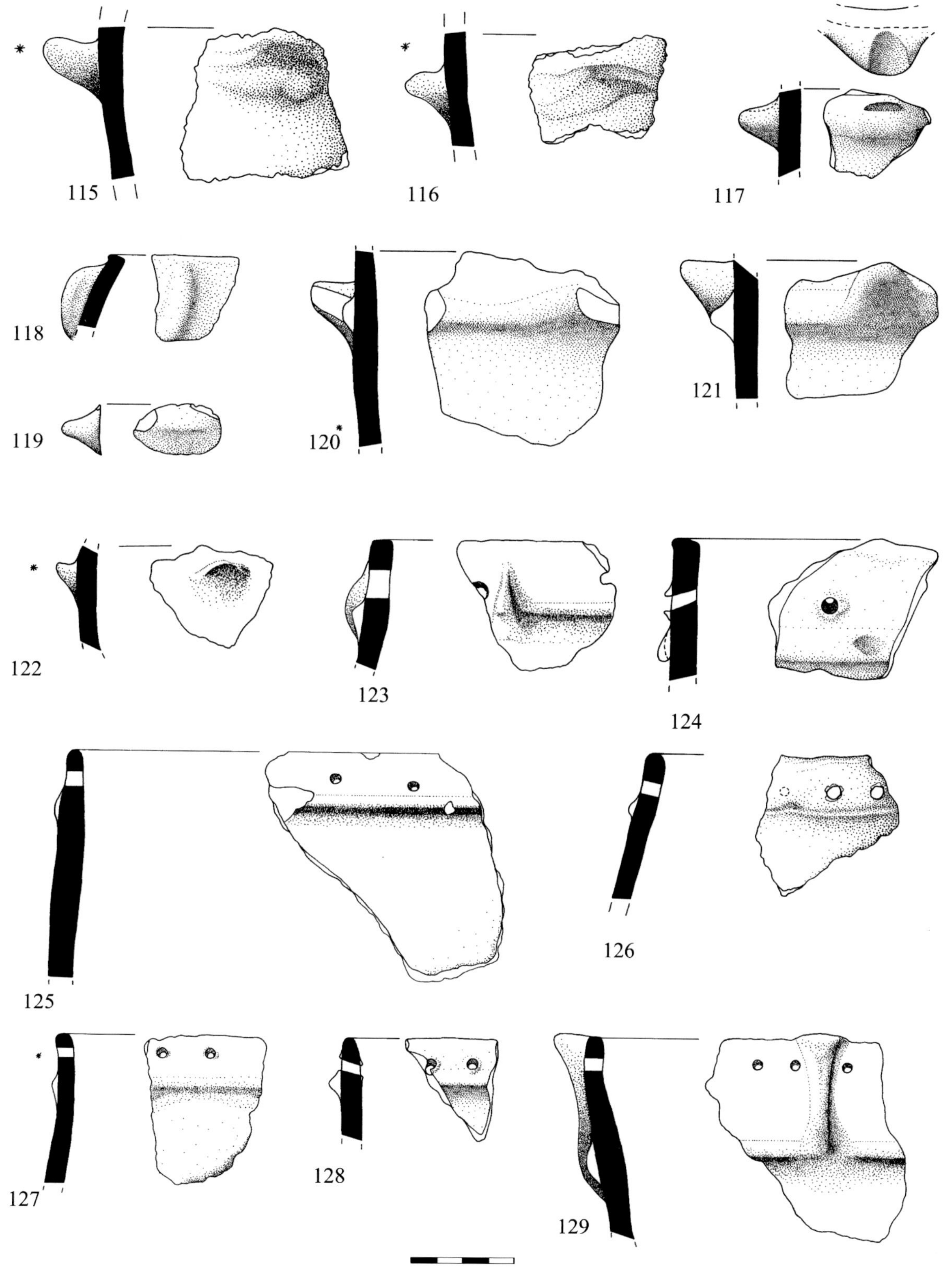
115
116
117
118
119
120*
121
122
123
124
125
126
127
128
129

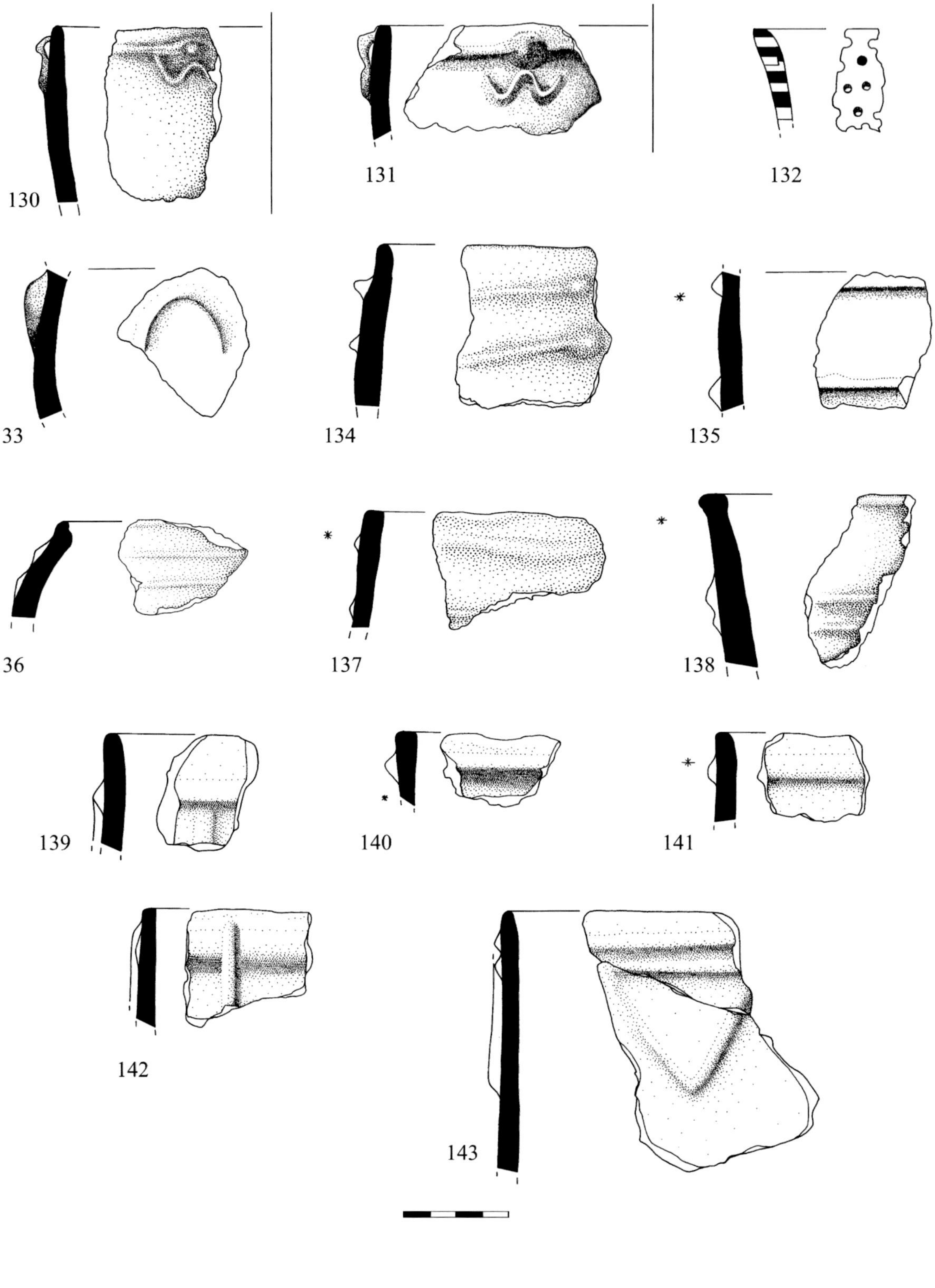
130
131
132
133
134
135
136
137
138
139
140
141
142
143

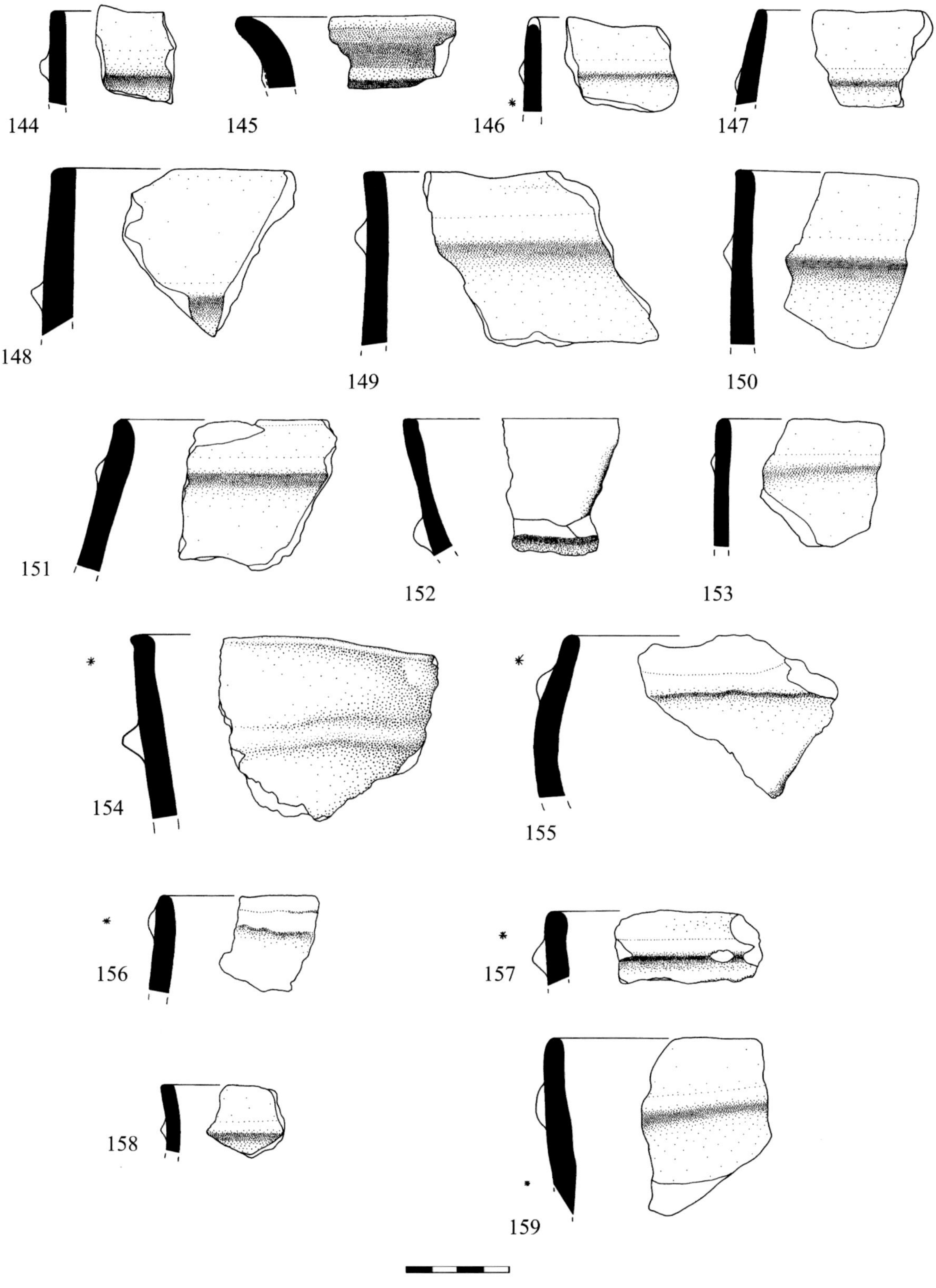
144
145
146
147
148
149
150
151
152
153
154
155
156
157
158
159

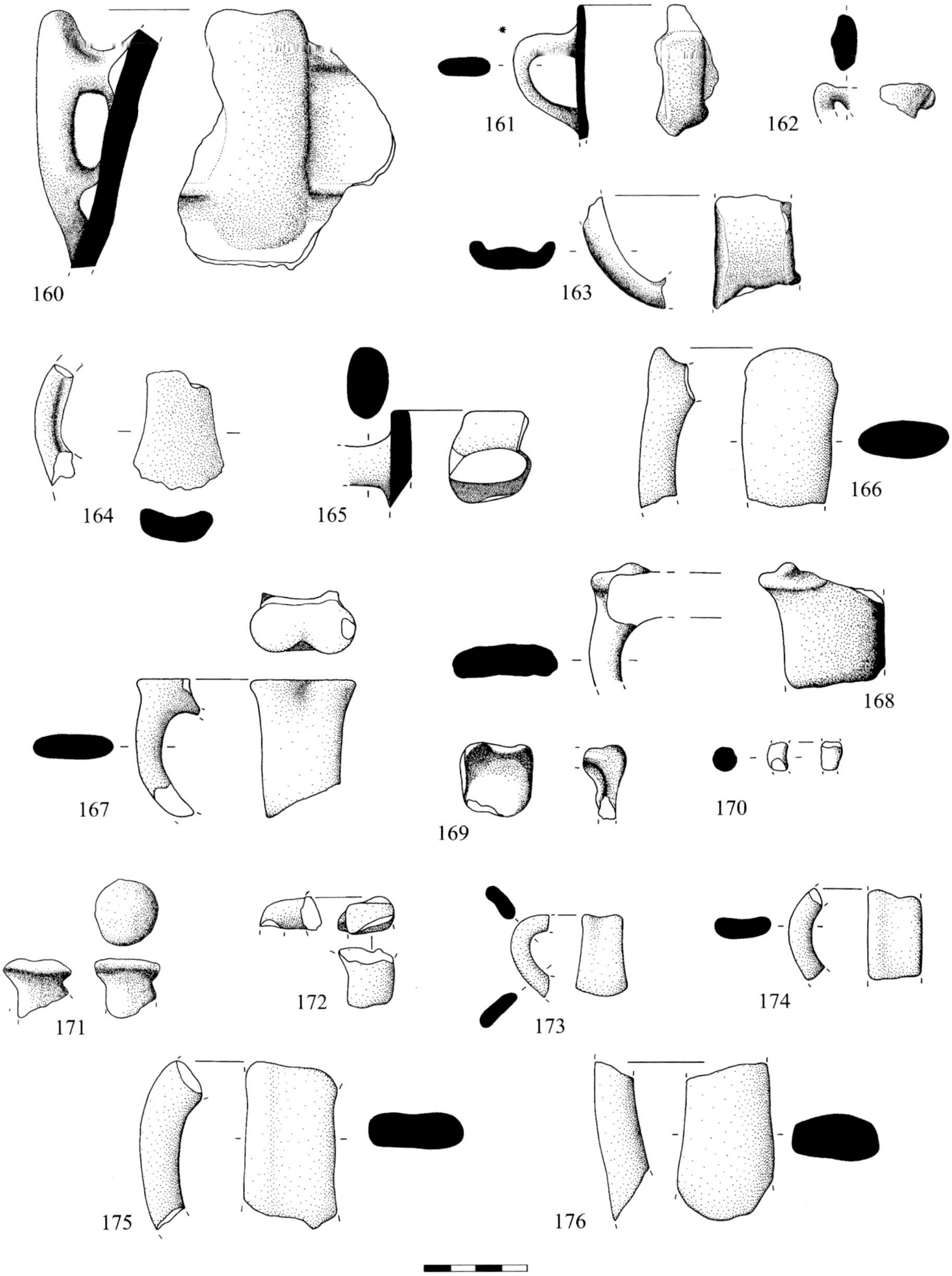
160
161
162
163
164
165
166
167
168
169
170
171
172
173
174
175
176

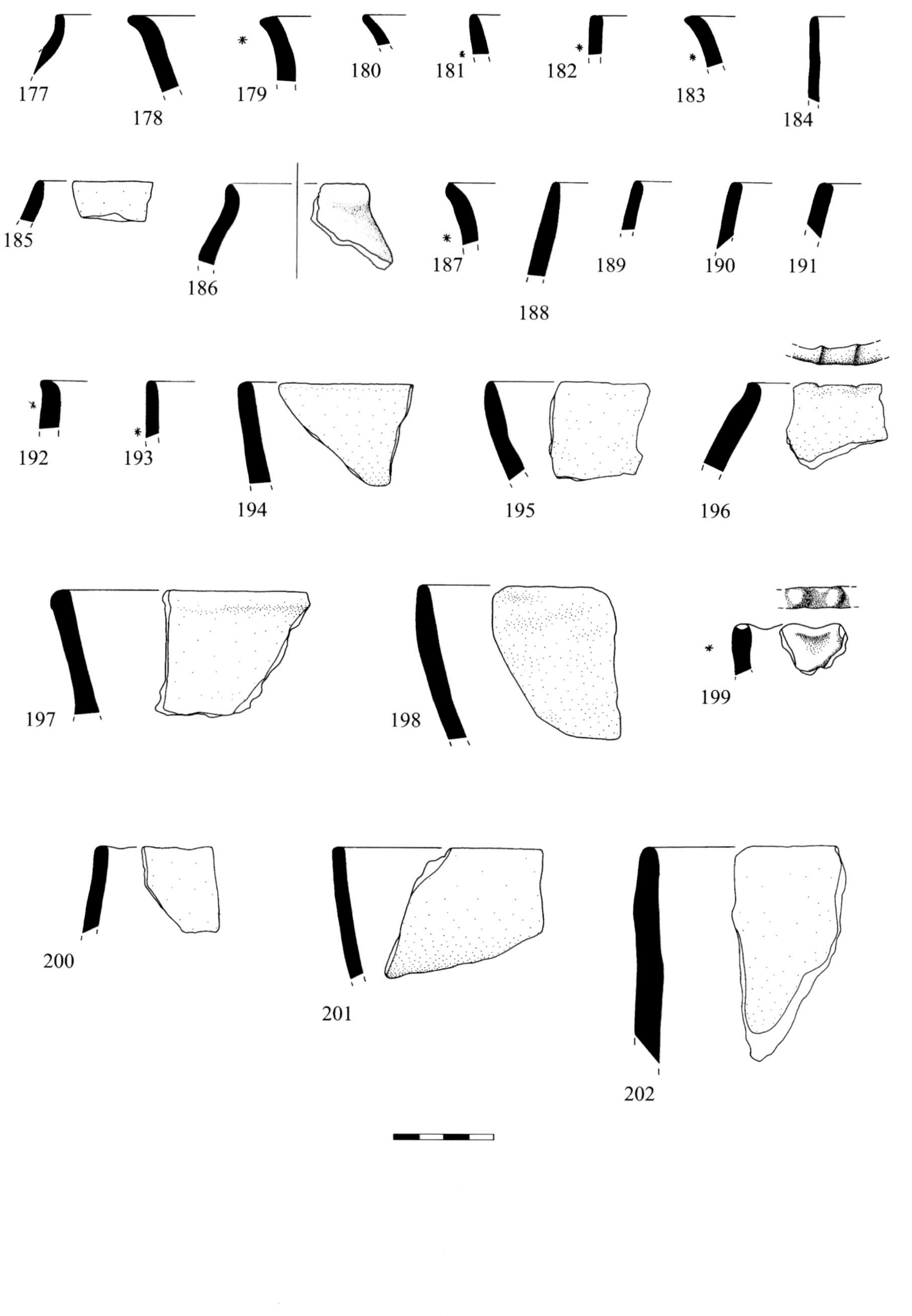
177
178
179
180
181
182
183
184
185
186
187
188
189
190
191
192
193
194
195
196
197
198
199
200
201
202

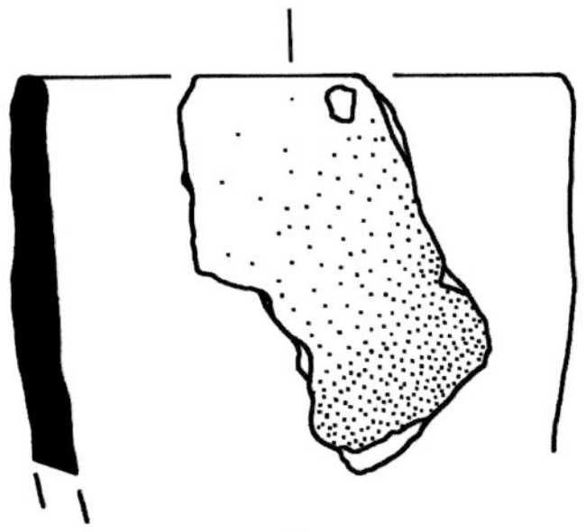

203

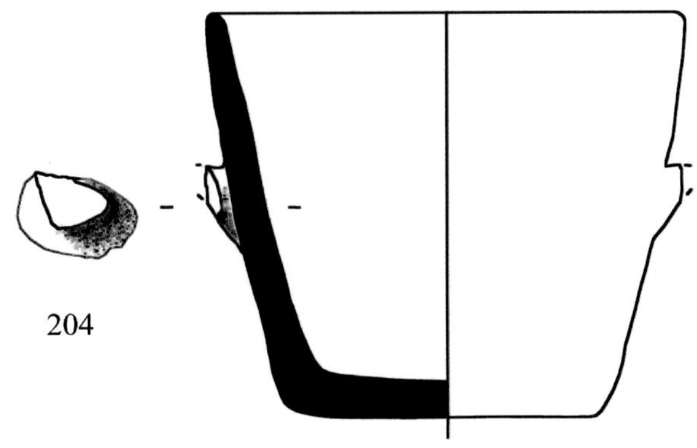

204

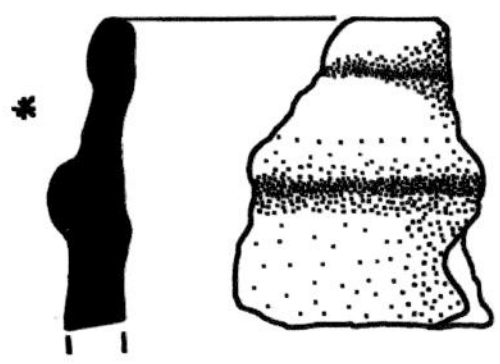

205

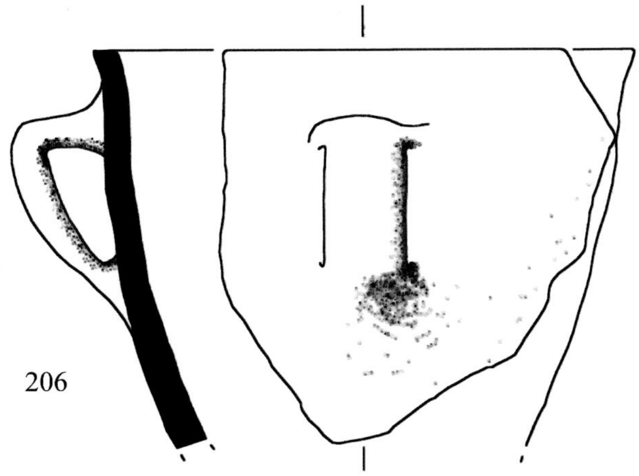

206

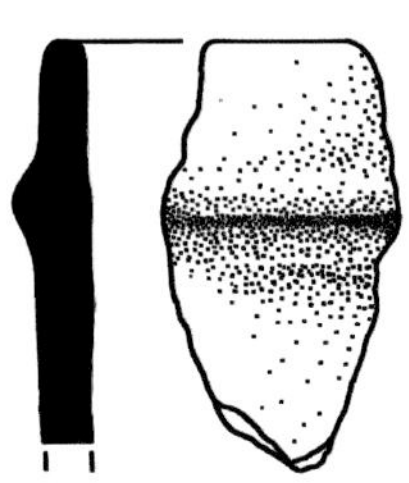

207

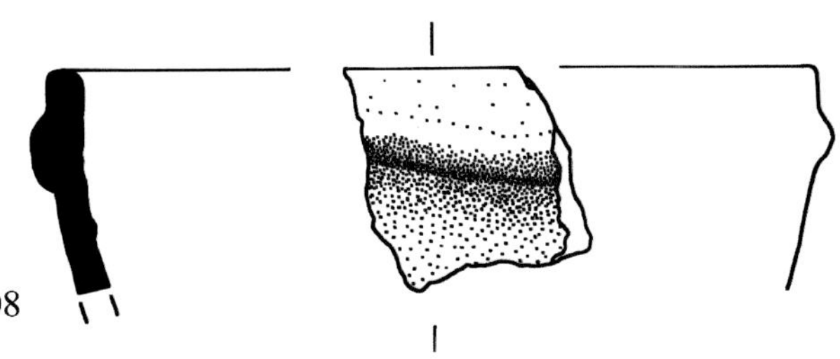

208

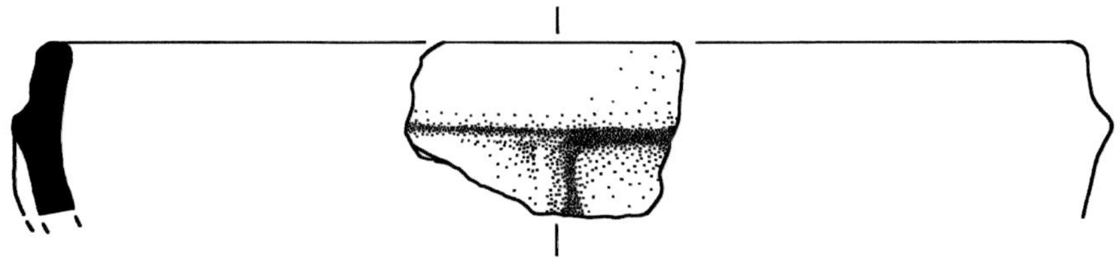

209

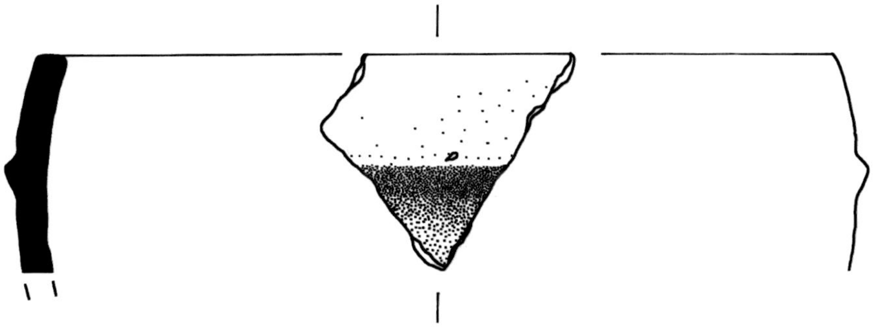

210

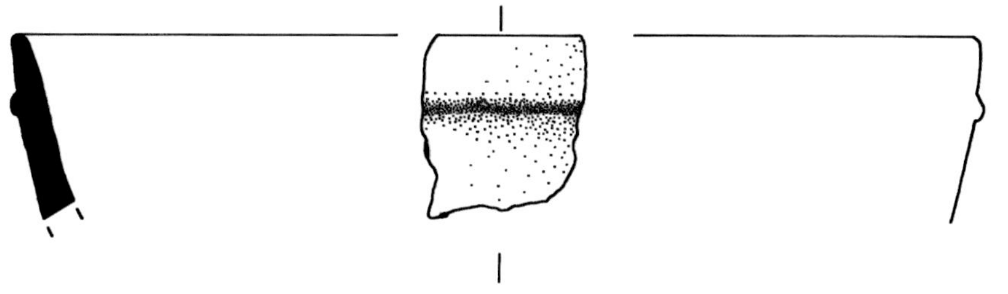

211

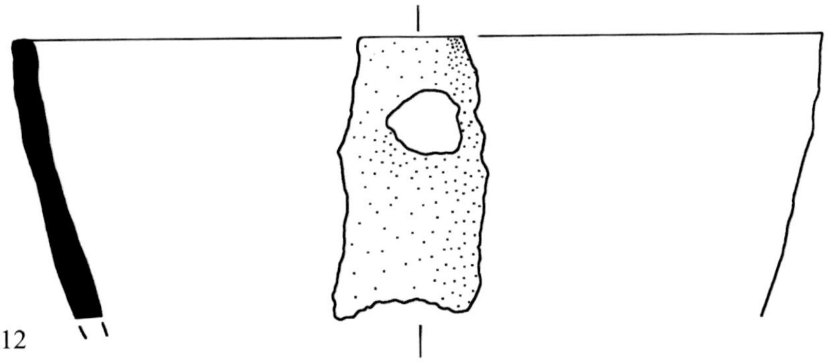

212

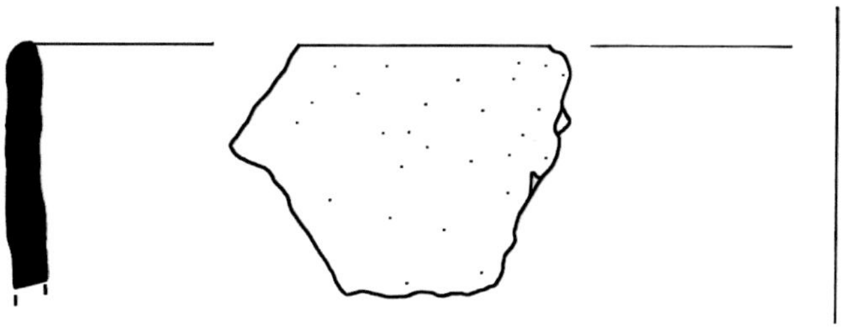

213

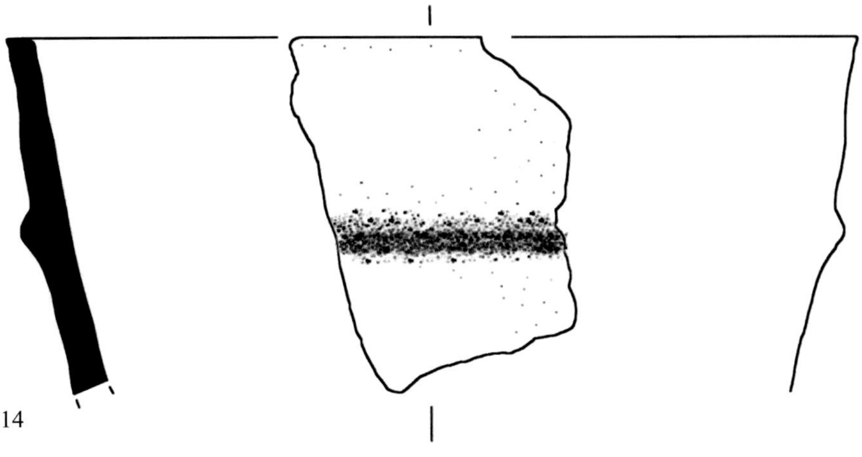

214

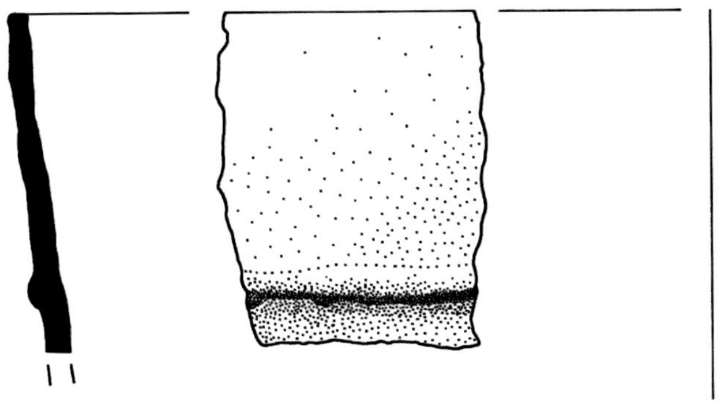

215

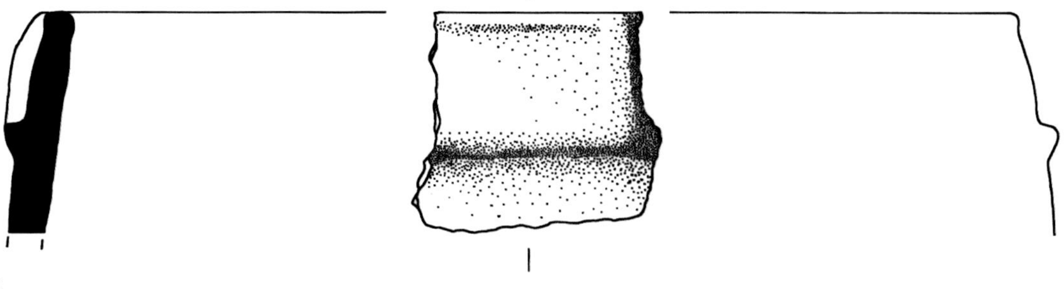

216

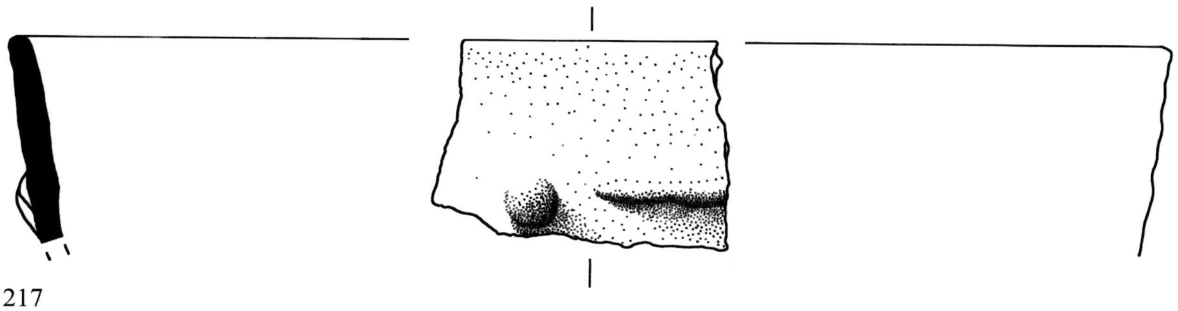

217

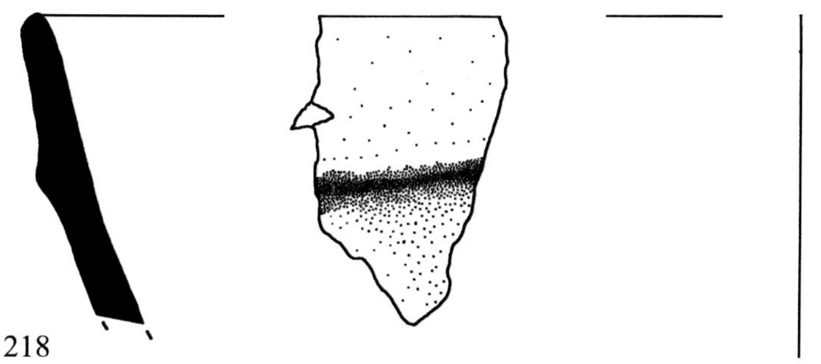

218

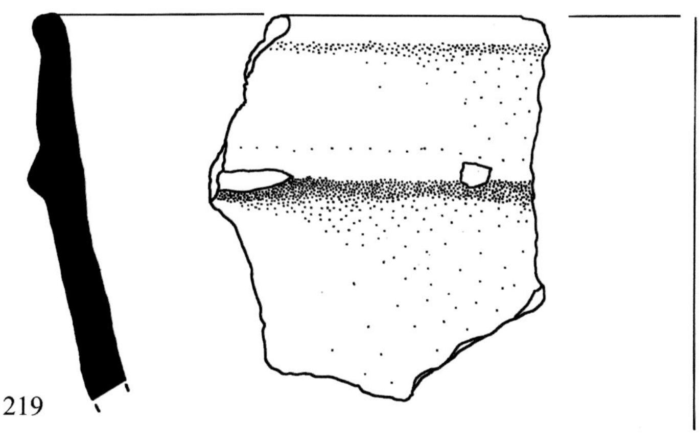

219

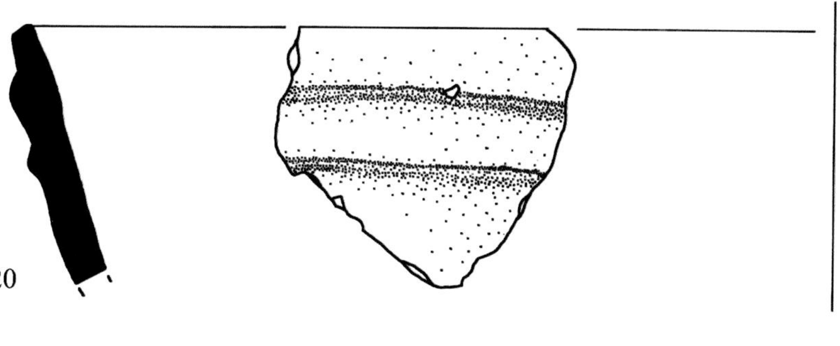

220

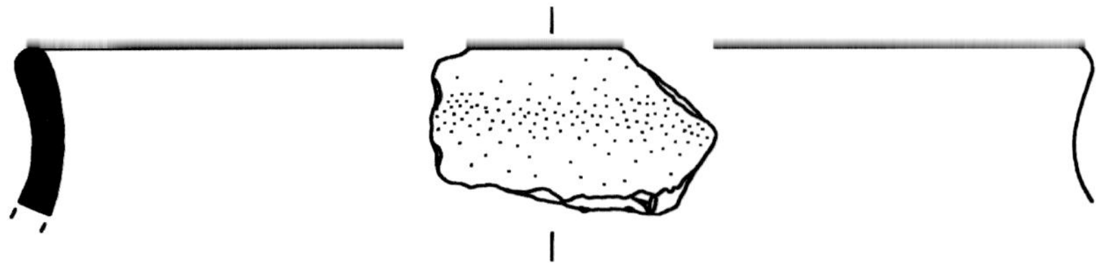

221

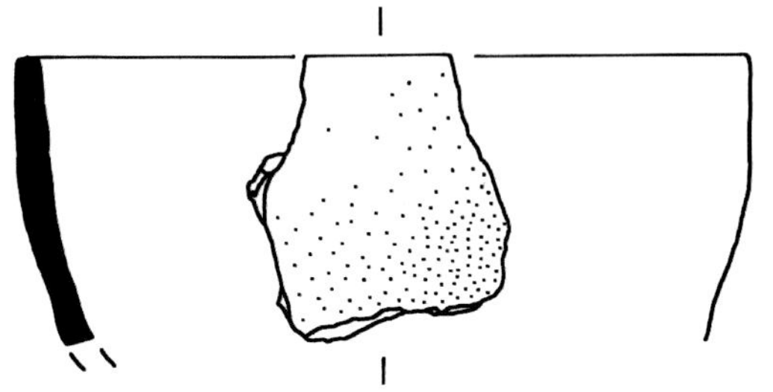

222

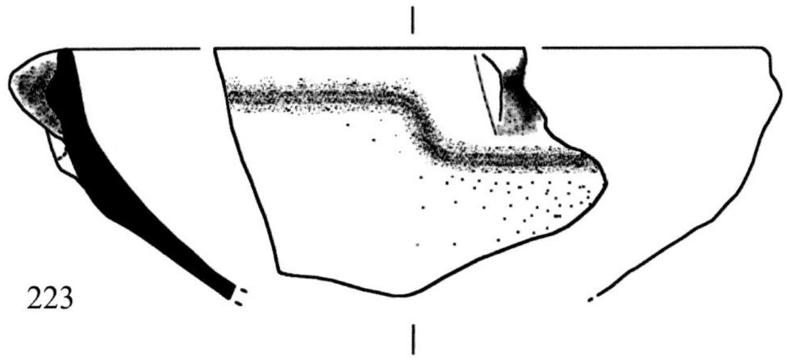

223

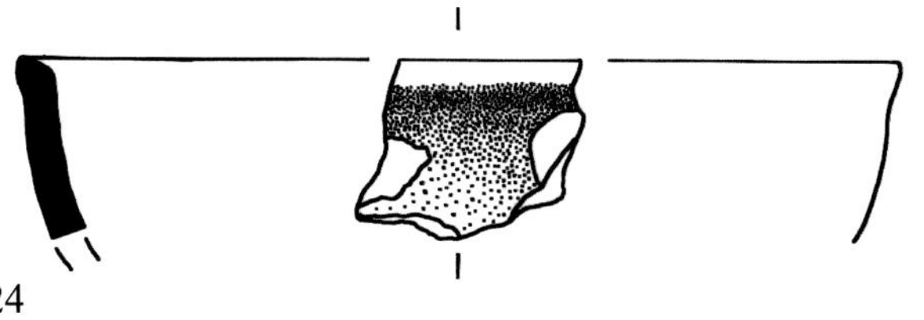

224

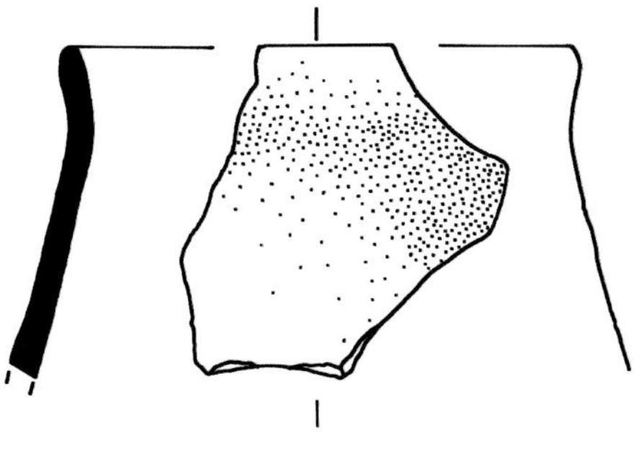

225

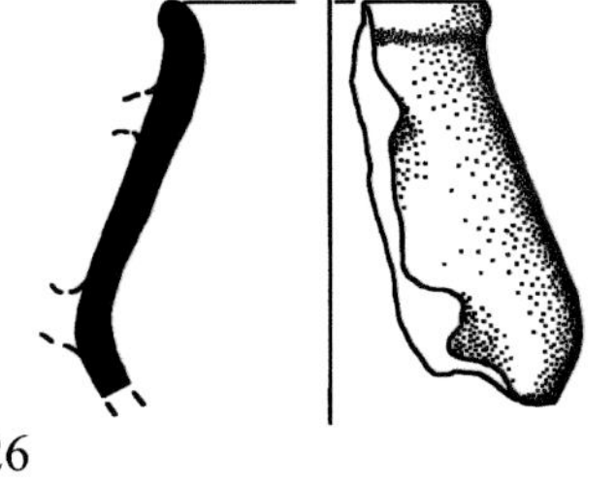

226

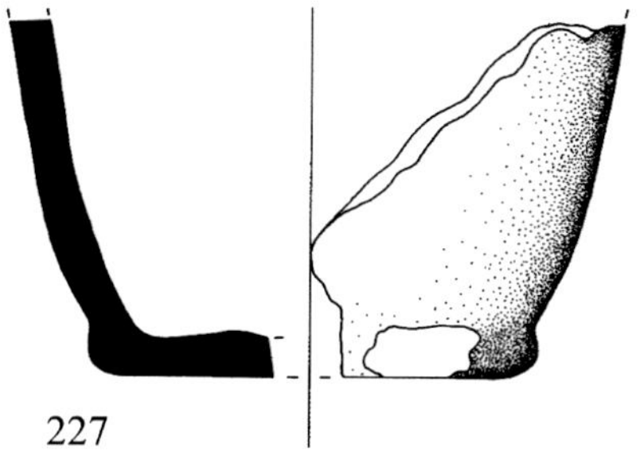
227

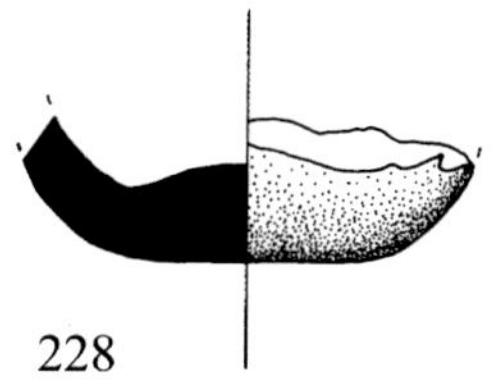
228

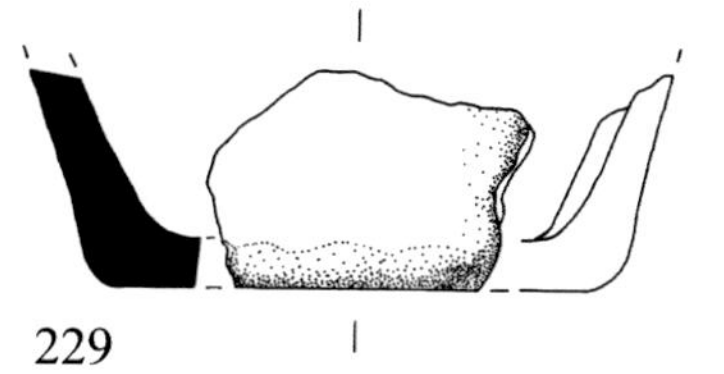
229

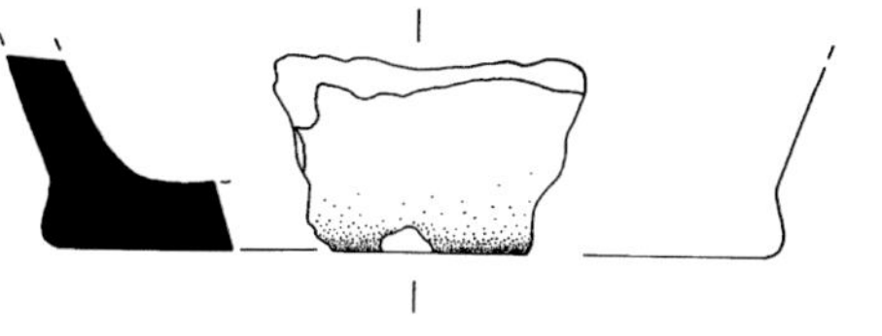
230

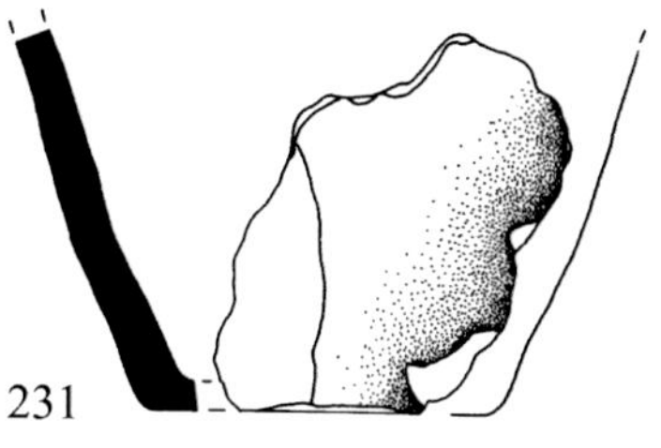
231

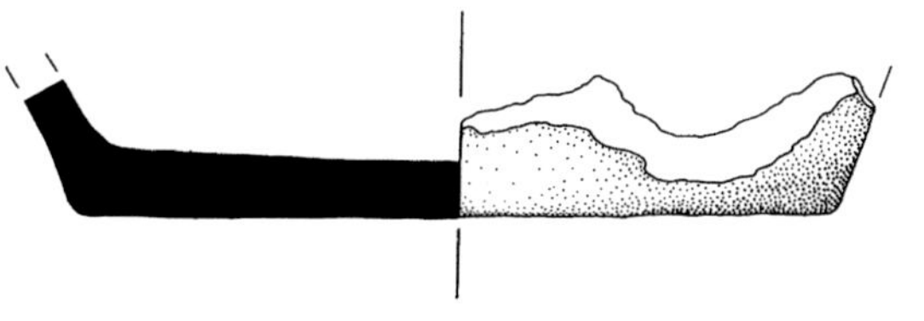
232

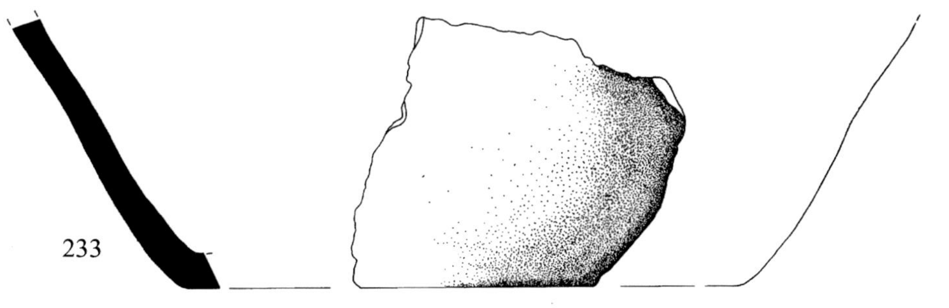
233

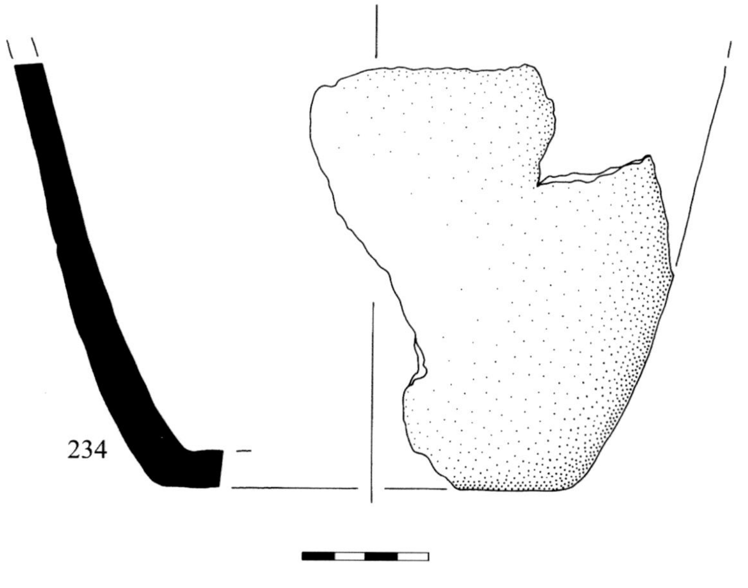
234

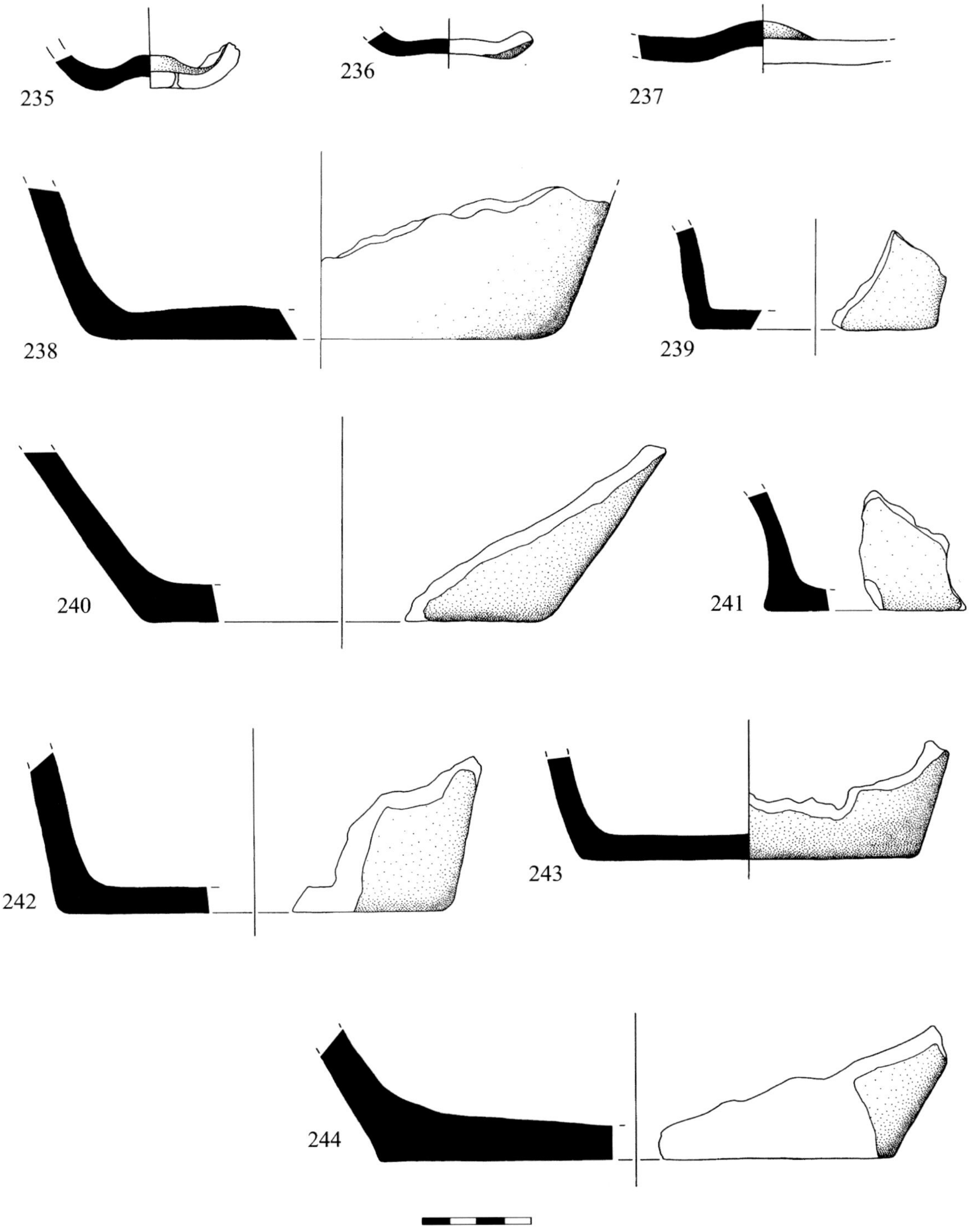
235
236
237
238
239
240
241
242
243
244

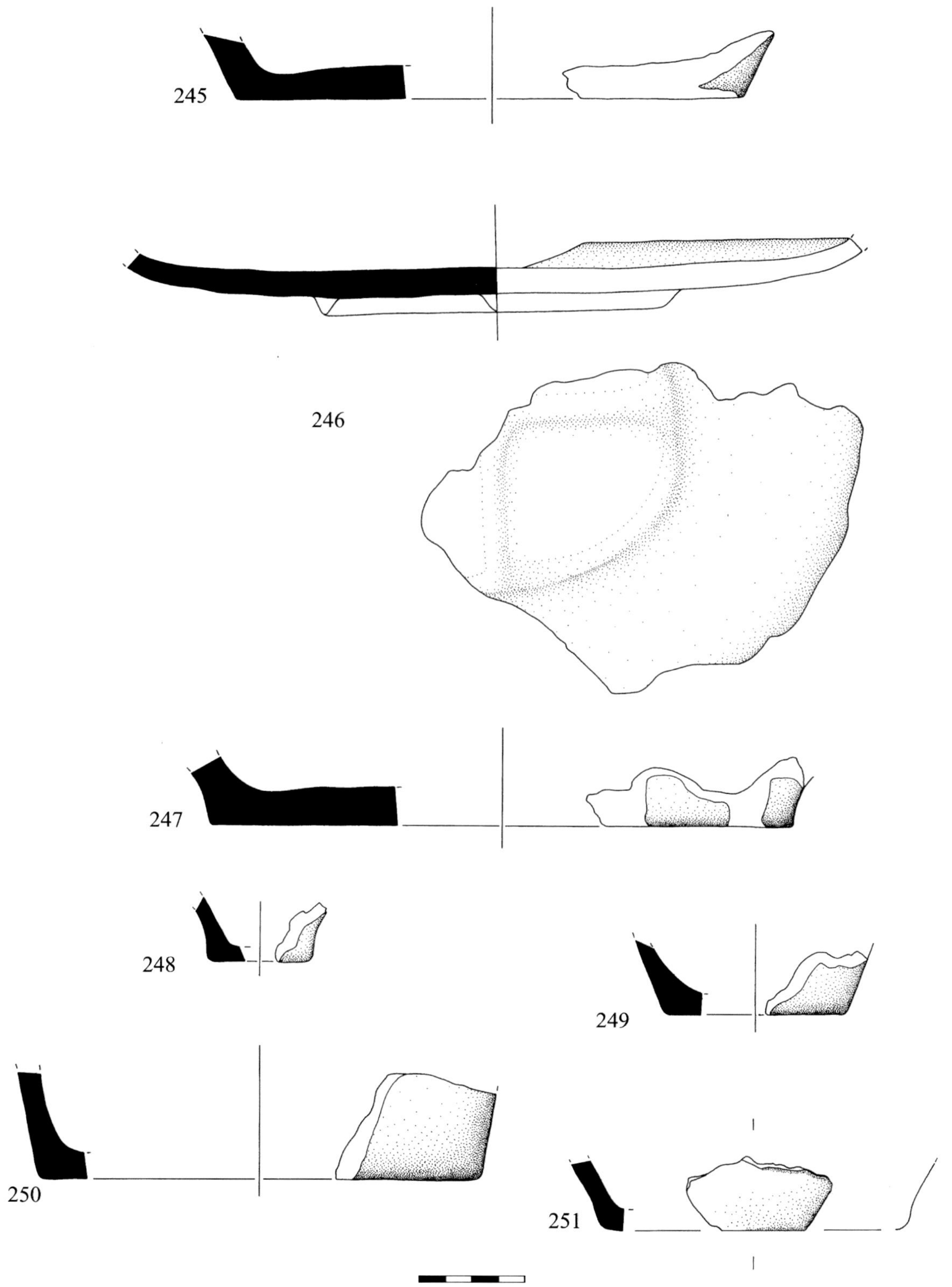
245
246
247
248
249
250
251

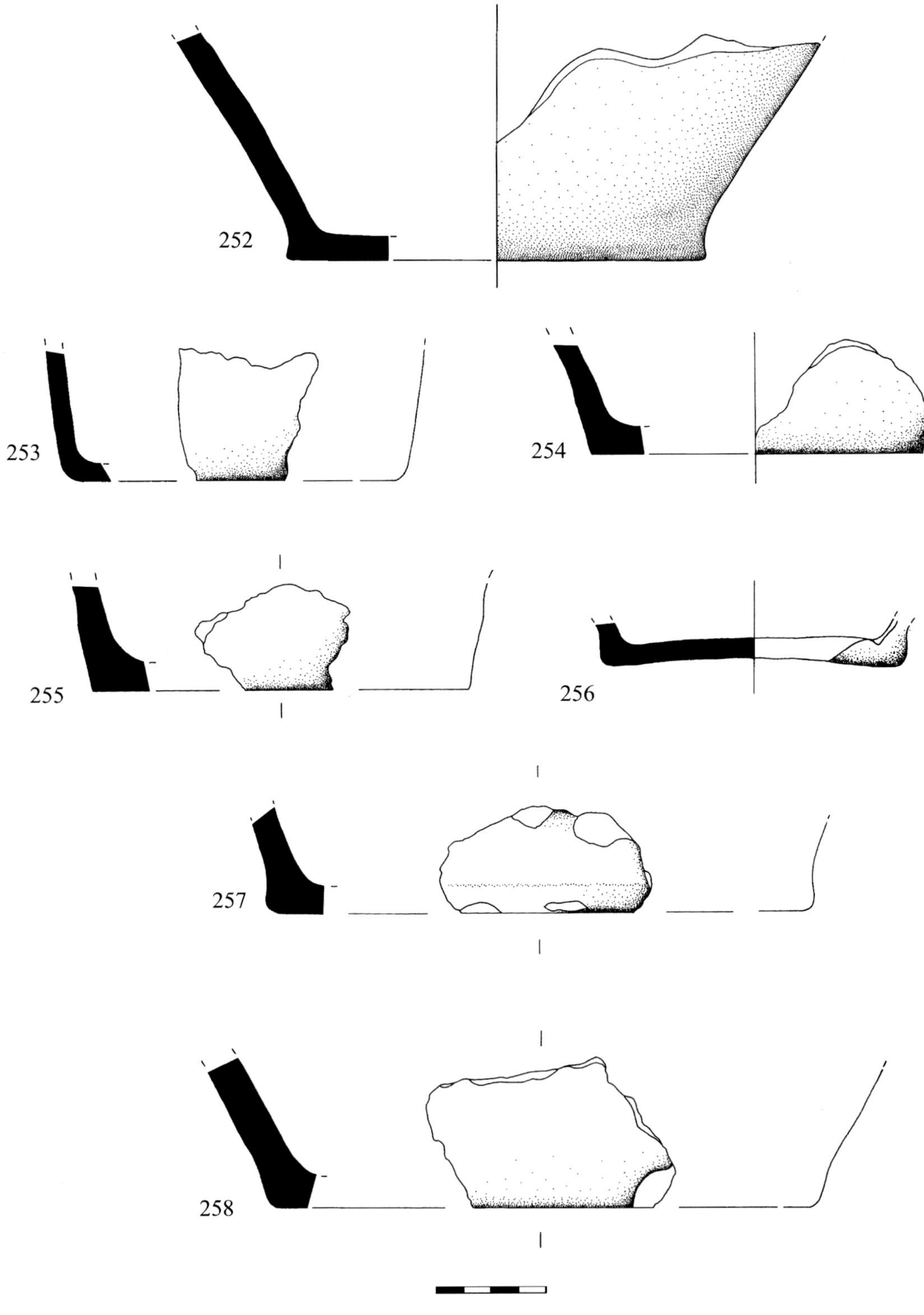
252
253
254
255
256
257
258

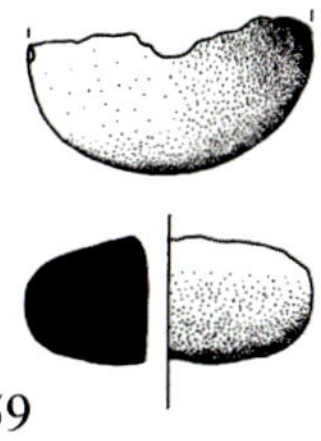
259

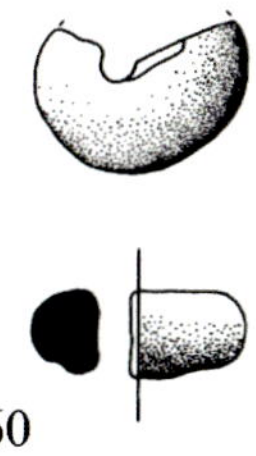
260

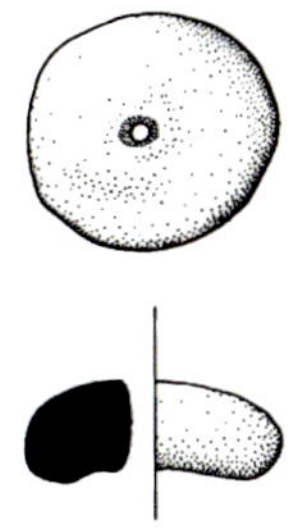
261

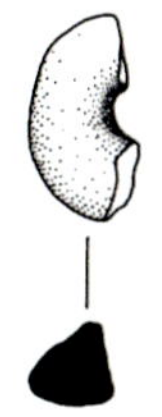
262

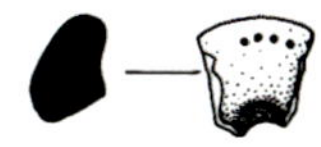
263

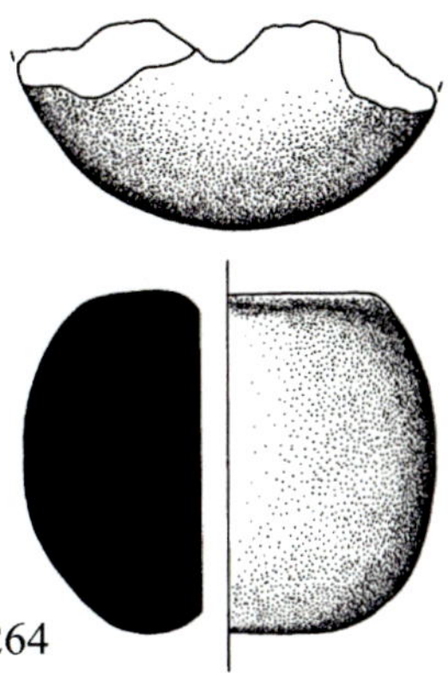
264

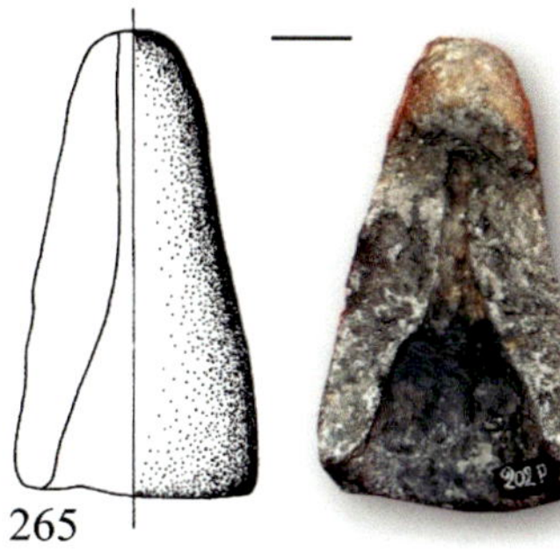
265

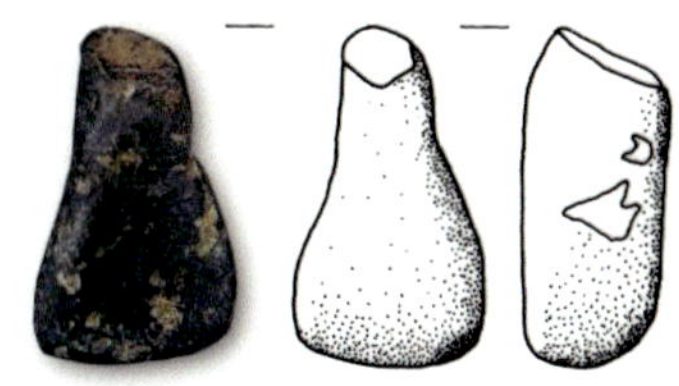
266

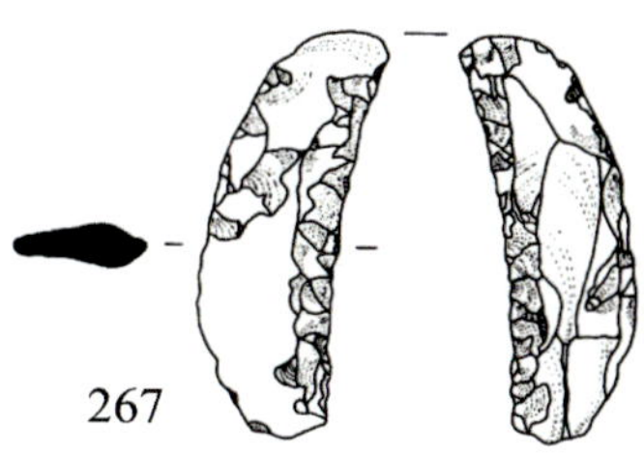
267

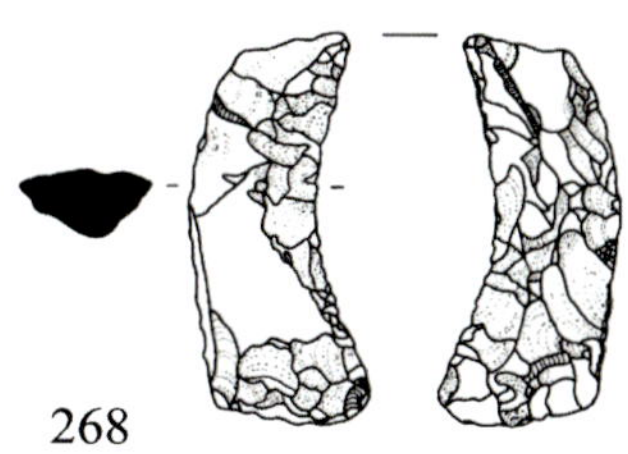
268

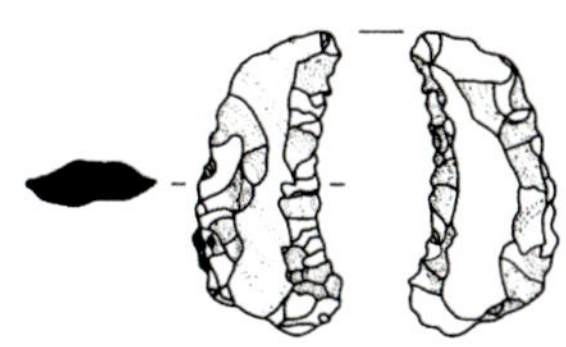
269

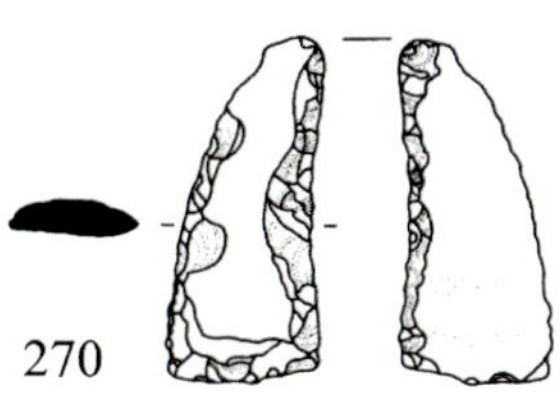
270

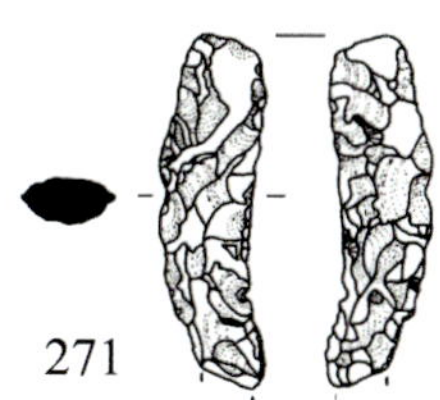
271

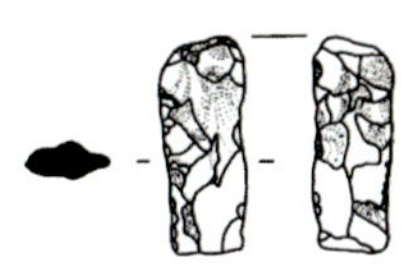
272

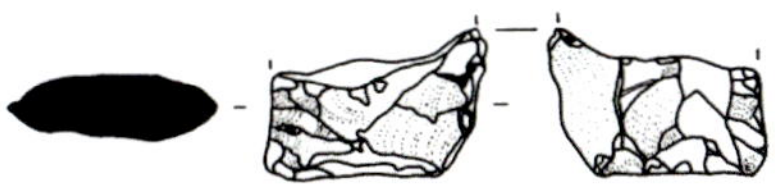
273

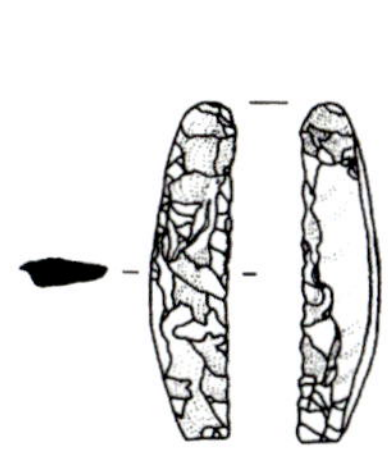
274

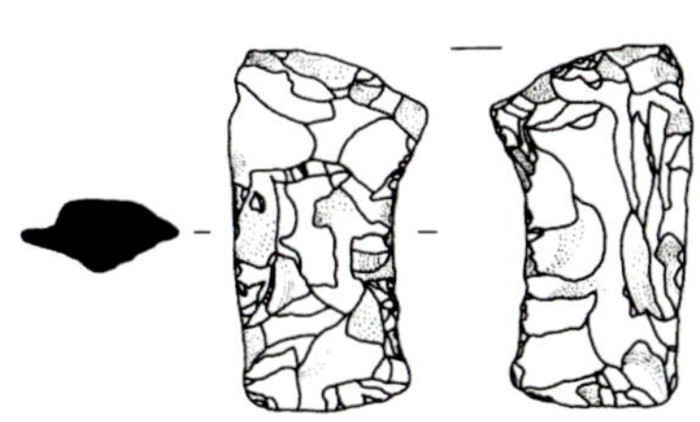
275

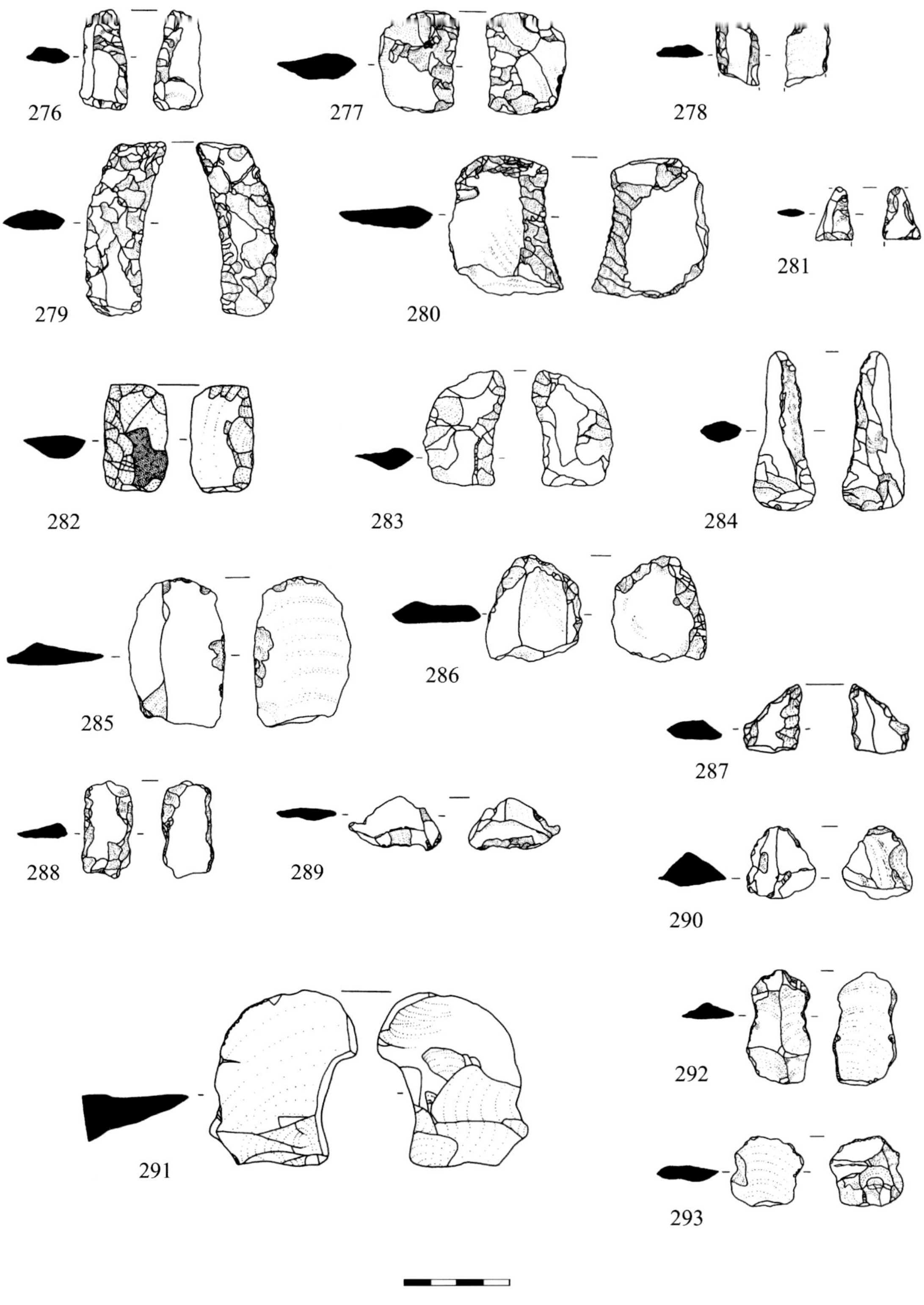
276
277
278
279
280
281
282
283
284
285
286
287
288
289
290
291
292
293

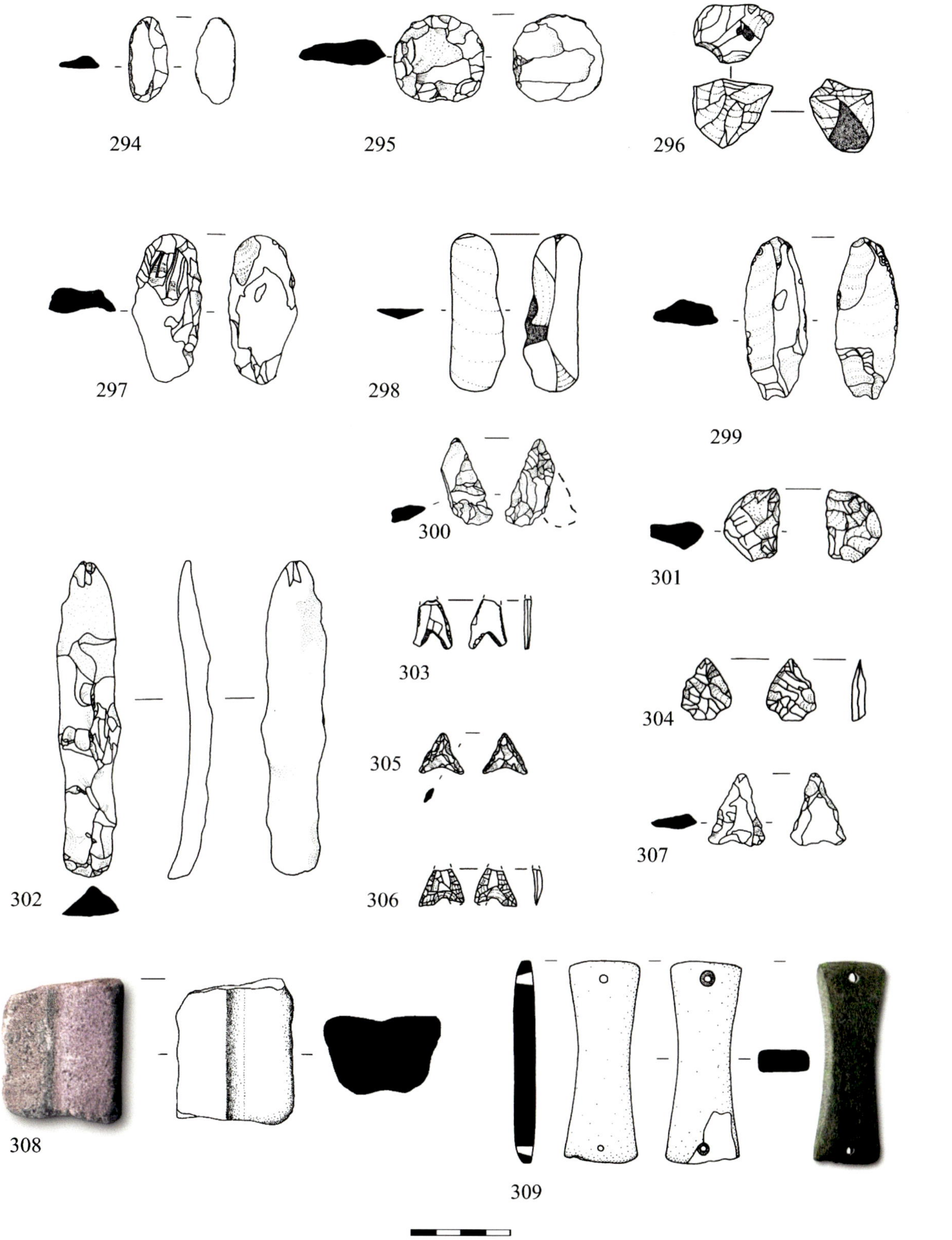
294
295
296
297
298
299
300
301
302
303
304
305
306
307
308
309

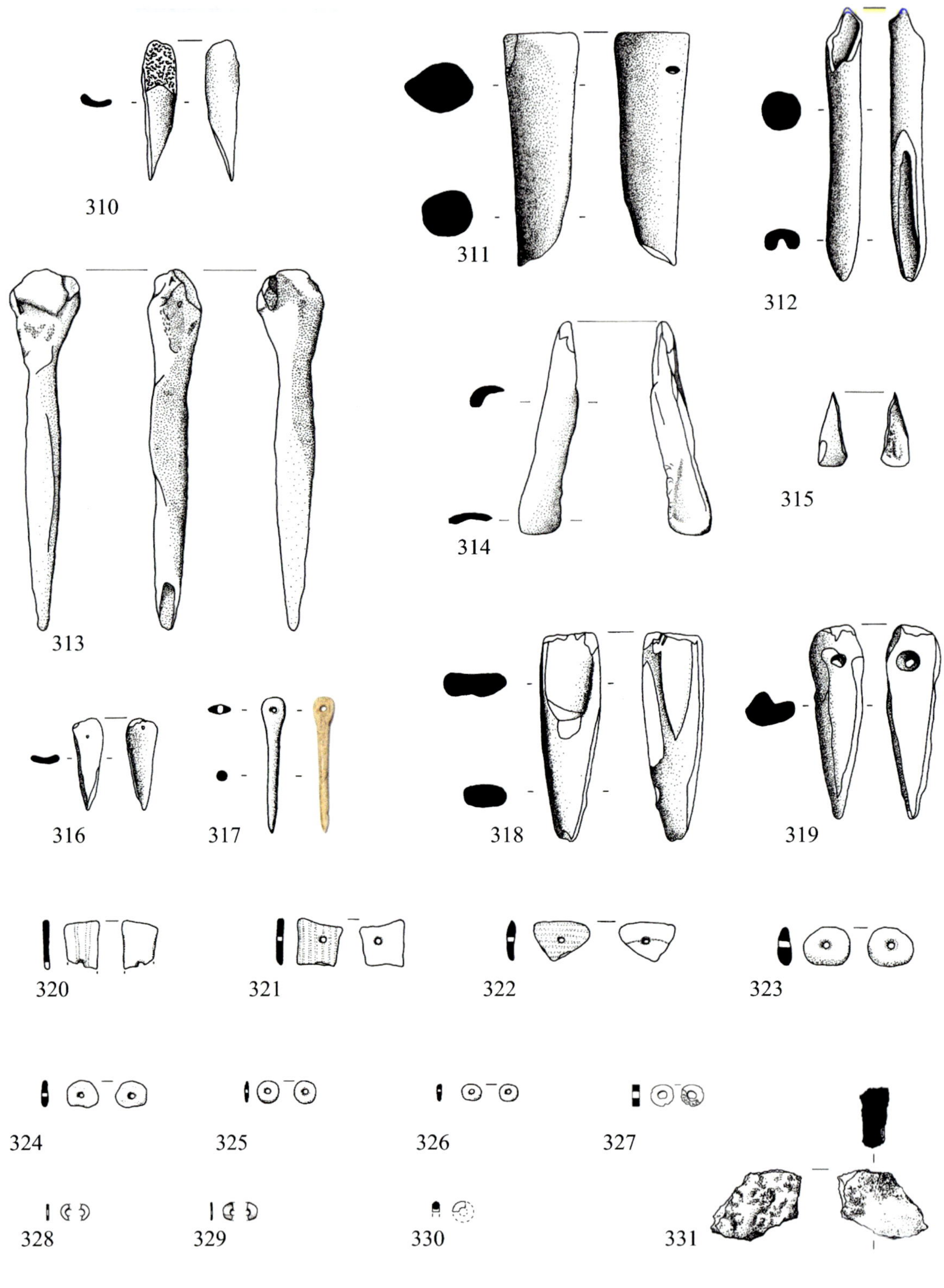
310
311
312
313
314
315
316
317
318
319
320
321
322
323
324
325
326
327
328
329
330
331

Appendix

Vessel classes

Given the high fragmentation index (very small potsherds) found in the site, it was not considered useful to refer to modern classification criteria which assign the vessel classes according to metric parameters, which are available in the case of archaeological sites with a low fragmentation index (that is in the presence of whole vases or at least potsherds large enough to enable the reconstruction of the vessels' profile).[1] We have thus adapted to the context in question the conventional system designed to classify the vessels of the site of Nössing (BZ),[2] dating back to the EBA. It is a useful reference system for defining vessel classes beginning with the morphology and diameter (where it can be measured with a certain approximation) of a single fragment. For this purpose some typological categories have been distinguished and selected which refer to the terminology proposed by Renato Peroni:[3]

Beakers, jars and dolia

Generally truncated cone or sub-cylindrical vessels with a diameter at the mouth always less than the depth of the vessel, at times with slightly convex walls which give an ovoid profile. They may have handles or lug handles and decorations. The rim, usually straight, may also have everted or inverted forms. Since there exists a formal *continuum* between beakers, jars and dolia, the distinction between them is here based conventionally on criteria of size. Two classes of intermediate size were also created, defined: '*Beakers to jars*' (or *beakers/jars*) and '*Jars to dolia*' (or *jars/dolia*). These differences in size must surely be connected to the similarly different functional categories. Those vessels of a greater size than the beakers probably did not have a drinking function but rather would have been used for food conservation or, in the case of '*Beakers to jars*', maybe even for cooking, whereas the function of larger vessels ('*Jars to dolia*' and dolia) must surely have been connected to storage and long term conservation of foodstuffs. The dolia in reality also include large vessels with convex and biconical closed forms and therefore large ollas have also been included in this category.

Bowls and large bowls

These are open vessels with a hemispherical or truncated cone form, sometimes handled or with lug handles, in which the diameter of the mouth is significantly greater than the height. In this case too there exists an evident formal *continuum* between the bowls and large bowls. The distinction between them is thus based conventionally just on the criterion of size. This implies, as was seen above for the class '*Beakers to jars*', an intermediate sized class between bowls and large bowls defined: '*Bowls to* large *bowls*' (or *bowls*/large *bowls*). Its function is certainly connected to food consumption or, in the case of the middle or large shapes, perhaps to cooking.

Mugs and ollas

Mugs and ollas are vessels in which the mouth is usually smaller than the depth and smaller also than the widest part of the body. In shape the profile is more or less *sinuous*, sometimes characterized by having carinations. The neck is sometimes distinct and the rims are generally everted. The mugs are always handled while the ollas often have plastic lug handles on the widest part of the body or handles placed on the upper part. Two intermediate categories have been distinguished: one

[1] Reference is made above all to pile-dwelling sites in the Gardesana area (De Marinis and Rapi 2017, p.31–38).
[2] Monograph in the process of being written by one of the authors of this volume (U.T.).
[3] Peroni 1994. The system developed by Tecchiati for Nössing has here been adapted to the site in question, also eliminating some vessel classes not present in the record of Castel Corno Caves.

defined *'Mugs to ollas'* (or *mugs/ollas*) and the others *'Ollas to dolia'* (or *ollas/dolia*). As already shown the greater sized ollas have been inserted in the category of dolia, in the variant which includes the more closed shapes.

The mugs can be considered vessels for the consumption of liquids while the ollas are suitable for the conservation of the same or, in the case of appropriate sized vessels, for the cooking of foodstuffs.

In order to distinguish the different typology, seven dimensional categories have been identified to which are connected the different vessel classes found at the site of the Castel Corno Caves:

Miniaturistic

Up to 7 cm in diameter at the mouth; up to 5 cm in diameter at the bottom
Vessel classes: Beakers, Bowls, Mugs

Small

From 7.5 cm to 15 cm in diameter at the mouth; from 5.5 cm to 10 cm at the bottom
Vessel classes: Beakers, Bowls, Mugs

Medium-small

From 15.5 cm to 20 cm in diameter at the mouth
Vessel classes: Bowls, 'Beakers to jars', 'Mugs to ollas'

Medium

From 20.5 cm to 30 cm in diameter at the mouth; from 10.5 cm to 15 cm at the bottom
Vessel classes: Jars, Bowls, Ollas

Medium-large

From 30.5 cm to 40 cm in diameter at the mouth
Vessel classes: 'Jars to truncated cone dolia', 'Bowls to large bowls', 'Ollas to biconical and convex dolia'

Large

From 40.5 cm to 50 cm in diameter at the mouth; from 15.5 cm to 20 cm at the bottom
Vessel classes: Dolia, Large bowls

Very large

Over 50 cm in diameter at the mouth; over 20 cm in diameter at the bottom
Vessel classes: Dolia, Large bowls

Quality classes

For the definition of the potsherd quality class reference was also made to the already mentioned conventional system devised for the site of Nössing (BZ).

The combined analysis of the fabric quality and surface treatment led to the identification, for the site of the Castel Corno Caves, of five distinct 'quality classes', which reassume in one single valutational criterion the sequence of actions involved in the manufacture of the vessel: selection of the raw material, preparation of the fabric, shaping, finishing and, lastly, firing.

Coarse

Fabrics with heterogeneous inclusions, with harsh edges of a large size (even the same as, or of greater thickness than, the walls). Irregular thickness. Surfaces slightly smoothed. Firing poorly controlled with friable fabrics and pulverulent surfaces or with varying colour.

Semi-coarse

Fabrics with more homogeneous inclusions and/or of smaller size. Thinner walls. Surfaces treated either freehand or with a stick, brush or cloth.

Semi-fine

Fabrics with lithologically homogeneous and isometric inclusions. Surfaces accurately smoothed with the use of a stick. Shine and waterproofing effects. Colour tending to be uniform.

Fine

Fabrics without inclusions or of fine grind, homogeneous and isometric. Thin walls. Shiny and waterproof surfaces smoothed with a sitck or a burnisher when the clay had dried to leather hardness. Firing well controlled, uniform colour.

Dark-burnished

Variety of fine pottery with brilliant surfaces obtained with a stick when the clay had reached leather hardness.

Bibliography

Aimar, A. and S. Gregoriani 2000. I manufatti in materia dura animale del sito di Lucone. Analisi Micromorfologica di superficie. *Annali del Museo Civico Archeologico della Valle Sabbia* 18: 1–127.

Andreazza, A. 1989. *Sacco e gli zattieri*. Rovereto, TN: Comune di Sacco.

Angelini, B., B. Bagolini and T. Pasquali 1980. Acquaviva di Besenello, *Preistoria Alpina* 16: 67–69.

Angelucci, D. 2016. La valle dell'Adige: genesi e modificazione di una grande valle alpina come interazione tra dinamiche naturali e fattori antropici, in V. Rovigo (ed.) *Il fiume, le terre, l'immaginario. L'Adige come fenomeno storiografico complesso, Memorie dell'Accademia Roveretana degli Agiati 4, Atti del Convegno, Rovereto, 21-22 febbraio 2013*: 9–43. Rovereto, TN: Edizioni Osiride.

Anzelini, R., F. Arioldi, C. Armani, V. Chiocchietti, L. Dal Rì, C. Gius, R. Lazzerini, A. Pisetta, M. Plotegher, G. Polidori, C. Ravagni, A. Rigotti, S. Rossi, G. Simonini, J.P. Stedile and G. Zanolli, 1972. Il ‚Colombo' di Mori. *Atti della Accademia Roveretana degli Agiati*. Atti A-B 1969 serie VI, volume IX, CCXIX anno accademico: 17–76.

Aspes, A. 1972. Materiali inediti dell'antica età del Bronzo da Cattaragna (Brescia) conservati al museo civico di storia naturale di Verona. *'Natura Bresciana', Annali del Museo Civico di Storia Naturale* 9: 13–34.

Aswani, O.K., A. Kumar 2018. Megalithic Religion: An Archaeological Review of Beliefs and Practices. *Heritage: Journal of Multidisciplinary Studies in Archaeology* 6: 647-668.

Ausserer, K. 1911. *Die Herren von Schloss und Gericht Castelcorno im Lagertale (Vallagarina)*. Wien.

Avanzini, M. 1985. Relazione inedita su Castel Corno, Museo Civico di Rovereto.

Avanzini, M. 1988. Castel Corno. Analisi della fauna. *Annali del Museo Civico di Rovereto* 4: 119–122.

Avanzini, R. 1990. Note su Castel Corno (Vallagarina, Trentino Occidentale). *Annali dei Musei Civici di Rovereto* 5 (1989): 24–40.

Avanzini, M., B. Bagolini, M. Capitanio, G. Chelidonio, T. Pasquali, G. Prosser and B. Robol 1985. Bersaglio di Mori. Dati e ricerche. *Annali del Museo Civico di Rovereto* 1: 23–66.

Avanzini, M., Avanzini, R., Carli, R., Pasquali, T., Pisetta, C., Scartezzini, A. 1987. Note su Castel Corno (Vallagarina – Trentino Occidentale). *Annali del Museo Civico di Rovereto* 3: 3–22.

Avanzini, M., R. Avanzini, R. Carli and A. Scartezzini 1988. Note su Castel Corno (Vallagarina – Trentino Occidentale). II parte. *Annali dei Musei Civici di Rovereto* 4: 55–78.

Bagolini, B. 1980. Il Neolitico nel territorio veronese, in L. Fasani (ed.), *Il territorio veronese dalle origini all'età romana (Contributi ed aggiornamenti di ricerca preistorica)*: 43–64. Verona: Fiorini.

Bagolini, B., G. Borgogno, R. Carli, F. Corazzola and T. Pasquali 1986. Nogarole di Mezzolombardo (Trentino occidentale). *Preistoria Alpina* 21(1985), Notiziario regionale 1982–1986: 277–81.

Bagolini, B., R. Carli, A. Ferrari, A. Messori, T. Pasquali and A. Pessina 1991. Il sepolcreto eneolitico del Dos de la Forca (Mezzocorona - Trento). *Preistoria Alpina* 25: 121–164.

Bagolini, B., L. Dal Ri and U. Tecchiati 1988. L'area megalitica di Velturno in Alto Adige, in D. Manfredi, R. Piccioli and E. Vecchi (eds) *La statuaria antropomorfa in Europa dal Neolitico alla Romanizzazione*: 331–348. La Spezia-Pontremoli: Istituto internazionale di Studi Liguri sezione Lunense.

Bagolini, B., M. Lanzinger, and T. Pasquali 1980. Paludei - Volano (Trento), *Preistoria Alpina* 14, Notiziario Regionale 1978–1979: 227–228.

Baioni, M. 2004. Relazione preliminare sulle ricerche archeologiche alla Corna Nibbia di Bione (BS). *Annali del Museo Civico Archeologico della Valle Sabbia* 19 (2001/2002): 59–78.

Baioni, M. 2017. *Bione, Corna Nibbia : 5000 anni fa in Valle Sabbia : Pubblicazione in occasione della mostra 17 settembre 2016 - 7 maggio 2017 Bione, Pieve Municipio Sala consiliare* (Archeologia e territorio 1). Salò: Edizioni della Sabbia.

Baioni, M., M.A Borrello, A. Feldtkeller and H. Schlichtherle 2003. I pesi reniformi e le fusaiole piatte decorate della Cultura della Lagozza. Cronologia, distribuzione geografica e sperimentazioni, in M. Bazzanella, A. Mayr, L. Moser and A. Rast-Eicher (eds) *Textiles. Intrecci e tessuti dalla preistoria europea*: 99–109. Trento: Provincia Autonoma di Trento, Servizio Beni Culturali, Ufficio Beni Archeologici.

Bandera, S. and U. Tecchiati 2020. I corredi funerari con elementi d'ornamento in conchiglia della necropoli biritualistica del Bronzo medio e recente di Scalvinetto (Legnago, VR) e alcune note su conchiglie forate e oggetti d'ornamento in conchiglia nell'età del Bronzo dell'Italia settentrionale, in L. Salzani (ed.) *La necropoli dell'età del Bronzo di Scalvinetto di Legnago (Verona)*: 425–430. Legnago: Fondazione Matilde Avrese.

Barbieri, S., A. Avanzini and S. Grimaldi 2014. La selce nel bacino atesino meridionale: caratterizzazione e diffusione. *Preistoria Alpina* 47 (2013): 27–37.

Barfield, L.H. 1974. Scavi nella stazione di Monte Covolo: seconda nota preliminare sulle ricerche condotte nel 1973. *Annali del Museo* 11: 5–15. Brescia: Museo Civico Gruppo Grotte Gavardo.

Barfield, L.H. 1976a. Bronze Age pottery, in L.H. Barfield and B. Bagolini, *The excavations on the Rocca di Rivoli-Verona. 1963-1968* (Memorie del Museo Civico di Storia Naturale di Verona, II serie, Sezione Scienze dell'Uomo 1): 54–64. Verona: Museo civico di storia naturale di Verona.

Barfield, L.H. 1976b. Worked bone, antler and teeth, in L.H. Barfield and B. Bagolini (eds) *The excavations on the Rocca di Rivoli-Verona. 1963-1968* (Memorie del Museo Civico di Storia Naturale di Verona, II serie, Sezione Scienze dell'Uomo 1): 125–131. Verona: Museo civico di storia naturale di Verona.

Barfield, L.H., S. Buteux and G. Bocchio 1995. *Monte Covolo. Una montagna e il suo passato. Ricerche archeologiche 1972-1994.* Birmingham: Birmingham University Field Archaeology Unit.

Barfield, L.H. 2007. Chapter 17. Beads and other necklace elements, in L.H. Barfield (ed.) *Excavations in the Riparo Valtenesi. Manerba 1976-1994* (Origines): 296–331. Firenze: Istituto Italiano di Preistoria e Protostoria.

Barich, B. 1971. Il complesso industriale della stazione di Polada alla luce dei più recenti dati. *Bullettino di Paletnologia Italiana*, Nuova Serie 22, vol. 80: 77–182.

Bassetti, M. and N. Degasperi 2007. Lavagnone (BS) – settore B. Osservazioni micromorfologiche su alcuni campioni di concotto, in R.C. de Marinis (ed.) *Studi sull'abitato dell'età del Bronzo del Lavagnone, Desenzano del Garda* (Notizie Archeologiche Bergomensi 10): 277–283. Bergamo: Civico museo archeologico di Bergamo.

Bassetti, M., N. Degasperi and F. Nicolis 2005. Volano prima della storia, in R. Adami, M. Bonazza and G.M. Varanini (eds) *Volano. Storia di una Comunità* (Terre): 277–283. Trento: Comune di Volano.

Battaglia, R. 1943. *La palafitta del lago di Ledro nel Trentino* (Memorie del Museo di Storia Naturale della Venezia Tridentina, anno XI, vol. VII). Trento: Museo di Storia Naturale.

Battisti, M. 1999. Il 'castelliere' dei Pizzini di Castellano. *Il Comunale* 29, anno XV, giugno 1999: 99–102.

Battisti, M. 2001. Il 'castelliere' dei Pizzini (Villalagarina, loc. Castellano) e l'antica età del bronzo in Vallagarina (Trentino meridionale). Unpublished dissertation, University of Bologna, Faculty of Conservazione dei Beni Culturali.

Battisti, M. 2004. Un piccolo villaggio di 4000 anni fa costruito sulla nuda roccia. Novità dagli scavi ai Pizzini di Castellano (Bronzo antico). *Il Comunale* 39–40, anno XX, giugno 2004: 17–28.

Battisti, M. 2010. L'antica età del Bronzo in Vallagarina, in L. Dal Ri, P. Gamper and H. Steiner (eds) *Abitati dell'età del Bronzo e del Ferro* (Beni Culturali in Alto Adige VI): 1–36. Trento: Temi.

Battisti, M. 2015. Le tavolette enigmatiche della Vallagarina (Rovereto, TN) nel contesto europeo. *Annali del Museo Civico di Rovereto* 30 (2014): 3–26.

Battisti, M. 2016. Manufatti in selce, in B. Maurina (ed.) *Richerche archeologiche a Sant'Andrea di Loppio (Trento, Italia). Il Castrum Tardoantico-Altomedievale*: 703–712. Oxford: Archeopress.

Battisti, M. and S. Cavalieri (in press). Patorizia tra Neolitico e romanità sul Monte Pasubio, in M. Avanzini and I. Salvador (eds), *Memorie di terre alte: archeologia di un paesaggio pastorale tra Pasubio e Piccole Dolomiti* (MUSE, monografie 7). Trento: Museo delle Scienze di Trento.

Battisti, M. and S. Cavalieri 2019. I ritrovamenti preistorici della Becchetta di Ronzo-Chienis (Tn). *Annali del Museo Civico di Rovereto* 34 (2018): 23–38.

Battisti, M. and S. Marconi 2004. La fauna dell'insediamento dei Pizzini di Castellano (TN) e l'allevamento nell'Italia nord orientale nel corso dell'antica età del bronzo. *Padusa*, anno XXXIX nuova serie (2003): 45–59.

Battisti, M. and U. Tecchiati 2003. Il sito dei Pizzini di Castellano (Villalagarina – TN), in *Atti della XXXV riunione scientifica dell'Istituto italiano di preistoria e protostoria: le comunità della preistoria italiana, studi e ricerche sul neolitico e le eta dei metalli. Castello di Lipari, Chiesa di S. Caterina, 2-7 giugno 2000: in memoria di Luigi Bernabò Brea*: 851–854. Firenze: Istituto Italiano di Preistoria e Protostoria.

Bazzanella, M., A. Mayr, L. Moser and A. Rast-Eicher 2003. *Textiles. Intrecci e tessuti dalla preistoria europea.* Catalogue of the homonymous exhibition, Riva del Garda 2003. Trento: Ufficio Beni Archeologici della Provincia Automa di Trento.

Bazzanella, M. and A. Mayr 2009. *I reperti tessili, le fusaiole e i pesi da telaio dalla palafitta di Molina di ledro.* Trento: Provincia Autonoma di Trento.

Bellintani, P. 1987. I materiali dell'insediamento dell'età del Bronzo di Canàr (Castelnovo Bariano-Rovigo): le raccolte di superficie. *Padusa,* Anno XXIII, 1-2-3-4: 147–187.

Bermond Montanari, G., A. Del Lucchese, P. Frontini, F.M. Gambari, G. Kaufmann, F. Marzatico, M. Montagnari Kokelj, F. Nicolis, G. Odetti, A . Pedrotti and L. Salzani 1996. Articolazioni culturali e cronologiche. L'Italia settentrionale, in D. Cocchi Genick (ed.) *L' antica età del bronzo: atti del congresso di Viareggio, 9-12 Gennaio 1995*: 57–78. Firenze: Octavo.

Bertoldi, R. 1968. Ricerche pollinologiche sullo sviluppo della vegetazione tardi glaciale e postglaciale nella regione del Lago di Garda. *Studi Trentini di Scienze Naturali*, sez. B, vol. XLV, n. 1: 87–162.

Bocchio, G. 1988. Saggio stratigrafico presso Lucone D. Polpenazze del Garda (BS). *Annali del Museo Archeologico della Valle Sabbia* 16 (1985–1988): 15–43.

Bonardi, S., S. Marconi, A. Riedel and U. Tecchiati 2002. La fauna del sito dell'antica età del bronzo del Colombo di Mori (TN), campagne di scavo 1881 e 1970: aspetti archeozoologici, paleoeconomici e paleo ambientali. *Annali del Museo Civico di Rovereto* 16 (2000): 63–102.

Bonardi, S. and U. Tecchiati 2005. Risultati delle ricerche 1994 e 1996 nel sito dell'età del Bronzo del Riparo del Santuario di Lasino in Val di Cavedine (TN). *Annali del Museo Civico di Rovereto* 20 (2004): 3–21.

Bonomi, F., T. Pasquali and V. Rosà 1986. Arco, Nago-Torbole e Mori (Trentino Sud-Occidentale). *Preistoria Alpina* 21(1985), Notiziario regionale 1982–1986: 181–190.

Borrello, M.A. and A. Girod 2008. Bivalves D'eau Douce, Matière Première Pour La Fabrication De Parures En Suisse, Du Néolithique à L'âge Du Bronze. *Annuaire d'Archéologie Suisse* 91: 108–115.

Bronk Ramsey, C. 2009. Bayesian analysis of radiocarbon dates, *Radiocarbon* 51(1): 337–360.

Camps, G. and E. Rostan 1982. Les poteries à perforations en ligne, à propos du faciès terrinien du Chalcolithique corse. *Bulletin de la Société préhistorique française* 79(8): 240–249, <doi: 10.3406/bspf.1982.5393>.

Capitanio, M. 1973. I resti scheletrici umani, riferibili agli inizi dell'età del Bronzo, finora ritrovati a Loch di Romagnano (Trento). *Preistoria Alpina* 9: 7–43.

Casini, S. 2005. Manufatti in pietra dalla palafitta del Lavagnone (Desenzano del Garda, Brescia). *Notizie Archeologiche Bergomensi* 11(2003): 79–116.

Castiglioni, E. and U. Tecchiati 2005. Archaeobotanical studies on the levels of the Late Calcolithic in Velturno-Tanzagasse in Val d'Isarco (BZ). *Atti dell'Accademia degli Agiati*, a. 255, ser. VIII, vol. V, B: 505–528.

Cattaneo Cassano, A. 1996. L'abitato dell'antica età del bronzo di Milzanello (Brescia). *Natura Bresciana, Annali del Museo Civico di Scienze Naturali di Brescia* 30(1994): 329–381.

Cazzella, A. 1989. *Manuale di Archeologia*. Laterza.

Cazzanelli, F. 2007. La fase del Bronzo Antico II nel Settore B, in R.C. de Marinis (ed.) *Studi sull'abitato dell'età del Bronzo del Lavagnone, Desenzano del Garda* (Notizie Archeologiche Bergomensi 10): 187–211. Bergamo: Civico museo archeologico di Bergamo.

Ceschin, N. 1985. Codice d'analisi della ceramica preistorica. Seconda edizione riveduta e ampliata. *Padusa* XXI: 5–51.

Chelidonio, G. 1990. Due acciarini per fuoco da Castel Corno (Vallagarina, Trentino Occidentale). *Annali dei Musei Civici di Rovereto* 5 (1989): 75–84.

Chiarenza, N. 2013. Liguria terra di confine. Influssi culturali e vie di percorrenza nell'età del Rame, in R.C. de Marinis (ed.) *L'età del Rame. La pianura Padana e la Alpi al tempo di* Ötzi: 277–292. Roccafranca: Compagnia della Stampa Massetti Rodella editori.

Chiocchetti, V. 1985. Zone archeologiche nel territorio dell'antico Comun Comunale. Le grotte di Castel Corno. *Il Comunale, Periodico culturale della destra Adige*, novembre 1985, 2: 6–10.

Chiusole, P. and S. Vettori 1972. *Sondaggio stratigrafico al riparo del 'Santuario' in 'Val Cornelio' nel Comune di Lasino (Trentino)*. Reovereto: Società Museo Civico di Rovereto.

Clément, N. 2020. Le prestige des guerriers: équipements d'archers campaniformes en Europe centrale, *Préhistoires Méditerranéennes* 8, viewed 19 July 2021. <http://journals.openedition.org/pm/2202>.

Colledge, S. 2007. Chapter 20. The Copper Age Carbonised Plant Remains, in L.H. Barfield (ed.) *Excavations in the Riparo Valtenesi. Manerba. 1976-1994*: 391–413. Firenze: Istituto Italiano di Preistoria e Protostoria.

Cooper, A., D. Garrow, C. Gibson and M. Giles 2019. Covering the Dead in Later Prehistoric Britain: Elusive Objects and Powerful Technologies of Funerary Performance. *Proceedings of the Prehistoric Society*, 85: 223–250. <doi:10.1017/ppr.2019.8>.

Corrain, C. and D. De Marchi 1980. Resti scheletrici umani dal riparo in 'Val Cornelio', comune di Lasino, e dalla grotta di Castel Corno, comune di Isera (Trentino). *Atti dell'Accademia Roveretana degli Agiati*, Anno 228–229, Serie VI, 18–19: 45–51.

Corrain, C. and G. Erspamer 1980. Gli scheletri tardo-neolitici giovanili di Volano presso Rovereto (Trento). *Preistoria Alpina 14* (1978): 197–203.

Costantini, L., M. Lauria and U. Tecchiati 2003. I resti carpologici dell'antica e media età del Bronzo del Riparo del Santuario di Lasino (Trento) - Scavi 1996. *Annali del Museo Civico di Rovereto* 17 (2001): 3–40.

D'Ercole, V. 1997. Grotte dell'Abruzzo con rinvenimenti delle età del rame e del bronzo, in M. Pacciarelli (ed.) *Acque, grotte e Dei. 3000 anni di culti preromani in Romagna, Marche e Abruzzo, Imola 11-12 January 1997*: 50–61. Imola: Musei Civici di Imola.

D'Oronzo, C. 2019. Le strutture di combustione: è tutta una questione di relazioni?, in A. Peinetti, M. Cattani and F. Debandi (eds) *Focolari, forni e fornaci tra neolitico ed età del ferro comprendere le attività domestiche e artigianali attraverso lo studio delle installazioni pirotecnologiche e dei residui di combustione (Abstract Book of the Sixth Annual Meeting of Prehistory and Protohistory, Università di Bologna, Dipartimento di Storia Culture Civiltà, 29 marzo 2019)*: 43–47. Firenze: Istituto Italiano di Preistoria e Protostoria.

Dal Ri, L., G. Rizzi and U. Tecchiati 2004. L'area megalitica dell'età del rame di Velturno - loc. Tanzgasse (BZ). Aggiornamenti sullo stato delle ricerche, in E. Bianchin Citton (ed.), *L'area funeraria e cultuale dell'età del Rame di Sovizzo nel contesto archeologico dell'Italia settentrionale*, (Quaderni di Archeologia Vicentina 1): 125–174. Vicenza: Museo Naturalistico Archeologico.

Dal Ri, L. and U. Tecchiati 1995. L'area megalitica e la statua-stele eneolitica di Velturno-loc. Tanzgasse (BZ). Contributo alla storicizzazione delle statue stele dell'area atesina. *Notizie Archeologiche Bergomensi* 2 (1994): 15–36.

Dal Ri, L. and U. Tecchiati 1996. Aspetti del popolamento dell'alto corso dell'Adige durante l'antica età del Bronzo, in D. Cocchi Genick (ed.) *L' antica età del bronzo: atti del congresso di Viareggio, 9-12 Gennaio 1995*: 532–533. Firenze: Octavo.

Dal Santo N., A. Ferrari, G. Morico and G. Steffè 2014. Bell Beaker in Eastern Emilia (Northern Italy), in M. Besse (ed.) *Around the Petit-Chasseur Site in Sion (Valis, Switzerland) and New Approaches to the Bell Beaker Culture, Proceedings of the International Conference held at Sion (Switzerland), October 27th-30th, 2011*: 205–236. Oxford: Archaeopress Archaeology.

De Marinis, R.C. 1999. Towards a Relative and Absolute Chronology of the Bronze Age in Northern Italy. *Notizie Archeologiche Bergomensi* 7: 23–38.

De Marinis, R.C. 2000. *Il Museo Civico Archeologico Giovanni Rambotti di Desenzano del Garda: una introduzione alla preistoria del lago di Garda*. Desenzano: Città di Desenzano del Garda.

De Marinis, R.C., M. Baioni, N. De Gasperi, C. Mangani, and L. Seragnoli 1996. Nuovi scavi al Lavagnone (Desenzano del Garda-Lonato) e considerazioni sull'antica età del Bronzo nell'Italia settentrionale, in D. Cocchi Genick (ed.) *L' antica età del bronzo: atti del congresso di Viareggio, 9-12 Gennaio 1995*: 257–271. Firenze: Octavo.

De Marinis, R.C. and A. Pedrotti 1997. L'età del Rame nel versante italiano delle Alpi centro-occidentali, in Atti della XXXI Riunione Scientifica, *La Valle d'Aosta nel quadro della preistoria e protostoria dell'arco alpino centro-occidentale, Courmayeur, 2-5 giugno 1994*: 247–300. Firenze: Istituto Italiano di Preistoria e Protostoria.

De Marinis, R.C. and M. Rapi 2016. Note sui criteri di classificazione della ceramica e sulla terminologia delle anse con sopraelevazioni. *Notizie Archeologiche Bergomensi* 24: 27–59.

De Marinis, R.C., M. Rapi, L. Salzani and G. Spinelli 2015. L'abitato dell'antica Erà del bronzo di Canàr (Castelnovo Bariano, Rovigo), in G. Leonardi and V. Tiné (eds) *Preistoria e Protostoria del Veneto. Atti del Convegno Studi di Preistoria e Protostoria*: 279–288. Firenze: Istituto Italiano di Preistoria e Protostoria.

De Marinis, R.C. and E. Valzolgher 2013. Riti funerari dell'antica età del Bronzo in area Padana, in R.C. de Marinis (ed.) *L'età del Rame. La pianura Padana e le Alpi al tempo di Ötzi*: 545–559. Roccafranca: Compagnia della Stampa Massetti Rodella editori.

Dörfler, W. 2015. The late 3rd millennium BC in pollen diagrams along a south-north transect from the Near East to northern Central Europe, in H. Meller, H.W. Arz, R. Jung and R. Risch (eds) *2200 BC - A climatic breakdown as a cause for the collapse of the old world? 7th Archaeological Conference of Central Germany October 23-26, 2014 in Halle (Saale)* (Tagungen des Landesmuseums für Vorgeschichte Halle 12/I): 321–332. Halle: Landesmuseum für Vorgeschichte.

Eliade, M. 2001. *Trattato di storia delle religioni*. Torino: Bollati Boringhieri. (Translated edition of *Traité d'histoire des religions*, 1948. Paris: Payot).

Eliade, M. 2018. *Arti del metallo e alchimia*. Torino: Bollati Boringhieri. (Translated edition of *Forgerons er alchimistes*, 1977. Paris: Flammarion).

Farina, J. 2016. Analisi di stratigrafia e strutture, catalogo dei materiali ceramici dell'antica età del bronzo e analisi dei resti faunistici del sito di Elvas (Huber 4) presso Bressanone. Unpublished dissertation, University of Trento, Faculty of Beni Culturali.

Fasani, L. 1980. La fine del Neolitico e l'età del Bronzo nel territorio veronese, in L. Fasani (ed.) *Il territorio veronese dalle origini all'età romana (contributi ed aggiornamenti di ricerca preistorica)*: 65–98. Verona: Fiorini.

Fasani, L. 1984. L'età del Bronzo, in A. Aspes (ed.) *Il Veneto nell'antichità. Preistoria e protostoria*: 481–504. Verona: Banca populare di Verona.

Fasani, L. 1990. La sepoltura e il forno di fusione de La Vela di Valbusa (Trento). *Preistoria Alpina* 24 (1988): 165–181.

Favole, A. 2003. *Resti di umanità. Vita sociale dei corpi dopo la morte*. Roma: Editori Laterza.

Fedele, F. and A. Fossati 2012. L'area cerimoniale di Anvòia a Ossimo, Valcamonica: i monoliti simbolici e il loro contesto. *Preistoria Alpina* 46: 189–199.

Festi F. and F. Prosser 1991. Nota sulla flora e vegetazione della zona del Castel Corno, in T. Pasquali (ed.) *Castel Corno in mostra*: 53–56. Isera.

Fokkens, H., Y. Achterkamp and M. Kuijpers 2008. Bracers or Bracelets? About the Functionality and Meaning of Bell Beaker Wrist-guards. *Proceedings of the Prehistoric Society* 74: 109–140.

Fontana, A. 2007. La fauna dell'antica età del bronzo delle grotte di Castel Corno (Isera-TN). Aspetti archeozoologici, paleo economici e paleoambientali. Unpublished dissertation, University of Parma, Faculty of Scienze Matematiche Fisiche e Naturali.

Fontana, A., S. Marconi and U. Tecchiati 2010. La fauna dell'antica età del Bronzo delle grotte di Castel Corno (Isera – TN). *Annali del Museo Civico di Rovereto* 25 (2009): 27–66.

Fontana, A., S. Marconi and U. Tecchiati 2012. I resti faunistici dell'Antica Età del Bronzo delle Grotte di Castel Corno - Isera (TN). Aspetti archeozoologici e paleoeconomici, in J. De Grossi Mazzorin, D. Saccà, C. Tozzi (eds) *Atti del VI Convegno Nazionale di Archeozoologia Parco dell'Orecchiella San Romano in Garfagnana, Lucca, 21-24 maggio 2009*: 137–144. Lecce: Associazione Italiana di Archeozoologia.

Forte, V. 2019. Skilled people or specialists? Knowledge and expertise in copper age vessels from central Italy. *Journal of Anthropological Archaeology* 55, <https://doi.org/10.1016/j.jaa.2019.101072>.

Frazer, J.G. 2016. *La paura dei morti nelle religioni primitive*. Milano: Il Saggiatore. (Translation of *The Fear of the Dead in Primitive Religions*, 1936. London: MacMillan).

Frisone, F. 1994. Rituale funerario, necropoli e società die vivi: una riflessione fra storia ed archeologia. *Studi di Antichità* 7: 11–23.

Genov, A. 2016. Megalithic and Rock-Cut Monuments as Ritual Structures Related to Notions of Life and Death and Belief in Eternal Life and Rebirth, in D. Spasova (ed.) *Megalithic Monuments and Cult Practices, Proceedings of the Second International Symposium Blagoevgrad, 12-15 October 2016*: 323–330. Blagoevgrad: Neofit Rilski University Press.

Gibelli, D., F. Collini, D. Porta, M. Zago, C. Dolci, C. Cattaneo and C. Sforza 2016. Variations of midfacial soft-tissue thickness in subjects aged between 6 and 18 years for the reconstruction of the profile: a study on an Italian sample. *Legal Medicine* 22: 68–74.

Girod, A. 2005. Importanza dei molluschi terrestri e d'acqua dolce in archeologia. *Preistoria Alpina* 40 (2004) - suppl. 1: 125–132.

Gorfer, A. 1992. L'identità atesina, in E. Turri and S. Ruffo (eds), *L'Adige. Il fiume, gli uomini, la storia*: 177–262. Verona: Cierre Edizioni.

Guerreschi, G. 1981. La stazione preistorica del lago Lucone (Brescia) – Scavi 1965–1971. *Annali del Museo* 15: 7–78. Brescia: Civico Museo di Gavardo.

Gurova, M., P. Andreeva, A. Nikolov, B. Barbov and M. Kostadinova-Avramova 2020. Heat alterations of flint artefacts: archaeological evidence, experiments and analyses. *Bulgarian e-Journal of Archaeology* 10.1: 111–141.

Hetzer, K. 1949. Ein Grab der Wieselburger Kultur aus Arbesthal. *Jahrbuch für Landeskunde von Niederösterreich* 30: 110–122.

Holst, M.K. 2013. Burials, in H. Fokkens and A. Harding (eds) *The Oxford Handbook of the European Bronze Age*: 102–120. Oxford: Oxford University Press.

Kashina, E. and N.Y. Petrova 2019. The Kargopol type ceramics - the first pottery of the northern part of the East European Plain?, *Documenta Praehistorica* XLVI: 174–182.

Kramer, N. 2017. Archaeological Textiles from the Roman Period in the Netherlands, in M. Bravermanová, H. Březinová, J. Malcolm-Davies (eds) *Archaeological Textiles. Links Between Past and Present* (NESAT XIII): 51–60. Prague: Technical University of Liberec, Faculty of Textile Engineering in cooperation with Institute of Archaeology of the CAS.

Lachenal, T., V. Rinalducci de Chassey, K. Georges and J.P. Sargiano 2010. Une tuyère du Bronze ancien à la Bastide Neuve II (Velaux, Bouches-du-Rhône). Un témoin d'activité métallurgique en contexte domestique en Provence occidentale? Remarques sur les tuyères en céramique d'Europe occidentale. *Bulletin de la Société préhistorique française* 107(3): 549–565.

Ledger, M.L., E. Anastasiou, L.M. Shillito, H. Mackay, I.D. Bull, S.D Haddow, C.J. Knüsel and P.D. Mitchell 2019. Parasite infection at the early farming community of Çatalhöyük. *Antiquity* 93 (369): 573–587.

Leeb, A. 1987. Überblick über die Chorologie, Typologie und Chronologie der Wieselburgkultur. 100 Jahre Forschungsstand. *Wissenschaftliche Arbeiten aus dem Burgenland* 75: 231–283.

Lelong, O., I. Arabaolaza, T. Booth, J. Exans, R. Evershed, S. Harris, H. Hollund, B.J. Keely, A. Lamb, M.D. Pickering, A.P. Pinder, S. Ramsay, P. Walton Rogers, L. Soberl, C. Wilson and L. Wilson 2014. Wrappings of power: a woman's burial in cattle hide at Langwell Farm, Strath Oykel. *Proceedings of the Society of Antiquaries of Scotland* 144: 65–131.

Leonardi, G., M. Cupitò, M. Baioni, C. Longhi and C. Martinelli, N. 2015. Northern Italy around 2200 cal BC. From Copper Age to Early Bronze Age: continuity and/or discontinuity?, in H. Meller, H.W. Arz, R. Jung and R. Risch (eds) *2200 BC - A climatic breakdown as a cause for the collapse of the old world? 7th Archaeological Conference of Central Germany October 23-26, 2014 in Halle (Saale)* (Tagungen des Landesmuseums für Vorgeschichte Halle 12/I): 283–304. Halle: Landesmuseum für Vorgeschichte.

Leonini, V. and L. Sarti 2006. Sepolture e rituali funerari nell'Eneolitico e al passaggio all'età del Bronzo in Italia, in F. Martini (ed.) *La cultura del morire nelle società preistoriche e protostoriche italiane* (Origines 3): 129–160. Firenze: Istituto Italiano di Preistoria e Protostoria.

Lincetto, S. and E. Valzolgher 1998. *Manufatti litici inediti provenienti da Scalucce di Molina e Campostrin (Monti Lessini) conservati nella collezione Chierici dei Civici Musei di Reggio Emilia* (Pagine di Archeologia 3). Reggio Emilia: Comune di Reggio Emilia, Civici Musei.

Lincetto, S. and E. Valzolgher 2002. Nuovi dati sulla sepoltura eneolitico di Peri (1887). *Annuario Storico della Valpolicella* 2001–2002: 267–270.

Lucentini, N. 1997. Le grotte della Gola del Sentino, in M. Pacciarelli (ed.) *Acque, grotte e Dei. 3000 anni di culti preromani in Romagna, Marche e Abruzzo, Imola 11-12 January 1997*: 36–49. Imola: Musei Civici di Imola.

Mangani, C. and C. Longhi 2008. Palafitte e conchiglie. Fonti di approvvigionamento di malacofauna nell'età del Bronzo, in M. Baioni and C. Fredella (eds) *Archeotrade. Antichi commerci in Lombardia orientale*: 127–140. Milano: Et.

Mannoni, T. and E. Giannichedda 1996. *Archeologia della produzione*. Torino: Einaudi.

Marconi, S., B. Proserpio, M. Battisti and U. Tecchiati (in press). I resti archeobotanici provenienti dalle Grotte di Castel Corno di Isera (TN). Ambiente ed economia del sito fra la fine dell'età del Rame e l'inizio dell'età del Bronzo. *Annali del Museo Civico di Rovereto* 38 (2022).

Marzatico, F. 1987. L'insediamento dell'età del bronzo del Dosso Alto di Borgo Sacco (Rovereto). *Annali del Museo Civico di Rovereto* 3: 47–76.

Marzatico, F. 2013. Il Dosso di San Bartolomeo di Ceole: riscoperta di un castelliere nell'Alto Garda, in G.P. Broglio (ed.) *APSAT 3. Paesaggi storici del Sommolago*: 117–137. Progetti di Archeologia, SAP.

Marzatico, F. and U. Tecchiati 2002. L'età del Bronzo in Trentino e Alto Adige/Südtirol. *Atti della XXXIII Riunione Scientifica dell'Istituto Italiano di Preistoria e Protostoria*: 45–92. Firenze: Preistoria e Protostoria del Trentino Alto Adige/Südtirol.

Mazzucchi, A., G. Bonelli, M. Battisti and U. Tecchiati 2020. Le sepolture preistoriche delle Grotte di Castelcorno di Isera (TN). *Annali del Museo Civico di Rovereto* 35 (2019): 3–31.

McMichael, A.J. 2012. Insights from past millennia into climatic impacts on human health and survival. *PNAS* March 27th 109(13): 4730–4737.

Mezzena, F. 1965. Barche di Bocchio e la Cultura di Polada, in *Atti della X Riunione Scientifica. In memoria di Francesco Zorzi*: 155–160. Verona 21–23 novembre 1965. Firenze: Istituto Italiano di Preistoria e Protostoria.

Morandi, R., A. Vigliardi and A. Zanini 1996. Iconografia e arti decorative, in D. Cocchi Genick (ed.) *L' antica età del bronzo: atti del congresso di Viareggio, 9-12 Gennaio 1995*: 361–383. Firenze: Octavo.

Mottes, E. 1996. L'insediamento e la necropoli dell'antica età del Bronzo dei Solteri di Trento, *L'antica età del bronzo,* in D. Cocchi Genick (ed.) *L' antica età del bronzo: atti del congresso di Viareggio, 9-12 Gennaio 1995*: 542–545. Firenze: Octavo.

Mottes, E., M. Bassetti and E. Silvestri 2011. The Bronze Age tumuli of Gardolo di Mezzo (Trento, Italy) in the Adige Valley in E. Borgna, E. Müller Celka (eds) *Ancestral Landscapes. Burial mounds in the Copper and Bronze ages (Central and Eastern Europe - Balkans - Adriatic - Aegean, 4th-2nd millennium BC), Proceedings of the International Conference held in Udine, 14-19 Mai 2008, TMO 61*: 517–526. Lyon: Maison de l'Orient et de la Méditerranée.

Mottes, E., N. Degasperi, D. Gaudio and M. Zana 2019. Nuova sepoltura dell'età del Rame a Nogarole di Mezzolombardo (Trento) in Valle dell'Adige. *Archeologia Delle Alpi* 2017–2019: 11–19.

Mottes, E. and F. Nicolis 1998. Aspetti del bicchiere campaniforme in Trentino, in F. Nicolis and E. Mottes (eds) *Simbolo ed enigma. Il bicchiere campaniforme e l'Italia della preistoria europea del III millennio a.C.*: 73–76. Trento: Provincia Autonoma di Trento.

Mottes, E. and F. Nicolis 2019. Forme della ritualità funeraria tra età del Rame e antica età del Bronzo nel territorio della Valle dell'Adige (Trentino Alto Adige, Italia settentrionale). Nota di aggiornamento, in F. Martini and L. Salzani (eds) *Un lungo percorso di scienza. Scritti in onore di Leone Fasani* (Memorie del Museo Civico di Storia Naturale di Verona 2. Serie. Sezione Scienze dell'Uomo 13, Millenni. Studi di Archeologia Preistorica 22): 191–219. Verona: Museo e istituto fiorentino di preistoria.

Mottes, E., F. Nicolis and U. Tecchiati 1999. Aspetti dell'insediamento e dell'uso del territorio nel III e nel II millennio a.C. in Trentino Alto Adige, in P. Della Casa (ed.), *Prehistoric Alpine Environment, Society and Economy; papers of the international colloquium PAESE 1997 in Zurich* (Universitätsforschungen zur prähistorischen Archäologie 55): 81–97. Bonn: Rudolf Habelt.

Munsell Soil Color Charts 1994 (revised edition). New Windsor (NY): Macbeth Division of Kollmorgen Instruments Corporation.

Nålebinding. Wikipedia <https://en.wikipedia.org/wiki/N%C3%A5lebinding> (website accessed on 20 February 2021).

Neugebauer, J.W. 1979. Das frühbronzezeitliche Gräberfeld von Bernhardsthal, Flur Unfrieden, Niederösterreich. *Fundberichte aus Österreich* 17.

Nicolas, C. 2019. The production and use of archery-related items as a reflection of social changes during the Late Neolithic and the Early Bronze Age in Europe, in S. Kadrow S. and J. Müller (eds), *Habitus? The Social Dimension of Technology and Transformation* (Scales of Transformation in Prehistory and Archaic Societies 3): 115–139. Leiden: Sidestone Press.

Nicolis, F. 1996. Strutture e riti funebri, in D. Cocchi Genick (ed.) *L' antica età del bronzo: atti del congresso di Viareggio, 9-12 Gennaio 1995*: 337–344. Firenze: Octavo.

Nicolis, F. 2001. Il culto dei morti nell'antica e media età del Bronzo, in M. Lazinger, F. Marzatico, A. Pedrotti (eds) *Storia del Trentino, I. La preistoria e la protostoria*: 337–366. Bologna: Istituto Trentino di Cultura, Il Mulino.

Nicolis, F. 2016. Le evidenze funerarie dell'antica età del bronzo in Italia settentrionale, in M. Besse and J. Desideri (eds), *Graves and funerary rituals during the late Neolithic and the early Bronze Age in Europe (2700-2000 BC)*: 111–145. Oxford: BAR Publishing.

Nisbet, R. 1984. Vegetazione e agricoltura durante l'età del Bronzo al Riparo Gaban (Trento). *Preistoria Alpina* 20: 301–310.

Nobelen, J. 2016. Untangling Wool. Fibre preparation for woollen threads in Dutch Early Bronze Age to Middle Iron Age. Unpublished dissertation, Leiden University, Faculty of Archaeology.

Oberrauch, H. 2014. Pigloner Kopf, un rogo votivo dell'età del Rame - Il rito di deposizione di oggetti in un'area sacra, in R.F. de Marinis (ed.), *Le manifestazioni del sacro e l'età del Rame nella regione alpina e nella Pianura Padana, Studi in memoria di Angelo Rampinelli Rota. Brescia, Palazzo Broletto, 23-24 maggio 2014*: 67–84. Brescia: Edizioni Euroteam.

Olsen, O. and I. Svanberg 2010. Nalbinding in the Faroe Islands?, *Annales Societatis Scientiarum Færoensis* 54: 190–199.

Orombelli, G. and C. Ravazzi 1996. The Late Glacial and Early Holocene: Chronology and paleoclimate. *Il Quaternario* 9: 439–444.

Orsi, P. 1882. La stazione litica del Colombo di Mori e l'età della pietra nel Trentino. *Bullettino di Paletnologia Italiana*, anno VIII, luglio, agosto e settembre 1882, 7-8-9: 106–218.

Pacciarelli, M. and G. Sassatelli 1997. Acque, grotte e Dei, in M. Pacciarelli (ed.) *Acque, grotte e Dei. 3000 anni di culti preromani in Romagna, Marche e Abruzzo, Imola 11-12 January 1997*: 10–19. Imola: Musei Civici di Imola.

Pacciarelli, M. and W.R. Teegen 1997. La grotta del Re Tiberio: resti di sepolture dell'età del Bronzo, in M. Pacciarelli (ed.) *Acque, grotte e Dei. 3000 anni di culti preromani in Romagna, Marche e Abruzzo, Imola 11-12 January 1997*: 29–35. Imola: Musei Civici di Imola.

Pajuelo Pando, A. and P.M. López Aldana 2016. Prestige indicators and Bell Beaker ware at Valencina de la Concepción (Sevilla, Spain), in E. Guerra Doce and C. Liesau von Lettow-Vorbeck (eds)

Analysis of the Economic Foundations Supporting the Social Supremacy of the Beaker Groups, Proceedings of the XVII UISPP World Congress (1–7 September, Burgos, Spain): 55–68. Oxford: Archaeopress.

Pals, J.P. and A. Voorrips 1981. Chapter III. Carbonised seeds, fruits and charcoal, in L.H. Barfield, G.W.W. Barker, J.T. Chesterman, J.P. Pals, and A. Voorrips (eds) *Excavations at Monte Covolo, Villanuova sul Clisi, Brescia (1972–73), Part II* (Annali del Museo, Gavardo 13): 31–40. Brescia: Geroldi.

Palumbo, C. 2012. Il 'Brassard' nell'Eneolitico. Tipologia e funzione, in M. Congiu (ed.), *NEOS - Progetto giovani Studiosi e Ricercatori. Atti dei Seminari di Studio*, I edizione. Sala degli Operatori del Museo Tripisciano Palazzo Moncada – Caltanissetta, gennaio – aprile 2012.

Pasquali, T. (ed.) 1991. *Castel Corno in mostra*. Catalogue of the homonymous exhibition. Rovereto: Museo Civico di Rovereto.

Pasquali, T. and B. Rauss 1987. I resti della cultura materiale rinvenuti a Castel Corno (Vallagarina-Trentino occidentale). *Annali del Museo Civico di Rovereto* 3: 23–46.

Pasquali, T. and B. Rauss 1988. I resti della cultura materiale rinvenuti a Castel Corno (Vallagarina-Trentino occidentale). *Annali del Museo Civico di Rovereto* 4: 79–118.

Pasquali, T. and B. Rauss 1990. I resti della cultura materiale rinvenuti nella parte bassa di Castel Corno e nelle zone limitrofe (Vallagarina-Trentino occidentale). *Annali del Museo Civico di Rovereto* 5: 41–74.

Pedrotti, A. 1982. L'Eneolitico e l'Età del Bronzo nella successione stratigrafica del riparo Gaban. Unpublished dissertation, University of Bologna, faculty of Lettere e Filosofia.

Pedrotti, A. 2001a. *Il Neolitico*, in M. Lanzinger, F. Marzatico and A. Pedrotti (eds) *Storia del Trentino. I. La preistoria e la protostoria*: 120–181. Il Mulino, Bologna: Istituto Trentino di Cultura.

Pedrotti, A. 2001b. L'età del Rame, in M. Lanzinger, F. Marzatico and A. Pedrotti (eds) *Storia del Trentino. I. La preistoria e la protostoria*: 183–253. Il Mulino, Bologna: Istituto Trentino di Cultura.

Peinetti, A., M. Cattani and F. Debandi (eds) 2019. *Focolari, forni e fornaci tra neolitico ed età del ferro comprendere le attività domestiche e artigianali attraverso lo studio delle installazioni pirotecnologiche e dei residui di combustione (Abstract Book of the Sixth Annual Meeting of Prehistory and Protohistory, Università di Bologna, Dipartimento di Storia Culture Civiltà, 29 marzo 2019)*. Firenze: Istituto Italiano di Preistoria e Protostoria.

Perini, R. 1971. I depositi preistorici di Romagnano-Loc II e IV. *Preistoria Alpina* 7: 7–106.

Perini, R. 1972. Il deposito secondario n°3 dei Montesei di Serso. Contributo alla conoscenza del Bronzo Antico nella Regione Trentino-Alto Adige. *Preistoria Alpina* 8: 7–30.

Perini, R. 1973a. Montesei di Serso-Lo scavo del 1968: settore VI. La successione cronologica dell'abitato dei Montesei di Serso. *Preistoria Alpina* 9: 91–111.

Perini, R. 1973b. Romagnano - Tof de la Val (Trento). *Preistoria Alpina* 9, Notiziario regionale: 247–250.

Perini, R. 1975. La necropoli di Romagnano-Loc III e IV. Le tombe all'inizio dell'età del bronzo nella regione Subalpina Centro-orientale. *Preistoria Alpina* 11: 295–315.

Perini, R. 1987. *Scavi archeologici nella zona palafitticola di Fiavé-Carrera. Parte II, Campagne 1969-1976. Resti della cultura materiale. Metallo - osso - litica - legno* (Patrimonio storico e artistico del Trentino 9). Trento: Servizio Beni Culturali della Provincia Autonoma di Trento.

Perini, R. 1988. Gli scavi nel Lavagnone. Sequenza e tipologia degli abitati dell'età del Bronzo. *Annali Benacensi* 9: 109–154.

Perini, R. 1994. *Scavi archeologici nella zona palafitticola di Fiavé-Carrera, Parte III, Campagne 1969-1976. Resti della cultura materiale. Ceramica* (Patrimonio storico e artistico del Trentino 10). Trento: Servizio Beni Culturali della Provincia Autonoma di Trento.

Perini, R. 2000. L'età del Bronzo Antico e Medio, in Lanzinger, M., Marzatico, F., Pedrotti, A. (eds) *Storia del Trentino. I. La preistoria e la protostoria*: 287–337. Il Mulino, Bologna: Istituto Trentino di Cultura.

Perna, G. 1974. Le frane glaciali e postglaciali nel Trentino Meridionale (Marocche e Laste). *Bollettino del Comitato Glaciologico Italiano*, ser. 2 (22): 59–66.

Peroni, R. 1996. *L'Italia alle soglie della storia*. Roma: Laterza.

Peŝka, J. 2016. Graves of metallurgists in the Moravian Beaker Cultures, in E. Guerra Doce and C. Liesau von Lettow-Vorbeck (eds) *Analysis of the Economic Foundations Supporting the Social Supremacy of the Beaker Groups, Proceedings of the XVII UISPP World Congress (1–7 September, Burgos, Spain)*: 1–18. Oxford: Archaeopress.

Pezzato, C., 2016. Manufatti in osso, in B. Maurina (ed.) *Richerche archeologiche a Sant'Andrea di Loppio (Trento, Italia). Il Castrum Tardoantico-Altomedievale*: 627–651. Oxford: Archeopress.

Pia, G.E., 1987. Le strutture archeologiche dell'insediamento dell'antica età del bronzo ad Ostiano (Cremona). *Natura Bresciana, Annali del Museo Civico di Scienze Naturali di Brescia* 23 (1986): 299–340.

Poggiani Keller, R. 2006. Santuari megalitici nelle valli lombarde, in A. Pessina and P. Visentini (eds) *Preistoria dell'Italia settentrionale. Studi in ricordo di Barnardino Bagolini, atti del Convegno, Udine 23–24 settembre 2005*: 243–266. Udine: Comune di Udine, Edizioni del Museo friulano di storia naturale.

Rageth, J. 1974. *Der Lago di Ledro im Trentino* (Bericht der Römisch-Germanischen Kommission, Band 55). Zurich: Juris

Rapi, M. 2007. Lavagnone di Desenzano del Garda (BS), settore B: la ceramica del Bronzo Antico I, in R.C. de Marinis (ed.) *Studi sull'abitato dell'età del Bronzo del Lavagnone, Desenzano del Garda* (Notizie Archeologiche Bergomensi 10): 109–185. Bergamo: Civico museo archeologico di Bergamo.

Rapi, M. 2013. Dall'età del Rame all'età del Bronzo. I primi villaggi palafitticoli e la cultura di Polada, in R.C. de Marinis (ed.) *L'età del Rame. La pianura Padana e le Alpi al tempo di Ötzi*: 525–544. Roccafranca: Compagnia della Stampa Massetti Rodella editori.

Rapi, M. 2020. *Il complesso del Lavagnone 3. Scavi dell'Università degli Studi di Milano (1989-2006)* (Palafitte 2.1). Quingentole (MN): SAP Società Archeologica.

Regola, E. 2005. Le grotte di Castelcorno. Cronologia e tipologia della cultura materiale nel quadro dell'antica Età del Bronzo in Italia Settentrionale. Unpublished dissertation, University of Parma, Faculty of Lettere e Filosofia.

Reimer, P.J., E. Bard, A. Bayliss, J.W. Beck, P.G. Blackwell, C. Bronk Ramsey, C.E. Buck, H. Cheng, R.L. Edwards, M. Friedrich, P.M. Grootes, T.P. Guilderson, H. Haflidason, I. Hajdas, C. Hatté, T.J Heaton, D.L. Hoffmann, A.G. Hogg, K.A. Hughen, K.F. Kaiser, B. Kromer, S.W. Manning, M. Niu, R.W. Reimer, D.A. Richards, E.M. Scott, J.R. Southon, R.A. Staff, C.S.M. Turney and J. van der Plicht 2013, IntCal13 and Marine13 radiocarbon age calibration curves 0–50,000 years cal BP, *Radiocarbon* 55(4): 1869–1887.

Reitberger, M.M. 2008. *Das frühbronzezeitliche Gräberfeld von Haid, Oberösterreich* (Studien zur Kulturgeschichte von Oberösterreich 20). Weitra: Bibliothek der Provinz.

Reiter, V. 2008. Die frühbronzezeitlichen Brandbestattungen von Franzhausen II und Ratzersdorf im Unteren Traisental. Unpublished dissertation, University of Wien.

Remotti, F. 2006. *Morte e trasformazione dei corpi. Interventi di tanatometamorfosi*, Mondadori.

Riedel, A. and U. Tecchiati 1992. La fauna del Riparo del Santuario (Comune di Lasino-Trentino): aspetti archeozoologici, paleoeconomici e rituali. *Annali del Museo Civico di Rovereto* 8: 3–46.

Rigotti, A. 1974. Giornale di scavo n.2, Sopralluogo e sondaggio a Castel Corno, Settembre 1974, unpublished document kept in Museo Civico di Rovereto.

Roberti, G. 1913a. La grotta sepolcrale detta 'La Cosina' a Stravino, *Bullettino di Paletnologia Italiana*, Anno XXXIX, n. 1–5.

Roberti, G. 1913b. La grotticella sepolcrale di Nogaredo, *S. Marco*, 4: 141–145.

Roden, C. 1988. Blasrohrdüsen: ein archäologischer Exkurs zur Pyrotechnologie des Chalcolithikums und der Bronzezeit. *Der Anschnitt. Zeitschrift für Kunst und Kultur im Bergbau* 40(3): 62–82.

Roncoroni, F. 2013. Le sepolture secondarie e collettive in ripari sotto roccia nel Bresciano, in R.C. de Marinis (ed.) *L'età del Rame. La pianura Padana e la Alpi al tempo di Ötzi*: 405–422. Roccafranca: Compagnia della Stampa Massetti Rodella editori.

Rottoli, M. 2001. Lettura del paesaggio antico della Pedemontana attraverso i dati archeobotanici, in *Archeologia e risorse storico-ambientali nella Pedemontana e nella Valli del Friuli occidentale, Atti del convegno di Meduno 6 e 7 ottobre 2000*: 13–18.

Salzani, P. 2010. *La necropoli dell'età del Bronzo di Bovolone* (Memorie del Museo Civico di Storia Naturale di Verona, 2a serie, Sezione Scienze dell'Uomo 10). Verona: Comune di Verona, Soprintendenza per i beni archeologici del Veneto.

Salzani, P. 2014. Il sito di Arano (Verona – scavi 2007) alla luce delle trasformazioni sociali, economiche, tecnologiche tra età del Rame e Bronzo Antico in Italia settentrionale. Unpublished dissertation, Scuola di dottorato in Studi Umanistici, Discipline Filosofiche, Storiche e dei Beni culturali, University of Trento.

Salzani, L., L. Salvadei and E. Valzolgher 2004. Nuove ricerche presso il riparo sepolcrale di Peri (Dolcé, Verona). *Padusa* XL, 40: 7–38.

Sangmeister, E. 1974. Zwei Neufunde der Glockenbecherkultur in Baden-Württemberg: ein Beitrag zur Klassifizierung der Armschutzplatten in Mitteleuropa, *Fundberichte aus Baden-Württemberg* 1: 103–156.

Schwarz, R. 2015. Kultureller Bruch oder Kontinuität? – Mitteldeutschland im 23. Jh. V. Chr., in H. Meller, H.W. Arz, R. Jung and R. Risch (eds) *2200 BC - A climatic breakdown as a cause for the collapse of the old world? 7th Archaeological Conference of Central Germany October 23-26, 2014 in Halle (Saale)*

(Tagungen des Landesmuseums für Vorgeschichte Halle 12/I): 671–713. Halle: Landesmuseum für Vorgeschichte.

Sebesta. G. 1996. *Il lavoro dell'uomo nel ciclo dei Mesi di Torre Aquila*. Trento: Provincia Autonoma di Trento.

Simoni, P. 1966. Prima campagna di scavo all'ex Lago di Lucone di Polpenazze (Brescia). *Annali del Museo* 6: 7–53. Brescia: Civico Museo di Gavardo.

Steadman, L., C. Palmer and C. Tilley 1996. The Universality of Ancestor Worship. *Ethnology* 35 (1): 63–76. <doi:10.2307/3774025>.

Steffè, G. 1984. Rinvenimenti dell'eneolitico e del bronzo antico a Casalecchio di Reno (Bologna). *Preistoria Alpina* 20: 147–154.

Straham, C. 1998. Il bicchiere campaniforme: fenomeno e cultura, in F. Nicolis and E. Mottes (eds) *Simbolo ed enigma. Il bicchiere campaniforme e l'Italia della preistoria europea del III millennio a.C.*: 20–44. Trento: Provincia Autonoma di Trento.

Stuiver, M. and P.J. Reimer 1993. Extended ^{14}C data base and revised CALIB 3.0 ^{14}C age calibration program, *Radiocarbon* 35, 1: 215–230.

Tecchiati, U. 1991. Il riparo del santuario in 'Val Cornelio' (Comune di Lasino-Trentino): una successione stratigrafica dall'Eneolitico recente al Bronzo finale. Unpublished dissertation, University of Trento, Faculty of Lettere e Filosofia.

Tecchiati, U. 1995. Indizi di attività metallurgica preistorica al santuario in 'Val Cornelio' (Comune di Lasino -Trentino). *Annali dei Musei Civici di Rovereto* X (1994): 3–16.

Tecchiati, U. 1996a. Dal Neolitico all'età del bronzo nel territorio dell'antico Comun Comunale Lagarino, in U. Tecchiati (ed.) *Dalle radici della storia. Archeologia del Comun Comunale Lagarino*: 61–70. Catalogue of the homonymous exhibition. Stella: Villalagarina (TN).

Tecchiati, U. 1996b. Il popolamento del Comun Comunale Lagarino nel II millennio a.C., in U. Tecchiati (ed.) *Dalle radici della storia. Archeologia del Comun Comunale Lagarino*: 107–122. Catalogue of the homonymous exhibition. Stella: Villalagarina (TN).

Tecchiati, U. 1997. L'industria su osso e su corno proveniente dai livelli dell'antica e media età del Bronzo del Riparo del Santuario (Lasino - Trento). *Atti dell'Accademia Roveretana degli Agiati* a. 247, ser. VII, vol. VII, A: 71–113.

Tecchiati, U. 2005. Le grotte di Castel Corno nella protostoria della Vallagarina. *Atti dell'Accademia Roveretana degli Agiati, Giornata di Studi in ricordo di Adriano Rigotti*, VIII, V, A, fasc. II: 109–120. Rovereto: Edizioni Osiride.

Tecchiati, U., E. Castiglioni and M. Rottoli 2013. Economia di sussistenza nell'età del Rame dell'Italia settentrionale. Il contributo di archeozoologia e archeobotanica, in R.C. de Marinis (ed.) *L'età del Rame. La pianura padana e le Alpi al tempo di Ötzi*: 39–52. Roccafranca: Compagnia della Stampa Massetti Rodella editori.

Terrasi, F., N. De Cesare, A. D'Onofrio, C. Lubritto, F. Marzaioli, I. Passariello, D. Rogalla, C. Sabbarese, G. Boriello, G. Casa and A. Palmieri 2008. High precision 14C AMS at CIRCE. *Nucl. Instrum. Methods Phys. B 266*: 2221–2224.

Tews, T. 2016. Os vasos perfurados sem fundo nas primeiras sociedades agro-pastoris na Península Ibérica e na Europa Central: perspetivas da arqueologia (experimental), arqueometria e etnografia, in I. Pinto Coelho, J. Bento Torres, L. Serrão Gil (eds) *Tiago Ramos, Entre ciência e cultura da interdisciplinaridade à transversalidade da arqueologia, Actas das VIII jornadas de jovens em investigação Arqueológica*. Lisbon: Universidade Nova de Lisboa.

Tirabassi, J. 2000. La tomba campaniforme di Ca' di Marco (Brescia). *Pagine di archeologia. Studi e materiali* 1(1999*), Musei Civici di Reggio Emilia*: 1–52.

Trinco, V. 2020. L'insediamento dell'Età del Bronzo di Dosso Alto di Borgo Sacco (Rovereto, TN), Unpublished dissertation, Inter-university of Quaternary, Prehistory and Archaeology (Ferrara, Modena, Reggio Emilia, Verona and Trento - Italy).

Turek, J. 2015. Bell Beaker stone wrist-guards as symbolic male ornament. The significance of ceremonial warfare in 3rd millennium BC Central Europe, in M.P.P. Martínez and L. Salanova (eds) *The Bell Beaker transition in Europe Mobility and local evolution during the 3rd Millennium BC*: 28–40. Oxford: Oxbow Books.

Turek, J. and V. Černý 2001. Society, gender and sexual dimorphism of the Corded Ware and Bell Beaker populations, in F. Nicolis (ed.) *Bell Beakers today. Pottery people, culture, symbols in prehistoric Europe, Proceedings of the International Colloquium, Riva del Garda (Trento, Italy), 1-16 May 1998*: 601–612. Trento: Provincia Autonoma di Trento, Servizio Beni Culturali, Ufficio Beni Archeologici.

Valzolgher, E. and S. Lincetto 2002. La necropoli eneolitica di Scalucce di Molina. Gli scavi De Stefani del 1883, in L. Salzani and A. Brugnoli (eds) *Stefano De Stefani. Pioniere della ricerca preistorica veronese. Le ricerche sui Monti Lessini e in Valpolicella. Atti del convegno (Fumane, 26 maggio 2001)*: 159–206. Fumane: Centro di documentazione per la storia della Valpolicella.

Valzolgher, E. and G. Quarta 2009. Date radiocarboniche AMS dal riparo di Peri (Dolcé, Verona). Commento e analisi bayesiana. *Bollettino del Museo Civico di Storia Naturale di Verona. Geologia Paleontologia Preistoria* 33: 84–113.

Verwers, G.J. 1964. A Veluvian bell beaker with remains of a cremation in a tumulus near Meerlo. *Analecta Praehistorica Leidensia* 1: 17–24.

Walker, P.L., R.R. Bathurst, R. Richman, T. Gjerdrum and V.A. Andrushko 2009. The causes of porotic hyperostosis and cribra orbitalia: a reappraisal of the iron-deficiency-anemia hypothesis. *American Journal of Physical Anthropology* 139: 109–125.

Wilkinson, C., 2004. *Forensic facial reconstruction*. Cambridge: Cambridge University Press.